The purpose of this book is to re-examine those basic issues in the study of *Midrash* which to some extent have been marginalised by current trends in scholarship and research. Irving Jacobs asks, for example, whether the early rabbinic exegetes had a concept of *peshat*, plain meaning, and, if so, what significance they attached to it in their exposition of the biblical text. He enquires if the selection of proemial and proof-texts was a random one, dependent purely upon the art or whim of the preacher, or rather if exegetical traditions linked certain penta-teuchal themes with specific sections of the Prophets (and particularly the Hagiographa), which were acknow-ledged by preachers and audiences alike. As *Midrash* in its original, pre-literary form, was a living process involving both live preachers and live audiences in the ancient synagogues of the Holy Land, to what extent, he asks, did the latter influence the former in the development of their art and skills? The answers he provides to these, and other, questions, represent a fresh approach to the peren-nial problem of the rabbis' awareness of plain meaning, and to the significance which they attached to it.

THE MIDRASHIC PROCESS

THE MIDRASHIC PROCESS

Tradition and Interpretation in Rabbinic Judaism

IRVING JACOBS

Former Principal, Jews' College London

CAMBRIDGE
UNIVERSITY PRESS

Published by the Press Syndicate of the University of Cambridge
The Pitt Building, Trumpington Street, Cambridge CB2 1RP
40 West 20th Street, New York, NY 10011–4211, USA
10 Stamford Road, Oakleigh, Melbourne 3166, Australia

© Cambridge University Press 1995

First published 1995

Printed in Great Britain at the University Press, Cambridge

A catalogue record for this book is available from the British Library

Library of Congress cataloguing in publication data
Jacobs, Irving.
The midrashic process: tradition and interpretation in rabbinic Judaism /
Irving Jacobs.
p.   cm.
Includes bibliographical references and index.
ISBN 0 521 46174 x (hardback)
1. Midrash – History and criticism.
2. Bible. O.T. – Criticism, interpretation, etc., Jewish.
I. Title.
BM14.J33 1995
296. 1'406–dc20   93–46182   CIP

ISBN 0 521 46174 x hardback

To my wife
Ann
whose unfailing support in all matters
made this book possible.

Contents

Preface   *page* xi
Abbreviations   xiii

1   What is *Midrash?*   1

2   Traditional motifs in early rabbinic exegesis I:
    Job and the Generation of the Flood   21

3   Traditional motifs in early rabbinic exegesis II:
    Job and Israel's early history as a nation   43

4   Popular legends and traditions I: the archetypal
    sage   79

5   Popular legends and traditions II: the archetypal
    priest-king   95

6   Popular legends and traditions III: the
    regenerating tree   133

7   The midrashic background for James 2:21–23   145

8   Elements of Near-Eastern mythology in rabbinic
    Aggadah   154

9   Conclusions   168

Appendices
1   Job and the Generation of the Flood   173
2   Job and Israel's early history as a nation   179
3   The archetypal sage   187
4   The archetypal priest-king   190

Select bibliography   193
Index of sources   199
Index of names   214
Index of subjects   217

Preface

This book has long been in the making! It is based initially on the years of study and research at Jews' College, under the powerful influence of Professor Naftali Wieder, who left his indelible mark upon every student who had the privilege of studying under him. A number of chapters in this work are based directly on those contained in the dissertation which I wrote under Professor Wieder's guidance, for the PhD degree of London University, entitled 'The Book of Job in Rabbinic Thought' (1971).

I attach almost equal significance to the contribution made by the generations of students to whom I have endeavoured to teach *Midrash* during the past twenty-seven years. I argue in this book that the midrashic process was profoundly influenced by a vital interaction between preacher and audience in the ancient synagogues of *Eretz Yisrael*. I have no doubts that a similar interaction between my students and myself has influenced and enriched my understanding of the midrashic process.

A book is not produced by the author alone. The sheer effort of churning out various versions of the manuscript must be acknowledged. I am happy, therefore, to express my thanks to Mrs Adele Lew, Mrs Annette Nissim and Mrs Linda Ofstein for their invaluable assistance in completing this arduous task. I must also express my gratitude to Mr Alex Wright, religious studies editor, Cambridge University Press, and particularly to Mrs Sherry Begner, who have done much to facilitate the publication of this book. Thanks are due also to Mr Ezra Kahn and his colleagues of the Jews' College Library, for the willing spirit with which they accommodated my every need.

Two chapters of this book have already appeared in print. 'The Midrashic Background for James 2:21–23' was published in *New Testament Studies* (vol. 22, pp. 457–464). 'Elements of Near-Eastern Mythology in Rabbinic *Aggadah*' appeared in the *Journal for Jewish Studies* (vol. 28, pp. 1–11). I am grateful to the editors of both these journals for kindly granting me permission to incorporate those articles into this volume.

I complete this work and sign this preface on my fifty-fifth birthday. I do so, confident in the knowledge that the last word on *Midrash* has not yet been written. It is my fervent hope that those who may one day write it, will find my contribution useful.

Abbreviations

JOURNALS AND TEXTS

ANET	*Ancient Near-Eastern Texts*
ARN	*Avot d'Rabbi Natan*
BT	Babylonian *Talmud*
EJ	*Encyclopaedia Judaica*
HUCA	*Hebrew Union College Annual*
JE	*Jewish Encyclopedia*
JJS	*Journal for Jewish Studies*
JQR	*Jewish Quarterly Review* (OS = Old Series; NS = New Series)
JSS	*Journal for Semitic Studies*
MGWJ	*Monatsschrift für Geschichte und Wissenschaft des Judentums*
PT	Palestinian *Talmud*

GENERAL ABBREVIATIONS

b.	*ben* (or *bar* = son of)
R.	Rabbi (Rav)

CHAPTER I

What is 'Midrash'?

In the context of a scholarly study, the question, what is *Midrash*, may appear to be trivial, if not irrelevant. For more than a century, *Midrash* has been the subject of intensive and extensive academic study and research. Its language and terminology have been analysed in detail. It has been exhaustively excavated as a mine of information relating to the religious beliefs and attitudes of the talmudic sages and to the political, social and economic conditions in which they lived. In more recent years, a new dimension has been added to the study of *Midrash*, through literary analysis. The phenomenon of *Midrash* has captured the attention of literary theorists, who have reinterpreted it in the light of the contemporary theory of intertextuality.[1] Consequently, this ancient corpus of specifically Jewish literature, which represents centuries of development as a living process in the ancient synagogues and school-houses of the Holy Land, retains its place in the forefront of modern scholarly interest.

Yet, despite this considerable and wide-ranging scholarly activity – or perhaps, in some measure, because of it – insufficient attention has been given hitherto, to one or two basic issues relating to the nature and the underlying rationale of the midrashic process. For example, what were the criteria upon which the selection of proemial and proof-texts was based? The early preachers frequently cite verses in support of their statements, or as the basis of a proem, with apparently scant regard

---

[1] For a résumé of the work currently being done in this field, see *Midrash and Literature*, ed. G. H. Hartman and S. Budick, Yale 1986.

for the plain meaning of their chosen text, or of the context from which it was taken. In many cases, no word of explanation is offered to justify the application of a particular verse from Job to Noah and the Generation of the Flood, or a specific quotation from the Psalms to Abraham or Moses. Have these midrashic expositions been transmitted defectively, omitting this crucial information which the compilers of midrashic texts, or subsequent generations of copyists, took for granted?

Although it is generally accepted that the material preserved in our extant midrashic works is derived from homilies and expositions which were actually delivered to live audiences in the ancient synagogues and study houses of the Holy Land, it is extremely unlikely that these have been preserved in an unedited form. This is particularly the case with the *petiḥot* or proems, which are a salient feature of the post-talmudic *midrashim*. In its simplest form, the proem consists of a 'distant' verse usually taken from the Hagiographa, which the preacher proceeds to relate to the *seder* verse, i.e. the opening verse of the weekly lection from the Torah according to the triennial cycle of the Holy Land. Frequently, the proems are very brief, containing little more than a germ of an idea, as will be seen from a number of *petiḥot* discussed subsequently. In such cases, we can safely assume that the living address on which the literary *petiḥah* is based, was originally more expansive. We cannot assume, however, that the congregants in the ancient synagogues were so familiar with the Hebrew Bible that they could recognise the source of a quotation instantly. Preachers probably prefaced their biblical quotations with stock phrases like כך אמר איוב, 'Thus Job said', or, in the case of Psalms and Proverbs, אמר שלמה, אמרו בני קרח, 'the Sons of Qoraḥ said', 'Solomon said'.

While this kind of simple device may have proved sufficient for an audience to identify the source of a quotation, were these early congregants able to recognise the relevance of the preacher's quotation for his chosen theme? Did congregation and preacher share an awareness of certain exegetical traditions, linking aspects of pentateuchal narratives with specific sections of other biblical books, so that the mere mention of Job in the context of a homily on the Flood, would have been sufficient to indicate the relevance of the source for the theme? Before attempting to answer this kind of question at length, as we propose to do in the following two chapters, it is necessary in our view, to begin by re-examining briefly the basic issue of what is *Midrash* and how did the midrashic process operate?

In simple terms, *Midrash* is the oldest form of Bible interpretation. For more than twenty centuries, the Bible has challenged the imagination and ingenuity of its interpreters. *Midrash* represents the response of the earliest generations of Jewish scholars to this challenge.

Clearly, the challenge of interpreting the Bible was not perceived in identical terms throughout the last two thousand years. For the great masters of the middle ages, like Rashi and Ibn Ezra, who laid the foundations of modern Bible scholarship, Bible exegesis was the pursuit of *peshat*. They saw it as their task to establish the plain meaning of the biblical text, primarily through a process of defining precisely the grammatical functions and structures of its language. This does not imply that the scholars of the talmudic period, who were capable of producing tolerably literal Aramaic translations of biblical texts, and who developed mishnaic Hebrew as a superb medium for their halakhic, midrashic and liturgical compositions, were incapable of appreciating the plain meaning of the biblical text.[2] Nor were they unaware of the 'mechanics' of its language, even though they did not develop a comprehensive technical terminology to describe them. On the contrary, as we shall endeavour to prove, they acknowledged plain meaning – *as they perceived it* – to be the boundary within which the midrashic process was obliged to function.

---

[2] However, this is an issue which has provoked considerable scholarly discussion and debate. See, for example, J. Z. Lauterbach, *Peshat*, *JE* vol. 9, pp. 652f; L. I. Rabinowitz, *Peshat*, *EJ* vol. 13, pp. 329–31; M. H. Segal, *Parshanut Ha-Miqra, S'qirah al Toldoteha v'Hitpathuta*, repr. Jerusalem 1980, pp. 7–9; E. Z. Melamed, *Mephar'shei Ha-Miqra*, Jerusalem 1978, vol. 1, pp. 5–8; B. J. Gelles, *Peshat and Derash in the Exegesis of Rashi*, Leiden 1981, pp. 1–8; also the literature cited by R. J. Loewe in his study, 'The Plain Meaning of Scripture in Early Jewish Exegesis', in *Papers of the Institute of Jewish Studies*, vol. 1 (ed. J. G. Weiss), Jerusalem 1964, pp. 140ff; and most recently, D. Weiss-Halivni, *Peshat and Derash*, Oxford 1991.

However, the determining factor in early Jewish scriptural exegesis, was the rabbis' perception of the Bible itself. They saw it as the revealed word of God, not only in terms of its eternal validity, but also with regard to the uniqueness of its language, which transcended the ordinary medium of human communication. In the context of this 'Divine Language', the most common-place terms and expressions – even particles of speech indispensable to the functioning of Hebrew – were to be regarded as 'containers' of deeper meanings, which the interpreter was required to unlock.[3] Consequently, the main challenge of the Bible, as perceived by the ancient Jewish exegetes, was to decode its messages, to reveal the inner significance of the text.

This might involve the most extrinsic forms of exegesis, which seem to transcend any concept of plain meaning, but were perceived by the rabbis as functioning within the permissible parameters of the text. This can best be illustrated by an unusual device developed by the early rabbinic exegetes, to which we will refer fairly frequently in the course of our subsequent discussions, climatic exegesis. This is based on the assumption that a scriptural expression, regardless of its usual connotation, or plain meaning, can absorb a new and quite unrelated meaning from the context or climate in which it occurs. A particularly good example of this device is preserved in *Leviticus Rabbah* 23:2 (p. 528) where, following on the assertion that God experienced the utmost difficulty in releasing Israel from Egypt because of their total assimilation, the *Amora*, R. Shemuel b. Naḥmani declared:

---

[3] The best-known example of this type of exegesis, particularly in the realm of *Halakhah*, is provided by the early *Tanna*, Naḥum of Gimzo, who interpreted every את and גם in the *Torah* as a ריבוי (an amplification or extension of the scope of the text) and every אך and רק as a מיעוט (a limitation). This method was adopted and propagated by his pupil, the outstanding exegete of the Yabneh period, R. Aqiva (see *Genesis Rabbah* 1:14 and the parallels cited by Theodor in his edition, p. 12). As is well known, this extrinsic treatment of the language of Scripture was not without its opponents, notably R. Aqiva's colleague and chief antagonist in halakhic debate, R. Ishmael, who insisted that the language of the *Torah* functioned in the same way as human speech (דברה תורה כלשון בני אדם; see, for example, *Sifrei Numbers* 15:31, 112 (p. 121); also *Genesis Rabbah* 1:14).

'Had God not bound Himself by an oath, Israel would not have been redeemed from Egypt! [As is implied in the following verse], "Wherefore (לכן) Say unto the Children of Israel: 'I am the Lord and I will bring you out from under the burdens of the Egyptians (Exodus 6:6).'" Now the expression לכן connotes an oath, as it is said, "And therefore (ולכן) *I have sworn* unto the house of Eli ... (I Samuel 3:14)".'

There are, however, many examples of midrashic exegesis which illustrate both the early rabbinic exegetes' awareness of plain meaning and their hermeneutic approach to the biblical text. While a number of these will be cited subsequently, it may be useful at this juncture, to analyse a few examples taken from well-known contexts.

(a) In the narrative of the *Aqedah*, related in Genesis 22, a comparatively rare term is used for the knife which Abraham took to slaughter his son, מאכלת. This expression occurs only four times in the Hebrew Bible, twice in Genesis 22 (verses 6 and 10) and again in Judges 19:29 and in Proverbs 30:14. The earliest midrashic commentary to the Book of Genesis, *Genesis Rabbah*,[4] records two views on the significance of this term:

R. Ḥanina said: 'Why is [a knife] called מאכלת? Because it renders food fit to be eaten.' The Rabbis said: 'Abraham's knife was so designated, because all the benefits which Israel enjoys in this world are on account of the merit of that knife.'

Despite the terseness of his comment, R. Ḥanina has presented his listeners with an effective definition of a rare term. Without recourse to grammatical terminology – which, in all probability, he did not possess – he has identified מאכלת as a present participle of the *hiph'il* of אכל, 'to eat', with the meaning of 'causing to eat', or simply, 'feeding'. Thus מאכלת is an implement which feeds, or allows food to be eaten, through the ritual act of slaughter. While modern grammarians might take issue with this,[5] R. Ḥanina has none the less addressed himself to the plain meaning of this term and has

[4] 56:3, p. 598.
[5] As מאכלת is usually taken as a feminine noun of the *maqtal* form (compare ממלכה and מלאכה).

offered a plausible explanation for designating a knife as מאכלת.

The anonymous rabbis cited in the same passage did not dispute R. Ḥanina's explanation; they too understood מאכלת to be an implement which feeds. However, they were looking beyond plain meaning to the inner implications of this term in its specific context. According to their view, Abraham's knife was called מאכלת to indicate its significance for the fate of all future generations of his descendents. Abraham's knife would 'feed' them in perpetuity with the benefits of his singularly meritorious deed.

(b) At the point when Abraham is about to slaughter Isaac, the angel intervenes, crying, 'Abraham, Abraham ...' (verse 11). This repetition of the patriarch's name provoked the following two comments, recorded once again in *Genesis Rabbah*:[6]

R. Ḥiyya taught: '[This repetition implies] affection and urgency.'
R. Eliezer said: '[This was addressed to Abraham] himself and to future generations, implying that there would be no generation without [a man] of the calibre of Abraham.'

Both the early teachers cited here were reacting to the same phenomenon, the repetition of a word in a text where any apparently superfluous term, or even a single letter, was intended to convey a message. However, R. Ḥiyya recognised that, in this instance, the repetition was to be interpreted in the light of its context. It was an effective means of expressing urgency at the crucial moment in a tense and dramatic situation, while at the same time, indicating God's especial affection for Abraham, which his supreme act of love had inspired. R. Ḥiyya's explanation of the phenomenon, therefore, is clearly in line with the plain meaning of the text as he perceived it. R. Eliezer, on the other hand, has interpreted the phenomenon in keeping with the broader concept of the Bible as the revealed word of God, which was intended to convey a message of both specific and eternal relevance. Thus, God addresses Himself both to Abraham in the immediate context

---

6 56:7, p. 602.

of the *Aqedah*, and to all future generations of his descendants, for whom that singular event would have eternal significance.

(c) *Exodus Rabbah*, the first part of which is an exegetical *midrash* like *Genesis Rabbah*, and may be of a similar age, records the following exposition of Moses' first encounter with the family of Jethro, narrated in 2:16–19:[7]

'Now the priest of Midian had seven daughters . . .' Does not God hate idolatry, yet He granted Moses refuge with an idolater?! However, our Rabbis have said that [originally] Jethro was a priest to idolatrous worship, but realising that it was without substance, he rejected it and considered repenting even before Moses' arrival. Consequently, he summoned his fellow-citizens and said to them, 'Until now I have served you, since I am now old, choose another priest!' Thereupon he arose, brought forth all the trappings of idolatry, and gave them everything. They arose and excommunicated him, so that nobody associated with him! They would not do any work for him, and they would not tend his sheep. He asked the shepherds to tend his sheep, but they refused, so that he was obliged to employ his own daughters. 'And they came and they drew water' – this indicates that they were coming [to the well] early, for fear of the shepherds!

'And the shepherds came and drove them away' – Is it possible that he was the priest of Midian, yet the shepherds were driving away his daughters?! This indicates that they had excommunicated him, and drove away his daughters like a divorced woman.

The passage appears to be purely an apologia, defending Moses' close association with an idolatrous priest, who would play an influential role in the life of the future leader and teacher of Israel. In reality, however, the anonymous aggadist was functioning within the parameters of plain meaning. He had focused his attention – and that of his listeners – on a serious problem presented by the text, for which no solution is offered in the biblical narrative. It had long been acknowledged by early Jewish exegetes that Jethro's title כהן, did not simply connote a religious functionary. He was a ruler or governor of the Midianites, a notion which was widely popularised in talmudic times and is no less acceptable today as a

---

[7] See *Exodus Rabbah* 1:32.

plausible interpretation of Jethro's role.[8] How was it possible, therefore, that his daughters were required to perform the menial task of tending his flocks and how could the shepherds have dared to assault their ruler's children? Our unknown exegete was clearly aware of this problem, for which he has endeavoured to provide a solution, by his reconstruction of the background to the biblical narrative.

(d) A seminal source for our discussion regarding the early rabbinic concept of plain meaning and its relationship to received traditions regarding the interpretation of a biblical passage, is *BT Shabbat* 63a. *Mishnah Shabbat* 6:4 records opposing views on the question of bearing arms on the Sabbath as an accessory to male attire. R. Eliezer (b. Hyrkanos) permitted the practice on the grounds that weapons may be regarded as an adornment. His colleagues, on the other hand, forbade it, declaring that weapons are intrinsically ignoble in function and purpose. Consequently, they are destined to be 'recycled' in the messianic age, as predicted by the prophecy of Isaiah (2:4): 'and they shall beat their swords into ploughshares, and their spears into pruning-hooks'. In the ensuing discussion among the *Amora'im* on these opposing views, the question was raised:

On what did R. Eliezer base his view that weapons are to be regarded as an adornment for a man? On the verse, 'Gird your sword upon your thigh, O mighty one, your glory and your majesty (Psalm 45:4)'. R. Kahana said to Mar, the son of R. Huna: 'This [verse] was written with reference to the words of the *Torah!*' He retorted: '*A verse does not lose its plain meaning* (אין מקרא יוצא מידי פשוטו).' R. Kahana said: 'When I was eighteen years old, I had already learned all the Six Orders [of the *Mishnah*], yet I did not know that a verse does not lose its plain meaning until now!'

The midrashic exegesis of Psalm 45 is the subject for special study in a later chapter.[9] Consequently, at this point, it is sufficient to note that there is adequate evidence both in *BT*

---

[8] On Jethro's role as a ruler and a judge in early sources, see R. Eleazar of Modi'in's interpretation of Exodus 18:1 in *Mekhilta d'Rabbi Ishmael, Yitro, Massekhta d'Amaleq* 1, p. 190, also *Targum Onqelos* to Exodus 18:1 and Josephus, *Antiquities* I, vii, 2.
[9] See pp. 95ff.

Shabbat – where this discussion is recorded – and in other
rabbinic sources, notably the Babylonian *Talmud*, to show that
this psalm, with its description of the physical attributes and
attire of a royal prince, was treated as an allegory alluding to
the sages and their pursuit of *Torah* learning. Our main
concern here is the precise implications of the maxim which
Mar, the son of R. Huna, cites.

We have taken פשוטו – like its cognate expression פשט – in
the usual sense of 'plain meaning', which was accepted already
in the middle ages.[10] However, this is not universally accepted
by modern scholars. Loewe, for example, suggests that in
talmudic sources, פשט connotes authoritative rather than
plain meaning.[11] Weiss-Halivni, on the other hand, argues that
the term connotes extension, continuation, hence context.[12] Is
it possible, therefore, to determine with any degree of certainty, what this crucial expression actually means here?

We should perhaps begin by asking what was the point at
issue between the two *Amora'im*? It is inconceivable that either
R. Kahana or Mar, the son of R. Huna, was unfamiliar with
the simple meaning of the Hebrew terms in Psalm 45:4, for
reasons we have stated above. Moreover, judging by Mar, the
son of R. Huna's unquestioning acceptance of R. Kahana's
assertion that the psalm is to be treated as an allegorical
description of the *Torah* and its sages, we can assume that he
was equally aware of this exegetical tradition, which was in
vogue in Babylon.

The point at issue between them, we would suggest, was the
implications of the traditional interpretation of a biblical
passage for its plain or simple meaning. R. Kahana had
assumed that the only meaning which might be legitimately
attached to a passage – or a verse – was that assigned to it by
tradition. The traditional exposition totally displaced its plain
meaning. Consequently, the term חרב in Psalm 45:4 no longer
connoted a sword. It had been completely divested of its plain

---

[10] See Weiss-Halivni, *Peshat and Derash*, pp. 79ff.
[11] 'The Plain Meaning of Scripture', p. 158.
[12] *Peshat and Derash*, pp. 53ff.

meaning and was purely an allegorical symbol for halakhic acumen, the cut and thrust of dialectical argument.

Mar, the son of R. Huna, on the other hand, insisted that plain meaning has an independent integrity and, therefore, cannot be obscured by traditional interpretation.[13] Consequently, as the text speaks of a sword in the most positive terms, it provides adequate scriptural support for R. Eliezer's view that such a weapon may be regarded as an adornment and not simply as an ignoble instrument of destruction.

However, Weiss-Halivni seeks support for his contention that פשט connotes extension or context from the use of the cognate Aramaic phrase פשטיה דקרא, which occurs notably in the Babylonian *Talmud*.[14] In a number of instances where this phrase is employed, the suggested 'plain meaning' of the text in question, would hardly be acceptable to the modern reader. For example, *BT Ḥullin* 6a records how R. Meir sent a disciple to purchase wine from the Cutheans (i.e. Samaritans). He encounters an old man who challenges him with Proverbs 23:2, 'and put a knife to thy throat, if thou be a man given to appetite'. The text continues:

To what does the *peshat* of the text relate? To a disciple sitting in the presence of his master. As R. Ḥiyya taught, 'When thou sittest to eat with a ruler, consider well him that sitteth before thee; and put a knife to thy throat if thou be בעל נפש (lit.: "a man given to appetite").' If a disciple knows that his master is able to give him a

---

[13] See Rashi's comment on this maxim in *BT Yevamot* 24a: 'Even though we may expound a verse midrashically, it cannot totally lose its plain meaning.' This source is of special significance as it cites the one case in the whole of Scriptures where this maxim does not apply, Deuteronomy 25:6. Referring to the child of a levirate marriage the text states: 'And it shall be that the first-born that she beareth shall succeed in the name of his brother that is dead, that his name be not blotted out in Israel.' According to its simplest meaning, the verse implies that the child should be given the name of its father's deceased brother. However, on the basis of a word analogy (גזרה שוה) with Genesis 48:6, 'they shall be called after *the name of their brethren* (על שם אחיהם)', the operative term שם is taken as a reference to the property of the deceased. In connection with this, Rava declared that contrary to the general rule of אין מקרא יוצא מידי פשוטו, the word analogy here has totally divested the verse of its plain meaning, leaving no residual obligation to name the child after the deceased (see Rashi, *BT Yevamot* 24a; see also *BT Yevamot* 11b).

[14] For a full review of all the relevant sources where this phrase occurs, see Weiss-Halivni, *Peshat and Derash*, pp. 63ff.

reasoned answer, then בִּין, ask [your question].[15] But if not, then 'consider well him that sitteth before thee; and put a knife to thy throat if thou art a master over thy desire'[16] – withdraw from him!

As Weiss-Halivni observes, R. Ḥiyya's exposition, which is presented here as *peshat*, is hardly closer to the plain meaning of the text than its supposedly midrashic use by the old man in the anecdote. Indeed, the latter appears to be more representative of the plain meaning. Therefore, to treat *peshat* as plain meaning here is inappropriate, Weiss-Halivni argues. R. Ḥiyya has provided and expounded the fuller context, or extension, of the text which the old man had quoted only in part.

An even more challenging example of פשטיה דקרא is recorded once again in *BT Ḥullin* (133a) in connection with Proverbs 25:20, 'As one that taketh off a garment in cold weather, as is vinegar upon nitre, so is he that singeth songs to a heavy heart.' The Babylonian *Amora*, Rava had forgotten a *halakhah* taught to him by his master, R. Joseph. Proverbs 25:20 is communicated to his colleague, R. Saphra, in a dream. The latter, who is disturbed by the implied criticism of the verse, is reassured by the news that it was intended for Rava, but was not communicated directly to him, as he was under a temporary ban. The passage continues:

Abbaye said to R. Dimi: 'To what does the *peshat* of the text relate?' He replied: 'To one who teaches an unworthy disciple'. For R. Judah said in the name of Rav: 'He who teaches an unworthy disciple, falls into Gehinnom.'

In reviewing this passage, Weiss-Halivni himself is obliged to admit that the standard text of the *Gemara* defies even the meaning of *peshat* as extension or context.[17] He suggests, therefore, that we accept the reading of MS Rome 2, the *Rif* and the *Rosh*, which cites only the opening clause of the verse in the context of R. Saphra's dream. The useless act implied in this

---

[15] For this rendering, see Rashi's commentary to the text.
[16] Although this rendering, which is clearly required by the context here, is the complete antithesis of its usual translation, 'a man given to appetite', it is entirely compatible with the plain meaning of בעל נפש.
[17] *Peshat and Derash*, p. 69.

first clause, Halivni argues, symbolises R. Joseph's imparting a
halakhah to Rava, which he failed to comprehend, while
Abbaye sought the meaning of the continuation of the verse,
which speaks of singing songs to a bad heart.

This approach, however, is hardly satisfactory. One cannot
attach too much significance to incomplete biblical quotations,
as these are a well-known feature of early rabbinic texts,
whether in printed or manuscript form. Very frequently, it is
precisely the relevant part of the verse that is omitted, which is
the case, we would suggest, in the sources Weiss-Halivni has
cited. Clearly, both the implied interpretation in the opening
anecdote and the subsequent *peshat* of Proverbs 25:20 allude to
a common theme, the instruction of a student. For the early
rabbinic exegetes, this was no doubt contained in the concluding words, 'so is he that singeth songs to a bad heart
(= לב רע)'. As is well known, לב in both biblical and
rabbinic sources connotes understanding. In addition, the biblical imagery of singing was treated midrashically as the study
of the *Torah*.[18] Thus the phrase as a whole was taken to mean
the teaching of *Torah* to a student either of poor intelligence or
of an evil mind or disposition, as we shall see subsequently.

None the less, this does not invalidate Halivni's basic contention that neither the implied interpretation of the verse nor its
subsequent *peshat* bear any resemblance to our concept of plain
meaning. However, this may be due to a basic principle of
hermeneutics, that an interpreter's approach to a text is profoundly influenced by what he perceives that text to be. Like
their modern counterparts, the early rabbinic exegetes recognised that the Book of Proverbs dealt with the nature and
character of חכמה. However, they did not share the modern
view that חכמה in this context connotes sagacity and worldly
wisdom. They regarded חכמה in biblical Wisdom Literature
as a technical term, referring specifically to the Wisdom of the
Torah, as is reflected in the widely recurring exegetical maxim,

---

[18] See, for example R. Ḥiyya's comment in connection with Lamentations 2:19 in *BT
Tamid* 32a: Anyone who occupies himself with the study of the Torah by night, the
Divine Presence is before him, as it is said, 'Arise, *sing* (רני, √רנן) by night ...
before the face of the Lord'.

'חכמה' connotes *Torah*.[19] This is not to be regarded purely as a midrashic device; it represents exegetical reality for the scholars of the talmudic period. Consequently, they perceived the 'plain meaning' of Proverbs 23 and 25 to be descriptions of *Torah* sages and their disciples.

Thus, in the earlier passage in *Ḥullin*, the application of Proverbs 23:1 to a context of eating and drinking was regarded as 'midrashic', while treating the verse as an allegorical description of a disciple's conduct towards his master was perceived to be *peshat*, plain meaning. The latter passage, however, does present a more serious problem, as both the implied interpretation in the anecdote and the subsequent *peshat* of Proverbs 25:20 actually refer to the teaching of *Torah* to disciples. We would suggest, therefore, that the *crux interpretum* here is the phase, לב רע. While in the anecdote, this was taken 'midrashically' to mean a student of poor or faulty understanding, the *peshat* appears to have been based on the use of the two terms in another biblical context. Both these expressions occur for the first time in *Genesis* 6:5, where their plain meaning is unmistakable, 'every imagination of the thoughts of his heart (לבו) was only evil (רע) continually'. Hence, R. Dimi perceived the plain meaning of לב רע to be 'evil heart', 'evil disposition'.

The midrashic process, however, did not consist purely of an interaction between a divinely inspired text and its authoritative interpreters. There was a third, equally indispensable component, the people for whom the text was intended. Consequently, the interpretation and exposition of Scripture were never regarded as exclusive activities, to be confined to the circle of the scholars and their disciples in the *Bet Ha-Midrash*. The sacred texts were the legacy of the entire nation of Israel, to whom their message was to be communicated. Therefore, at a very early stage, the midrashic process was assigned a prominent public role, both in the form of the *Targum* and the expositions of the weekly scriptural lections.

---

[19] See below, p. 82. Similarly, in connection with identification of the ruler in *Proverbs* 23:1 with the *Torah* sage, see below, pp. 105f.

In chapters 4–6, we will examine the implications and ramifications of the public role of the midrashic process. At this point we would merely call attention to a fairly obvious, but none the less crucial factor, which has not been given sufficient consideration hitherto, the important role of the audience in a public activity such as teaching or preaching.

In his efforts to influence his audience, a preacher/teacher is almost invariably influenced by them. His choice of theme is often determined by the circumstances and conditions of his listeners, who also exercise a formative influence on the manner of his presentation. He relies upon their collaboration, their comprehension and presumed knowledge, which allow him to leave things unsaid, or to be referred to by mere allusion, thus establishing that rapport with an audience which any public speaker will readily recognise and appreciate. These factors, we shall endeavour to prove, played an integral role in the selection and interpretation of scriptural texts preserved in our extant *midrashim*.

In the remaining two chapters of the book, we look beyond the purely rabbinic context of the midrashic process and its exegetical traditions to gain some insight into their antiquity. It has long been acknowledged that the early teachers of the Church not only took possession of the Jewish Bible as its primary text, they also inherited a highly developed and comprehensive interpretative process, which they adapted for their own purposes. In chapter 7, we will examine just a single but significant example of a midrashic statement preserved in a New Testament source, in order to illustrate how aspects of the exegetical methodology characteristic of rabbinic *Midrash*, were being employed by early non-rabbinic exegetes even before the beginning of the current era.

One of the perennial problems of *Midrash*, for which there is no comprehensive solution, is posed by the corpus of traditions which the early rabbinic exegetes have interpolated into their expositions of the biblical text. How old are these traditions? What was their original source? Biblical narrative frequently presumes a considerable knowledge on the part of the reader. For example, he is given no information regarding the early life

of a crucial personality like Abraham, who will figure prominently in our subsequent discussions. Similarly, a cataclysmic
event such as the Flood is recorded with an absolute economy
of detail regarding the conduct and conditions of the Antediluvians, which lead to God's returning the world to primeval
chaos.

In both rabbinic and non-rabbinic sources dating back to
the second century BCE, this sparse information is augmented
by a rich store of legends and traditions, as can be seen from the
material cited subsequently. While one may suspect that these
sources preserve elements of the ancient narratives only partially recorded in the Bible, which survived for centuries in an
oral form, it is impossible to identify them with any certainty.

However, there is one aspect of early rabbinic exegesis where
it is possible to identify the traditions which the rabbis have
introduced into their expositions of the text, as being of great
antiquity. As a result of archaeological discoveries, modern
scholars have long been able to identify biblical parallels for
the creation drama and combat myth preserved in other
ancient Near-Eastern texts. In chapter 8, we will endeavour to
prove that the earliest rabbinic exegetes – unlike their succes-
sors in the middle ages – were fully aware of the real significance of these allusions in the biblical text, which they
amplified in the light of their exegetical traditions.

With regard to the sources cited in this book, the recently
revised edition of Strack's important hand-book on talmudic
and midrashic literature will provide the reader with an adequate introduction to virtually all the major and minor
works.[20] None the less, before proceeding to discuss the first of
our topics, traditional motifs in early rabbinic exegesis, some
brief, general observations regarding the major midrashic
works to which we will refer most frequently in the ensuing
pages, may prove useful.

The oldest known literary format of rabbinic *Midrash* is the
exegetical *Midrash* which comprises a commentary to all, or a

[20] See H. L. Strack and G. Stemberger, *Introduction to the Talmud and Midrash*, trans.
Markus Bockmuehl, Edinburgh 1991.

major part of a biblical book. To this major category belong the tannaitic or halakhic *Midrashim*, the *Mekhiltot* of Rabbi Ishmael and Rabbi Shimon b. Yoḥai to the Book of Exodus, the *Sifra* to Leviticus and the *Sifrei* to Numbers and Deuteronomy.[21] It is generally assumed that these works were already in existence during the talmudic period, although not necessarily in their current form. They are, presumably, the literary representatives of a much older, oral process which dates back long before the beginning of the Christian era.[22]

For generations, teachers expounded the text of the Torah for their disciples in the school-houses of the Holy Land. In the course of time, leading expositors may have developed their own methodology and terminology, which became characteristic of their school. As is well known, the two great halakhic exegetes among the *collegeum* of scholars at Yabneh, R. Aqiva and R. Ishmael, were noted for their distinctive methods of exegesis and there was a tendency in the scholarly world to assign our extant halakhic *Midrashim* to the school of either one or other of these scholars. While so precise an identification may be difficult to substantiate, there is evidence for the theory of different schools of redactors, which may have produced our extant *Midrashim*.[23]

After the close of the talmudic period, the exegetical format was retained for a number of major midrashic works, which were produced in the Holy Land. The oldest of these post-talmudic *Midrashim*, is *Genesis Rabbah*, the largest, most comprehensive midrashic commentary to any individual book of the Bible. Its apparent dependence on the *Yerushalmi* – although not necessarily our extant version – and its extensive use of Greek and Latin loan-words, points to the fifth or sixth century as the most plausible dating for its compilation, that is to say, prior to the Arab conquest of the Holy Land, which displaced the Byzantine administration and its official languages.

---

[21] See Strack, *Introduction*, pp. 269ff; also Ch. Albeck, *Mavo l'Talmudim*, Tel Aviv 1969, pp. 79ff.
[22] See Albeck, *Mavo l'Talmudim*, pp. 87ff; also his *Mavo l'Mishnah*, Tel Aviv 1959, pp. 40f.
[23] For a review of the problem, see Strack, *Introduction*, pp. 270ff.

Although there are a number of major differences between
Genesis Rabbah and the older, halakhic *midrashim*, two are of
special significance, the one literary, the other linguistic.
Firstly, there is the *petiḥah* or proem referred to earlier. All the
ninety-nine chapters of this midrashic *magnum opus* open with
one or more of these homiletical units.[24] While the structure of
the proem is regular and easily recognisable, its precise function is a matter of scholarly debate. However, whether we
regard it as a prelude to the weekly lection from the *Torah*, or
as an introduction to the rabbi's exposition of the *seder* on the
Sabbath afternoon,[25] its provenance was the synagogue rather
than schoolhouse and was intended primarily for a popular
rather than a scholarly audience.

The 'popular' origin of much the material in *Genesis Rabbah*
is further indicated by the extensive use of Palestinian – or
Galilean – Aramaic, which constitutes the major linguistic
difference between the halakhic and post-talmudic *midrashim*.
Aramaic is employed for the many popular stories and anecdotes, which are a feature of *Genesis Rabbah*. This suggests once
again that the popular sermons and expositions of the ancient
synagogues, in whatever form they were recorded,[26] were a
major source for the material in *Genesis Rabbah*.

In almost every respect, *Leviticus Rabbah*, which is cited
frequently in the following chapters, is a companion volume to
Genesis Rabbah. There is considerable evidence to suggest that
they emanate from the same era, from the same area and
possibly from the same circle of compilers. They share the same

24 As the *petiḥah* is essentially a feature of the homiletical *Midrash*, *Genesis Rabbah* is
technically a hybrid work, combining the characteristics of both the exegetical and
homiletical *midrash*.
25 On the function of the proem, see J. Heinemann, 'The Proem in the Aggadic
Midrashim', in *Studies in Aggadah and Folk-Lore Literature* (eds. J. Heinemann and D.
Noy) Jerusalem 1971, pp. 104ff.
26 That collections of aggadic material existed in talmudic times is suggested by
references in Palestinian sources to '*Aggadah* books', ספרא דאגדתא or חד ספר
דאגדה (*PT Shabbat* 16, 15c) and even ספר תילים אגדה, an aggadic work on
Psalms (*PT Ketubot* 12:3, 35a). We can only assume that such works, including
collections of *petiḥot*, were available to the compilers of our extant *Midrashim*, as well
as to their contemporaries, the early *payyetanim* of the Holy Land, like Yannai, to
whom we will refer subsequently, who made extensive use of midrashic material in
their compositions.

languages, predominantly Hebrew, with Aramaic being used in stories, parables and anecdotes taken from the life of the people. Both *midrashim* are rich in Latin and particularly Greek loan-words. The compilers have employed the same terminology and evidently had access to the same sources. There is a noteworthy correspondence between the two works with regard to the scholars whose statements are cited. The same *Tanna'im* and *Amora'im* either figure prominently in both works, or are not found at all. Both *Midrashim* have much material in common; in some cases the parallel passages are virtually identical.

The significant difference between these two works lies in their literary format. *Leviticus Rabbah* is possibly the earliest example of a major development in the format of the literary *Midrash* in the post-talmudic period. Unlike an exegetical *Midrash* like *Genesis Rabbah*, which comments on virtually every verse in a *seder*, *Leviticus Rabbah* is a homiletical *Midrash*. Each chapter consists of a highly developed homily based on the opening verse, or verses of the *seder*. Every homily opens with a proem, the majority of homilies having several proems, notably of the complex pattern. As with *Genesis Rabbah*, the great majority of the proemial verses have been taken from the Hagiographa. Although in their extant form the homilies of *Leviticus Rabbah* – and of its companion work, *Pesiqta d'Rav Kahana* – are literary entities, none the less, we can assume once again that much of the content is based on sermons and expositions which were originally delivered to live audiences. As the format of *Leviticus Rabbah* represents a departure from the existing format of the exegetical *Midrash*, it is probably a little younger than *Genesis Rabbah* and may be assigned to the sixth century at the latest.

A further, major homiletical *Midrash* of which we have made extensive use, is the *Tanḥuma*, or *Yelammedenu*.[27] This work which, we can assume, is Palestinian in origin and contains homilies relating to the whole of the Pentateuch, presents its own peculiar problems. It is extant in two editions, which represent two different textual recensions, (a) the Ordinary, or Standard edition, first printed at Constantinople; and (b) the Buber Edition, based primarily on MS Oxford Neubauer 154, together with four other manuscripts.

In the middle ages, however, the name *Tanḥuma* appears to be interchangeable with *Yelammedenu*, a name clearly derived from the distinctive feature of this *Midrash*, the halakhic exordium or introduction to its homilies, which usually opens with the stereotyped formula ילמדנו רבנו, 'let our master instruct us'. The compiler of the *Yalqut*, on the other hand, evidently regarded *Tanḥuma* and *Yelammedenu* as two separate works. Moreover, there are many quotations in medieval sources in the name of the *Yelammedenu*, which cannot be found in either version of the *Tanḥuma*. This strongly suggests that there was an independent *Midrash Yelammedenu* which is no longer extant, which is the assumption we have adopted in this study. None the less, the problem remains a complex one, which cannot be adequately discussed in this context. As to the dating of the *Midrash Tanḥuma/Yelammedenu*, the view originally expressed by Zunz, that it belongs to the first half of the ninth century, is still widely, but by no means universally accepted.[28]

Two further works which deserve special mention, as we will have frequent recourse to them in the following pages, are the *Yalqut* and *Midrash Ha-Gadol* (*MHG*).[29] These are not *midrashim* in the classical sense. They are comparatively late midrashic anthologies or, more accurately commentaries, the former to the whole of the Bible, the latter to the Pentateuch, whose compilers have drawn their material from older sources, some of which are no longer extant, like the lost *Midrash Yelammedenu* referred to earlier. Consequently, both contain material which is to be found in no other source. Their main value, however, is as a source of accurate readings. In this respect, *MHG* is of special significance. While the compiler of the *Yalqut*, who lived in Franco-Germany, used MSS which we may regard as being part of the European tradition, the compiler of *MHG* lived in Yemen and used MSS which were extra-European in provenance and background. Therefore, a reading which is supported by *Midrash Ha-Gadol*, is usually given additional weighting.

A word in conclusion regarding the presentation of the material which follows. This is essentially a text-based study, comprising a detailed analysis of the early rabbinic exegesis of the *Hebrew* Bible. While we have endeavoured to restrict the use of original Hebrew and Aramaic texts to a practical minimum, in order to do justice to the subject, there can be no economising on the material to be discussed. None the less, in order to avoid lengthy and cumbersome foot-notes, we have adopted a simple system of appendices to a number of chapters, which contain a detailed evaluation of specific texts and topics.

CHAPTER 2

Traditional motifs in early rabbinic exegesis 1: Job and the Generation of the Flood

THE SELECTION OF PROEMIAL AND PROOF-TEXTS IN THE AGGADIC *MIDRASHIM*

Although there is a corpus of scholarly literature devoted to the origin, structure, place and purpose of the proem in the aggadic *Midrashim*,[1] the problems presented by the actual selection of proemial verses have not been fully explored. As we observed above, the characteristic feature of the proem is the opening quotation – usually from the Hagiographa – which may have no apparent relevance for the lection of the day. Yet the preacher proceeds to relate this remote verse to some aspect of the *seder* – or *haphtarah* – often without explaining his choice of text, or justifying its application to his theme from the pericope.

Frequently, the association between the proemial and *Seder* verses is an obvious one, based upon an easily recognisable verbal link. In many cases, however, the choice of proemial verses appears entirely arbitrary, as will be seen from the examples cited subsequently, leaving the modern reader to wonder what prompted the preacher to select his verse, and how his audience recognised its relevance for the morning's lection.

According to the view advocated by a number of scholars, notably Bloch,[2] Bacher[3] and, more recently, J. Heinemann,[4]

---

[1] See J. Heinemann, 'The Proem in the Aggadic Midrashim – A Form-Critical Study', in *Scripta Hierosolymitana* (*Studies in Aggadah and Folk-Lore Literature* – eds. J. Heinemann and D. Noy), Jerusalem 1971, p. 100.

[2] 'Studien zur Aggadah', *MGWJ* vol. 34 (1885), pp. 258f.

[3] *Die Proömien der alten jüdischen Homilie*, Leipzig 1913, p. 7.

[4] 'The Proem', p. 101.

the early preacher enjoyed complete freedom, both in his choice of proemial verse, and in the manner of its interpretation. Although the congregation might recognise the preacher's purpose in citing his 'remote' verse, since they were familiar with the morning's lection, they would not know how he intended to establish the midrashic link between the proemial and *Seder* verses. In his ingenious exposition of his proemial text with reference to the morning's lection, the preacher manifested his art and skill. Moreover, in Heinemann's view, an unexpected, or unobvious proemial verse would frequently be selected, 'for the elements of surprise and tension – he asserts – are a prominent feature of the proem-form'.[5]

In complete contrast to this view, Mann developed the theory that the selection of proemial verses was determined exclusively by verbal links, not with the *sedarim* of the triennial cycle, however, but with their corresponding *haphtarot*.[6]

Neither of these approaches is completely satisfactory. The main weakness of Mann's thesis, as has been noted by several scholars, becomes apparent in his treatment of those homilies based on proemial verses which have no links whatsoever with the known *haphtarot* of the triennial cycle. In such cases, Mann simply conjectures appropriate alternative *haphtarot* which provide the necessary verbal links, thus creating an imaginative superstructure of prophetic readings, unsubstantiated by any external evidence.

Similarly, the more generally accepted view that the preacher relied primarily upon his expositional skills to establish the midrashic link between his proemial verse and the pericope cannot stand unchallenged. There is substantial evidence in our sources to show that the early preachers, when

[5] 'The Proem', pp. 101–03. Heinemann readily acknowledges that the selection of proemial verses was by no means random. He asserts that it was 'selected mainly because of some inner link or association with the theme of the pericope on which it throws new light'. However, in citing the example from the *Pesiqta d'Rav Kahana* of the proem based on Canticles 5:1, relating to the erection of the Tabernacle, Heinemann attached no significance to the well-established tradition that this book is a commentary on Israel's experiences in Egypt, at the Exodus and in the wilderness (see note 7).

[6] See *The Bible as Read and Preached in the Old Synagogue*, vol. i, Cincinnati 1940, pp. 12ff.

dealing with certain pentateuchal themes, resorted consistently
to the same specific sections of other biblical books for their
proemial and proof-texts. This would suggest that there were
exegetical traditions linking pentateuchal with prophetic, and
particularly hagiographic texts, which were acknowledged,
presumably, by both preachers and audiences alike. Consequently, many proemial verses which may astonish the
modern reader by their apparent irrelevance, did not necessarily surprise an ancient audience, who may have recognised
the appropriateness of the preacher's text in the light of an
established tradition linking the source of his quotation with
the theme of his homily.

The most obvious example of this type of exegetical tradition
is provided by the midrashic treatment of Canticles. As is well
known, this poetic work was generally acknowledged by both
Tanna'im and *Amora'im* to be an allegory on the early history of
the Israelite nation, and was widely interpreted as such in
talmudic-midrashic sources. As might be expected, we find
numerous verses from Canticles cited in proems relating to
various aspects of Israel's experiences in Egypt, at the Exodus,
and in the wilderness.[7]

While, in such cases, the audience may not have known how
the preacher intended to expound his chosen text, it is highly
probable that they at least recognised the relevance of his
opening quotation, because of the accepted interpretation of
the source from which it was taken. This important aspect of
aggadic exegesis, which is by no means limited to the traditional interpretation of Canticles, still requires an exhaustive

---

[7] If examples are necessary to illustrate this, then the following, incomplete list of
proemial verses taken from only one midrashic source, *Tanhuma* (ed. Buber) should
suffice:

  1:3 (2, p. 69)
  1:15 (2, p. 95)
  2:4 (4, p. 13)
  3:7 (4, p. 32)
  4:1 (2, p. 58)
  5:1 (2, p. 37)
  6:8–9 (2, p. 20)
  7:3 (2, p. 103)
  7:6 (2, p. 96)

evaluation which is beyond the scope of this present study. It is possible, however, to offer one or two substantial examples of exegetical traditions which were established already in tannaitic times, relating to a major work of the Hagiographa, the Book of Job.

From an analysis of the abundant exegetical material relating to Job preserved in talmudic-midrashic sources, it is clear that specific sections of this book were consistently associated with certain pentateuchal themes by both *Tanna'im* and *Amora'im*. Moreover, there is explicit evidence to suggest that the Book of Job as a whole, shared a unique relationship with the Pentateuch in early rabbinic tradition. According to a *baraita* preserved in both the Palestinian and Babylonian *Talmudim*, Moses actually wrote the Book of Job, as well the Torah:[8] 'Moses wrote his own book, the section dealing with Balaam and [the Book of] Job.'

A tradition of even greater antiquity assigns Job himself to the age of Moses. Of the numerous views regarding the dating of Job recorded in our sources, the oldest and most fully developed is that which assigns him to the earliest phase of Israel's history. Writing in the second century BCE, Aristeas refers to the tradition that Job is identical with Jobab, king of Edom, 'the fifth from Abraham', which would place Job in the same generation as Amram, Moses' father.[9] This tradition

---

8 See *BT Bava Batra* 15a, and *PT Sotah* 5:8 (20d). This tradition regarding the Mosaic authorship of Job is found also in Christian sources (see Ginzberg, *The Legends of the Jews*, Philadelphia 1909–55, vol. 5, p. 382, note 3) and may also account for the phenomenon regarding the fragment of the Book of Job from the Qumran Caves. This – like certain fragments of the Pentateuch found at Qumran – is written in the archaic Canaanite Script. Driver (*The Judaean Scrolls*, Oxford 1965, p. 414) suggests that this script may have been used for Job as it was deemed appropriate to patriarchal period, which is the historical setting suggested by the book. It is conceivable, however, that the Dead Sea Covenantors were familiar with the tradition regarding the Mosaic authorship of Job, and therefore, reserved for this book the same script as for the Pentateuch itself.

We may also note that in a *piyyut* for *Shevuot* from the Genizah, attributed to Qaliri, the poet refers to the *six* volumes of the Written Law given by God to Moses, possibly an allusion to the Pentateuch plus the Book of Job; See M. Zulay, **הלל ושמאי? אחים?**, *Melilah* vol. 5 (1955), p. 70; also N. Wieder, *The Judean Scrolls and Karaism*, London 1962, p. 232, note 1.

9 See Eusebius, *Praeparatio Evangelica* ix, 25 (ed. E. H. Gifford, vol. 1, pp. 540ff); also J. Freudenthal, *Hellenistiche Studien*, Breslau 1874–75, pp. 136ff; and Z. Frankl, 'Die

forms the basis of the Job legend in the pre-Christian Testament of Job, a work of considerable importance for the background of rabbinic *Aggadah*, which may have its origins early in the second century BCE.[10]

Early tannaitic sources also elaborate on this tradition. In the oldest chronological work of post-biblical times, *Seder Olam*, Job's life-span – like that of Jochebed, Moses' mother – is presented as coincidental with the 210 years of Israel's sojourn in Egypt.[11] According to the early *Tanna*, R. Ishmael, Job actually occupied a position of importance in Pharaoh's household.[12] This notion, which may have gained wide currency in talmudic times, coincides with the view of R. Ishmael's colleague, R. Aqiva, that Elihu b. Buzi, the most mysterious of Job's friends, is none other than the pagan prophet and archenemy of Israel, Balaam.[13] According to a late tannaitic source, both Job and Balaam were members of Pharaoh's council, who were consulted on the issue of the massacre of the Israelite children.[14]

Zusatze in der LXX zu Hiob', *MGWJ*, (1872), p. 313. This tradition may have gained wide currency outside the Holy Land, as it was incorporated into the Colophon to the LXX on Job.

10 The text of this significant apocryphal work has been published with an introduction and translation by K. Kohler in the *Kohut Memorial Volume*, Berlin 1897, pp. 264–338. See also M. R. James' edition of the *Testament*, published – with an introduction – on the basis of a Paris MS in *Apocrypha Anecdota*, Cambridge 1897, pp. 104–37, and the most recent edition, which takes account of the Slavonic evidence for the text, published S. P. Brock, in *Pseudepigrapha Veteris Testamenti Graece*, vol. 2, Leiden 1967. For an evaluation of the contents, character and dating of this work, see my article, 'Literary Motifs in the Testament of Job', *JJS*, vol. 21 (1970), pp. 1ff.

11 Chapter 3, ed. Ratner, pp. 13–14; also *Mekhilta d'R. Shimon b Yoḥai* to Exodus 12:40, ed E. Z. Melamed, p. 34; *PT Sotah* 5:8 (20c); *Genesis Rabbah* 57:4 (p. 615); also *BT Bava Batra* 15a.

12 See *PT Sotah* 5:8 (20c); also *Targum Pseudo-Jonathan* to Exodus 9:20:
    Job was one of Pharaoh's servants and one of the senior members of his retinue, as it is written, 'He that feared (הירא) the Lord among the servants of Pharaoh ... (Exodus 9:20)' and it is written concerning him, 'that man was whole-hearted, and upright, and one that feared (ירא) God, and shunned evil (Job 1:1)'.

13 See *PT Sotah* 5:8 (20d).

14 See *BT Sotah* 11a:
    R. Simai said: 'Three people were involved in that consultation, Balaam, Job and Jethro. Balaam, who advised [that the children should be killed], was slain. Job, who was silent, was condemned to suffering. Jethro, who fled, merited that his descendants should sit in the Hewn-stone Chamber [of the Temple as members of the Sanhedrin].'

These two early, cognate traditions were by no means
formulated in a vacuum. As we shall endeavour to prove, the
Mosaic authorship of Job, and the Exodus period as the *Sitz im
Leben* of its hero, is clearly presupposed by the interpretation of
the book as a whole during the talmudic period.

JOB AND THE GENERATION OF THE FLOOD

The following proem is preserved in *Genesis Rabbah* 31:2 (p.
278) in conjunction with Genesis 6:13:

בין שורותם יצהירו (lit.:'They make oil[15] between their [neigh-
bours'] rows [24:11]') – [this implies] that they were making minia-
ture olive-presses[16] (which could be carried secretly into their
neighbours' olive groves). יקבים דרכו ויצמאו [which means] 'even
though they tread the winepresses (*viz.* containing stolen grapes)
none the less, they suffer thirst (Job, *ibid.*)'. R. Aibu said, 'Why do
"they tread the winepresses, yet suffer thirst"? Because a curse blights
the efforts of a wicked man'. Moreover, because they were steeped in
robbery,[17] they were obliterated from the world, as it is said, 'And
God said to Noah: "[The end of all flesh has come before Me, for the
earth is filled with robbery on account of them; and behold, I will
destroy them together with the earth.] (6:13)".'[18]

The preacher's theme reflects the well-known tendency in both
rabbinic and non-rabbinic literature, to amplify the wicked
conduct of the Generation of the Flood in order to portray
them as archetypes of evil. His choice of proemial verse,
however, calls for some clarification, as Job 24:11 contains no
obvious link, verbal or thematic, with the Genesis account of
the Generation of the Flood. This, apparently, would tend to

In Amoraic sources, Job is actually assigned a crucial role in the Exodus itself. His
suffering at the hands of Satan, according to R. Ḥanina b. Hamma, was God's
means of diverting the attention of the Accuser while Israel secured their passage
across the Red Sea in safety (see *Exodus Rabbah* 20:7).

[15] Associating יצהירו here with יצהר. Alternatively, יצהירו was taken as יצעירו
from צער, to be small, hence the reference to small olive-presses.

[16] Reading, with Jastrow (s.v. בדידה) בדידות; see also the variant readings cited by
Theodor, *Genesis Rabbah* p. 278.

[17] The criminal conduct of the Antediluvians is a widely recurring theme in talmudic-
midrashic sources, as can be seen from the material we have cited in this chapter.
See also the additional sources cited in Appendix 1 below, pp. 173ff.

[18] On this usage of the term חמס, see Appendix 1, p. 174.

support Heinemann's thesis that the early preachers frequently selected an unobvious text in order to surprise their audiences, and so capture their attention.

Yet the application of a verse from Job to the Generation of the Flood may not have been regarded as either unusual or surprising to a congregation in the talmudic period. Already in tannaitic times, Judah the Patriarch assigned to Job the special role of the expositor of the Flood-story.[19] In keeping with this tradition, aggadic exegetes from the beginning of the second century CE, sought a scriptural basis for their legends and traditions relating to the Generation of the Flood, particularly from chapters 21 and 24, as can be seen from the following sources.

In order to illustrate the overbearing arrogance of the Generation of the Flood towards God, the early *Tanna*, R. Aqiva, cites a verse which figures prominently in aggadic sources relating to the Antediluvians, Job 21:15:[20]

It is stated לא ידון רוחי באדם לעולם (Genesis 6:3). [This implies that] God said, 'They have not considered themselves, that they are merely flesh and blood, but they have behaved presumptuously towards heaven!'– as it is said, 'They said to God: Depart from us, for we desire not any knowledge of Your ways.'

R. Aqiva's association of Job 21:15 with the very early tradition of Antediluvians' rejection of Divine Authority,[21] which is a major theme in rabbinic aggadah, may presuppose a more

---

19 See *Genesis Rabbah* 26:7 (p. 255): 'Had Job come into the world for the sole purpose of recording for us the details of the story of the Generation of the Flood, it would have sufficed him!' The early *Amora*, R. Joḥanan b. Nappaḥa extended this tradition to include also Job's three companions, Eliphaz, Bildad and Zophar who, he asserts, are the אנשי השם, the 'men of renown', referred to in Genesis 6:4, who recorded in detail the Antediluvians' deeds (see *Genesis Rabbah* 26:7). However, it is open to question whether R. Joḥanan's view is simply an extension of the earlier tradition formulated by Judah the Patriarch. R. Meir, who lived a generation earlier, applied verses from Eliphaz's speeches in chapters 4 and 22 to the Antediluvians, without indicating the appropriateness of his proof-texts (see further the material cited in Appendix 1, pp. 174f). It is possible, therefore, that R. Joḥanan's view reflects an older, more comprehensive exegetical tradition connecting the Generation of the Flood with sections of Job other than the speeches of its hero.

20 See *Avot d'Rabbi Natan*, Version A, chapter 32 (p. 93).

21 See I Enoch 8:2–3, also 5:6f; II Enoch 34:1–2 (recensions A and B). As to early rabbinic sources, we have included most of the relevant material in this chapter and in Appendix 1, pp. 174ff.

comprehensive exposition of a whole series of verses from chapter 21, which occurs widely in tannaitic sources. The detailed account of the well-being of the wicked contained in verses 9–13 was regarded by early rabbinic exegetes as a record of the considerable prosperity bestowed by God upon the Generation of the Flood, who responded with an arrogant denial of their Benefactor's authority:[22]

The Generation of the Flood behaved arrogantly only on account of the beneficence which God bestowed upon them in abundance! What is written concerning them? 'Their houses are safe without fear, neither is the rod of God upon them (v. 9).' It is written further, 'Their bull genders and does not fail, their cow calves and does not cast its calf (v. 10)' and it is written, 'They send forth their little ones like a flock, and their children dance (v. 11).' It is written further, 'They sing to the timbrel and the harp, and rejoice to the sound of the pipe (v. 12)' and it is written, 'They spend their days in prosperity, and peacefully they go down to the grave (v. 13).' This is what induced them to say to God, 'Depart from us, for we desire not the knowledge of Thy ways! What is the Almighty that we should serve Him, and what profit should we have if we pray to Him? (vv. 14–15)' 'We have no need of Him – they declared – save for a mere drop of rain. We have rivers and springs to supply our needs!' Whereupon God said, 'You provoke Me to anger through the very benefit which I have bestowed upon you in abundance, consequently I shall punish you thereby!'

R. Aqiva is also our earliest authority to employ a verse from Job 24, in his discourses on the Generation of the Flood. When this scholar expounded on the fate of the Antediluvians to a congregation in the Median city of Ginzak (= Gazaka) he

---

[22] This translation is based on the fuller text of this homily recorded in a *Baraita* in *BT Sanhedrin* 108a; see also *Midrash Tanna'im*, ed Hoffmann, p 36, and the parallels cited there.

Both the notion expressed in this passage, and the context in which it occurs, suggest that it has a polemical colouring, as has already been noted by Marmorstein ('The Background of the Aggada', *HUCA* vol. 4 (1929), pp. 158ff). In most of the sources which record this *Aggadah*, the Generation of the Flood is bracketed with the Tower-builders and the Sodomites, in order to demonstrate that these offenders brought catastrophe upon themselves, by provoking God with their wickedness. This was no doubt directed against Gnostic criticisms of God's justice in His treatment of these and other biblical personalities who incurred divine punishment. The preacher endeavours to deflect such criticisms, by emphasising God's beneficence towards His creatures, who repay Him with arrogance.

failed to evoke any sympathy from his audience for this wicked generation. Whereupon he applied to them 24:20:

ישכחהו רחם מתקו רמה עוד לא יזכר וגו׳ (lit.: 'The womb forgetteth him; the worm feedeth sweetly on him; he shall be no more remembered.'). ישכחהו רחם [means that] they forgot mercy towards their fellow-creatures, consequently, God forgot His mercy towards them. מתקו רמה [means] the worms fed sweetly on them ...[23]

Presumably, R. Aqiva was alluding here to another ancient tradition, recorded in earliest apocryphal sources, regarding the lawless and violent character of the Antediluvians.[24] This theme is developed more extensively in conjunction with the opening verses of chapter 24, in the following two passages. The first, recorded in *Midrash Tanḥuma* (ed. Buber 1, p. 54) commences with the tradition formulated by R. Judah the Patriarch, assigning to Job the role of expositor of the Flood-story. The second passage, preserved in a Genizah fragment of the lost *Midrash Yelammedenu*, is an amplification of the same *Seder* verse with which our original proem was connected, Genesis 6:13 and is devoted to the same theme, the insidious and unscrupulous methods employed by the Antediluvians in the perpetration of their crimes.[25] Despite the obvious parallels

---

[23] See *Genesis Rabbah* 33:5 (p. 310). R. Aqiva's rendering of this verse presumably gained wide currency in talmudic times, as it is reflected in the *Targum* to Job 24:20.

[24] See the sources quoted at the beginning of note 21; also *Jubilees* 7:20ff, and particularly *Sybilla* i, 177–201.

[25] As A. Büchler has suggested, this motif, which also forms the basis of R. Ḥanina's homily cited in Appendix 1 (p. 173) may reflect the conditions prevailing in the Galilee in talmudic times, which the rabbinic scholars were obliged to combat (see *The Political and Social Leaders of the Jewish Community of Sepphoris in the Second and Third Centuries*, London 1909, pp. 43ff). Prominent among these social evils, Büchler suggests (*Political and Social Leaders*, pp. 42–3, and note 2) was the abuse of the poorer members of the community by their wealthier co-religionists, particularly in money matters. This may be reflected not only in imagery employed at the conclusion of Passage B, but also in the following exposition of Job 35:9, 'By reason of the multitude of oppressions they cry out; they cry for help by reason of the arm of the mighty', recorded in *Genesis Rabbah* 31:4 (p. 297). According to an anonymous preacher, it was the interclass strife which ultimately sealed the fate of the Antediluvians. The imagery in this passage is reminiscent of the terminology employed by R. Pinḥas b. Yair, who complains of the eclipse of scholars and free men through the emergence of 'violent and insolent men' (see *BT Sotah* 49a):
מרב עשקים יזעיקו, 'Amid their contentiousness (= מריב) the oppressed cry out [audaciously]' – this refers to the oppressed; 'while they cry out on account of

between them, both passages exhibit a number of distinctive features, and appear to be independent adaptations of a traditional exposition of a biblical text, with which both authors were familiar:

| *A* | *B* |

You find that the deeds of the Generation of the Flood are expounded, while those of the Generation of the Separation of the Tongues (= the Tower-builders) are not. Job has expounded the deeds of the Generation of the Flood, as it is said, 'They remove land-marks, they seize a flock and feed it. They drive away the ass of the orphan, they take the widow's ox in pledge (24:2–3).' What does 'They remove land-marks' imply? [It implies that] they were entering into one another's boundaries [illicitly]. 'They seize a flock and feed it' [indicates] that they were stealing each other's sheep. 'They drive away the ass of the orphan' – when they would see an ass in the possession of an orphan, they would deprive him of it forthwith. 'They take the widow's ox in pledge' – if a widow's husband died and left her an ox, and she would go out to feed it, they would immediately take it from her! 'They lie all night naked without clothing (v. 7)' – when

'The Lord tries the righteous (Psalm 11:5)' – this alludes to Noah, whom the Lord examined and found to be righteous, as it is said, 'Noah was a righteous man, he was perfect (Genesis 6:9).' 'But His soul hates the wicked man and the lover of robbery (Psalms *ibid.*)' – this alludes to the Generation of the Flood, all of whom were stealing from each other and were addicted to robbery, as it is said, 'And God said to Noah: "The end of all flesh has come before Me, for the earth is filled with robbery on account of them (Genesis 6:13)."'' If one of them possessed a field and his friend had the adjacent field, he would steal from the boundary little by little, until he had appropriated the entire field, as it is said, 'They remove land-marks (v. 2).' Similarly if a man possessed sheep, his friend would go and take them one by one, until he had appropriated the entire flock, as it is said, 'They seize a flock and feed it (*ibid.*).' Similarly, if a poor orphan

their might quarrelling (= רבים) [with the poor]' – this refers to the oppressors. Thus both the oppressed and the oppressors were quarrelling with each other, the former with the latter on account of their violence in money matters, and the latter with the former on account of their violence in speech, until their fate was sealed!

people saw that they were doing such things to them, they stripped of their garments and went about naked! acquired an ass's foal, as soon as he had reared it, one of them would come and drive it away from him, as it is said, 'They drive away the ass of the orphan (v. 3).' Moreover, if a widow acquired a calf and reared it, as soon as it had grown into an ox, one of them would come and take it away from her, as it is said, 'They take the widow's ox in pledge (*ibid.*).' Similarly, if a poor man entered into litigation, they would turn the verdict against him, as it is said, 'They divert the poor from the path of justice (v. 4).'

The concluding reference in passage A to the nudity of the Generation of the Flood, appears to be an adaptation of a much older tradition relating to the Antediluvians' immoral practices. One of the principal offences of the Generation of the Flood, according to R. Meir and R. Judah the Patriarch, was the public display of their nudity,[26] alluding, no doubt, to the practices of the Graeco-Roman world. In the following passage, this tradition, which may have its origins in pre-Christian times,[27] is associated appropriately with Job 24:7:[28]

The Generation of the Flood were imbued with a spirit of arrogance, on account of which, they were uprooted from the world. As it is said, 'They said to God: "Depart from us etc. . . . (Job 24:14)".' What did they do? They would strip of their clothes leaving them on the ground and walk about naked in the market-place, as it is said, 'They went

[26] See particularly *Targum Pseudo-Jonathan* to Genesis 6:2 (from its inclusion in a *Targum*, we may presume that this tradition presumably gained wide currency in talmudic times); see also the lurid descriptions of the practices of the Generations of Kain, attributed to R. Meir and R. Judah the Patriarch in *Pirqei d'Rabbi Eliezer* 22. In his translation of this text (London 1916, p. 158, note 7), G. Friedlander suggests that the allusion here may be to an obscure Christian sect. However, it is more plausible to assume that the comments of these two *Tanna'im* presuppose the practices of the Graeco-Roman world.

[27] See Jubilees 7:20, where Noah is depicted as admonishing his children to avoid the practice of uncovering the flesh. Ginzberg (*Legends*, vol. 5, p. 193, note 67) suggests that this phrase may only be an inaccurate translation of an original Hebrew גלוי עריות (*viz.* unchastity). However, in the light of the author's strong views on the subject of uncovering oneself after the fashion of the gentiles, the prohibition of which, he regards as being inscribed on the 'heavenly tablets' (*viz.* of the highest authority; see 3:30), we may presume that the reference to uncovering the flesh in 7:20 may be taken in its literal sense.

[28] See *Eliyahu Rabbah* 31 (ed. Friedmann 29, p. 158, and the parallels cited there).

about naked without any garb (v. 7).' Therefore, God made them
float like skin-bottles upon the face of the waters, as it is said, 'The
decree was that [their destruction should be] upon the face of the
waters (v. 18)', and it is said, 'Be you afraid of the sword, for wrath
brings the punishment of the sword, that you may know שדון (*ibid.*,
19:29)' – do not read שדון, but שדין, [meaning] that there is justice
above!

The unknown author in this passage has simply cited Job
24:18 as a proof-text in connection with the destruction of the
Generation of the Flood, without indicating how the verse was
to be interpreted in this context. However, a full exposition of
24:18 has been preserved in older rabbinic sources, in conjunction with a further motif of great antiquity, the Antediluvians'
licentiousness and fornication,[29] which is highly developed in
aggadic literature.[30] In the following proem, preserved in
Genesis Rabbah 30:2 (pp. 270f) in connection with Genesis 6:9,
an anonymous preacher has interpreted 24:18 to suggest that
the death and eternal ignominy of the Generation of Flood was
the direct result of their refusal to engage in normal sexual
practices:

'These are the generations of Noah (6:9)': It is written, קל הוא על
פני המים תקלל חלקתם בארץ לא יפנה דרך כרמים (lit.: "He is
swift upon the face of the waters; their portion is cursed in the
earth; he turneth not by the way of the vineyards."). קל הוא על
פני המם [means] that it was decreed that they should perish through

---

[29] See the sources cited in note 21; also Jubilees 7:20ff; and *Sybilla* i, 204ff.

[30] Apart from the sources we have cited in this chapter, see also the statements of
R. Ḥiyya, R. Simai, R. Jose and Bar Kappara in *Leviticus Rabbah* 23:9 (pp. 538ff);
also *Genesis Rabbah* 26:5 (pp. 248–9, and the parallels cited there). In all probability,
the graphic list of sexual offences attributed to the Generation of the Flood in
rabbinic *Aggadah*, homosexuality, animalism, the practice of *ius primae noctis*, reflects
the prevailing mores of the pagan world during the talmudic period. These
practices, so abhorrent to the rabbis, who constantly feared for the moral welfare of
their own flock, have left an indelible imprint on both their halakhic and aggadic
utterances. See *Sifra* on Leviticus 18:3 (p. 85b) for the reference to the long-standing
custom of both Egypt and Palestine for homosexual and lesbian marriages, polyan-
dry and incest; and *Tosephta Avodah Zarah* 3:2 (p. 463) which clearly indicates the
rabbis' worst fears regarding the depravity of the pagan population of Palestine;
also *BT Sanhedrin* 19a, the enactment of R. Jose b. Ḥalaphta on his arrival in
Sepphoris, that a boy should not walk behind his mother in the street (see Rashi
who, perhaps, somewhat innocently suggests that this was to protect the mother
from any abuse which results from the kidnapping of the child).

water.[31] תקלל חלקתם בארץ, [means] their portion is to be for a curse on earth, [hence the formula,] 'May He who exacted punishment from the Generation of the Flood etc. . . .'[32] Why was this so? Because, לא יפנה דרך כרמים, [which means] that it was not their intention 'to plant vineyards' (*viz.* to procreate).[33] Noah's intention, however, was to propagate and to multiply in the world, and to produce progeny, as it is said, 'These are the generations of Noah . . .'

The midrashic interpretation of 24:18 on which this proem is based, is recorded in *PT Yevamot* 6:5 (7c) in the name of the late *Amora*, R. Judah b. R. Simon.[34] It is interesting to note, therefore, that this same scholar has also interpreted 24:21 with

---

[31] קל has been equated with גזירה, 'a decree', on the basis of Daniel 4:28, וקל מן שמיא נפל (see MS Paris and the MS commentary on *Genesis Rabbah* quoted by Theodor, where this proof-text is actually incorporated into the text of the *Midrash*).

[32] For the full text of this formula, see *Mishnah Bava Meziah* 4:2: מי שפרע מאנשי דור המבול ומדור הפלגה הוא עתיד להפרע ממי שאינו עומד בדיבורו. 'May He who exacted punishment from the Generation of the Flood and from the Generation of the Separation [of the Tongues], ultimately exact punishment from one who does not abide by his word!'

In *BT Sanhedrin* 108a–b, 24:18 forms the basis of a homily by R. Jose of Caeserea, according to whom Methuselah (and not Noah, as found in printed editions; see Rabbinowicz, *Diqduqei Sopherim*, *Sanhedrin*; also *Midrash Ha-Gadol* to Genesis 6:13, pp. 155–6) tried vainly to induce the Antediluvians to repent of their evil ways, warning them of the advent of the flood. However, when they heard that this event would be delayed until the birth of a favoured one, they resolved to refrain from cohabiting with their wives.

[33] None of the sources which cite this phrase to indicate the Antediluvians' unwillingness to propagate actually states how this phrase was made to yield such a meaning. We may note initially that the use of the verb נטע, to plant, in the sense of 'to procure young', has its parallels in rabbinic literature. See, for example, *PT Yevamot* 1:1 (2b): 'He planted (נטע) five saplings (i.e. he fathered five children).' This alone, however, does not shed any light on the exposition of Job 24:18. I reproduce, therefore, the explanation I received from my revered teacher, Professor Naftali Wieder, many years ago. He suggested that in all the above sources, the expression כרם has been invested with the meaning of 'a woman', an imagery which presumably gained wide currency in talmudic times, in view of the rendering of Numbers 20:17, לא נעבר בשדה ובכרם, by both *Targum Pseudo-Jonathan* and the fragmentary *Targum*, 'We shall not set upon the *virgins* . . . nor shall we violate the *married women*!' (see also *Targum Pseudo-Jonathan* to Numbers 21:22). We may add that in keeping with this agricultural imagery, the expression גן has also been invested with the meaning of 'a woman', אין גן אלא אשה (see *Pirqei d'Rabbi Eliezer* chapter 21). As to the term דרך, this has been taken as a euphemistic synonym for the expression ביאה, 'sexual intercourse', as is explicitly stated in *BT Qiddushin* 2b, ביאה איקרי דרך, 'Intercourse is termed דרך'. Thus the phrase לא יפנה דרך כרמים, was presumably taken to mean, 'They did not turn to intercourse with women.'

[34] שלא היתה ביעלתם לשום בנים, 'Their sexual act was not for the purpose of procreation!'

reference to the Antediluvians' sexual improprieties, namely their abuse of the legal provision for polygamy purely for sexual gratification:[35]

'And Lemech took for himself two wives, the name of the one was Adah, and the name of the other was Zillah (Genesis 4:19).' R. Azariah said in the name of R. Judah b. R. Simon: 'This is what the generation of the Flood used to do. Each one of them would take for himself two wives, one for the purpose of procreation, the other purely for intercourse. The one reserved for procreation would sit like a widow in her husband's life-time,[36] while he would give a root-drink to the one reserved for intercourse to render her sterile and she would sit beside him bedecked like a harlot! – as it is written, "He tendeth to the barren women that she should not bear,[37] and doeth not good to the widow (Job 24:21)." Moreover, you may know that this was so, for the choicest[38] among them was Lemech, yet he took two wives, "the name of the one was Adah" – implying that she became pregnant by him[39] – "and the name of the other was Zillah" – which implies that she used to sit in his shadow.'[40]

---

[35] See *Genesis Rabbah* 23:2 (pp. 222–3).

[36] *Viz.* בחיי בעלה. Although this reading is most appropriate, it is not found in any of the MSS, the majority of which read: בחייה, 'during her own lifetime' (MSS Oxford 1 and 2 read בזויה, so Rashi on Genesis 4:19). Our reading, however, occurs in the *Arukh* and *Mayan Gannim* to Job verse 24 (ed. Buber, p. 79), and is substantiated further by the extra-European source, *Midrash Ha-Gadol* to Genesis 4:19, pp. 125–6.

[37] Presumably, R. Judah has taken לא תלד as a final, rather than a relative, clause.

[38] Or, 'the strongest', see Lieberman's comments on the expression ברור and cognate forms in talmudic-midrashic sources (*Greek in Jewish Palestine*, New York 1942, p. 51, note 122); also Zulay's observations on the meaning of ברור in the writings of the early *payyetan*, Yannai ('*Iyyunei Lashon be-Phiyyutei Yannai*', in *Studies of the Research Institute for Hebrew Poetry in Jerusalem*, vol. 6 (1945), pp. 178–9). The reading ברור is supported by both MSS Oxford, *Yalkut* and early printed editions. MS Stuttgart reads המובחר, and MS Munich, המוטב. Both these readings are probably explanatory glosses for the more unusual הברור.

[39] Connecting עדה with the Aramaic עדי, 'to carry', hence 'to become pregnant'.

[40] Connecting צלה with צל (see Rashi on Genesis 4:19). Once again, the rabbinic homily may presuppose a practice that may have been in vogue in talmudic times. This is indicated by the advice given by Judah the Patriarch to his son not to take a second wife, lest it be rumoured that 'the one was his wife, the second his harlot!' (see *BT Ketubot* 62b). If such polygamous unions did exist, they were probably beyond the financial scope of the poorer classes, and were more likely the prerogative of the wealthier elements of the community. See S. W. Baron, *A Social and Religious History of the Jews*, vol. 2, pp. 223ff; L. M. Epstein, *Marriage Laws in the Bible and the Talmud*, Cambridge (Mass.) 1942, p. 17; also S. Lowy, 'The Extent of Jewish Polygamy in Talmudic Times', *JJS* vol. 9, pp. 115ff.

One further tradition of pre-Christian origin was linked with a verse from Job 24, the Antediluvians' practice of witchcraft, which already figures in the list of the cardinal offences of the Generation of the Flood, recorded by the author of I Enoch.[41] The *Amora*, R. Eleazar b. Pedath, found an allusion to these malevolent practices in verse 13:[42]

R. Eleazar[43] said: 'They used to bring down the sun and the moon and practise witchcraft with them, as it is said, המה היו במורדי אור (lit.: "These are of them that rebel against the light"). However, do not read, במורדי אור, but, במוּרידי אור (*viz.* "who bring down the luminaries").'

One further, recurring theme in talmudic-midrashic sources which has been associated almost exclusively with two verses from Job, 6:17 and 22:20, is the punishment of the Generation of the Flood by fire. Although this motif is a comparatively late one, without any basis in the biblical narrative,[44] and occurring only in amoraic sources, it is none the less well developed, occurring in a variety of aggadic settings. As we have seen from the material cited earlier, the rabbis ascribed three major crimes to the Antediluvians, the three 'cardinal sins' in Jewish tradition, blasphemy – or the rejection of divine authority – violence and immorality.[45] It is interesting to note, therefore, that a fiery doom is prescribed in our sources for each one of these major offences.

---

[41] 8:2–3.
[42] See *Midrash Ha-Gadol* to *Genesis* 6:5 (ed. Margulies, p. 141); *Tanhuma* (Old Version) *Bereishit*, 12; the fragment of the lost *Midrash Yelammedenu* published by Wertheimer (*Batei Midrashot*, vol. 1, p. 148); also *Mayyan Gannim* to Job 24:13 (ed. Buber, p. 77).
[43] See the variant readings cited by Margulies in *Midrash Ha-Gadol*.
[44] However, see below, Appendix 1, pp. 177f.
[45] These occur already in Jubilees 7:21 as the major cause for the onset of the Deluge. The actual term used in this source is 'uncleanliness', *viz.* טומאה, which Ginzberg identifies as טומאת עבודה זרה, 'defilement through idolatry', a notion which occurs several times in biblical sources (see *Legends*, vol. 5, p. 173, note 17; also Ezekiel 20:7 and 18). Similarly, the author of ii Enoch (34:1–2, Recension B) depicts the world as quaking with the 'injustice, wrongs (= violence) and fornication and idolatry' of the Antediluvians. In rabbinic sources, the *Amora*, R. Levi found an allusion to the idolatry, immorality and bloodshed which filled the earth at the time of its destruction, in the single expression חמס (Genesis 6:11; see *Genesis Rabbah* 31:6, p 280; also Ginzberg, *Legends*, vol. 5, p. 173, note 17, for the variant traditions in rabbinic sources).

The following is an excerpt of a lengthy homily by R. Levi, elaborating upon the implications of Leviticus 6:2, הִיא הָעֹלָה עַל מוֹקְדָה, which he evidently rendered as 'who so goeth up – *viz.* behaves arrogantly – is set upon the conflagration'. To illustrate this notion that arrogant blasphemy incurs the punishment of fire, he adduces a number of biblical examples, commencing with the Generation of the Flood:[46]

R. Levi said: 'The Generation of the Flood, because they behaved arrogantly and said, "What is the Almighty that we should serve Him? And what profit should we have if we pray unto Him? (Job 21:15)", were punished by fire, as it is said, "What time they are incinerated it is forever[47] (*ibid.* 6:17)".'

According to an anonymous teacher, whose statement is preserved in an extract of the lost *Yelammedenu*,[48] the Antediluvians' violent acts of robbery led to their destruction by fire, as indicated in Job 22:20: 'The Generation of the Flood who were robbers (חוֹמְסִים) were punished by fire, as it is written, "Surely their substance is cut off, and their abundance the fire hath consumed".'

Of special interest is the following excerpt, where the tradition of the Antediluvians' punishment by fire is linked once again with Job 6:17. Although it is post-tannaitic – being essentially an aggadic exposition of *Mishnah Eduyot* 2:10 – it echoes a notion which has its origins in high antiquity. As a result of their unnatural practices and vices, the Antediluvians were likewise subjected to an unnatural punishment, involving the opposing elements of fire and snow:[49]

---

[46] See *Leviticus Rabbah* 7:6 (p. 161); also *Tanhuma*, ed. Buber, 3, p. 13 (Old Version, Ẓav 2, where both 6:17 and 22:20 are cited); *Yalqut Samuel* 161; and *Midrash Tehillim* to Psalm 11:6 (p. 100).

[47] Lit.: 'What time they wax warm, they vanish'. However, the midrashic rendering of clause A is indicated by the following comment found in printed editions: בְּעֵת יְזֹרְבוּ עֻצְמָתוּ – R. Joshua b. Levi said: 'This [phrase] implies that their incineration was to be forever. נִצְמָתוּ [having the same meaning] as לִצְמִיתֻת לַקֹנֶה ["and the house ...] shall belong for ever to him who bought it"' (Leviticus 25:30; see both *Targumim* to this verse, which render לִצְמִיתֻת as לַחֲלוּטִין).

[48] See *Yalqut Isaiah* 508.

[49] See *Tanhuma*, ed. Buber, 1, p. 23, and the parallels cited by Buber.

For what reason did [the author of the *Mishnah*] compare the punishment of the wicked in Gehinnom to the punishment of the Generation of the Flood? For just as the punishment of the former is by means of fire and snow,[50] so the punishment of the latter was by means of fire and snow. Whence do we know that they were punished by means of fire? Because it is said, 'Through His fire they were destroyed out of their place. (Job 6:17).' Whence do we know that they were punished by means of snow? Because it is said, 'And the water was upon the face of the earth (Genesis 7:12)'.[51] Why was this so? Because according to the measure of a man's own conduct, is punishment meted out to him![52] See what is written concerning them (Genesis 6:2): 'And the sons of the mighty saw the daughters of men that they were goodly' – this refers to the virgins[53] – 'and they took wives' – this refers to married women[54] – 'from wherever they chose' – which implies that they consorted even with males and beasts.

[50] See *Tanhuma* (Old Version) 12 (end). Our passage is preceded in ed. Buber by a graphic description of the suffering to which the wicked are subjected in fire and snow (see further *Pesiqta d'Rav Kahana*, ed. Friedmann, p. 97b, also the parallels cited by Mandelbaum in his edition, p. 165).
    The notion that fire and snow are reserved for those who indulge in unnatural vices, has a very early background. Enoch is shown the place of torment in the Third Heaven, where he sees fire, frost and snow, and is informed that this place is reserved particularly for those 'who dishonour God and sin against nature, which is child corruption after the Sodomite fashion' (II Enoch 10:1–6; see also the Testament of Levi 3:2). It is possible that this notion of the conflicting elements as a punishment of the wicked, was inspired by the third plague brought on the Egyptians, hail mingled with fire (see Exodus 9:24).
[51] Presumably this is based upon the phrase עַל הָאָרֶץ, *viz.* the water remained *upon* the earth, in the form of snow.
[52] The notion that the Antediluvians' punishment was related to their degenerate conduct reflects a tendency which occurs already in earliest rabbinic sources. R. Johanan b. Zaccai related the duration of the flood to the Antediluvians' adulterous behaviour (see *Genesis Rabbah* 32:5, p. 292). In the following generation, both R. Eliezer b. Hyrkanos and R. Joshuah b. Hananiah declared that God changed the cosmic order to bring about the deluge, because the Generation of the Flood perverted their actions (*BT Rosh Ha-Shanah* 11b-12a). In a *baraita* of the School of R. Ishmael, the waters of the flood are likened to the seminal fluid with which the Generation of the Flood sinned (see note 66). In a similar vein, the *Amora*, R. Levi declared that just as the Antediluvians employed their seminal ducts degenerately, so God changed the natural order in bringing about the flood (*Genesis Rabbah* 32:7, p. 294). Finally, according to the R. Jose b. Durmaskith, the floodwaters issued from the upper and the lower regions, because the Antediluvians sinned with their upper and their nether 'eyes' (see *Sifrei Deuteronomy* 43, p. 93, and the parallels cited there).
[53] See *Genesis Rabbah* 26:5, p. 248, on the basis of which the text here is emended.
[54] Taking אשה in this context in the more restricted sense of אשת איש.

In one or two sources, the element of fire appears not as an independent punishment relating to specific crimes, but merely as a means of reinforcing the effects of the deluge in order to secure the total destruction of the Generation of the Flood. Echoing the early tradition that the Antediluvians were a race of giants,[55] R. Berechiah observed that, on account of their size, they would not have succumbed to the flood waters alone. Therefore God brought down upon them a celestial fire in order to reduce them, as indicated by Job in 22:20:[56]

R. Berechiah said: 'The Antediluvians were exceedingly strong and of great stature. Consequently, had God not punished them from above, then the waters alone would not have prevailed against them! Thus Job said, אם לא נכחד קימנו ויתרם אכלה אש. What does this imply? When God saw that they did not perish in the watery depths from below, He brought down upon them celestial fire and burned them! Thus it is said, "If they were not destroyed [by the waters] because of their height,[57] then fire consumed what remained of them (*viz.* above the waters)."'[58]

In connection with this same verse from Job, R. Eleazar b. Pedath proposed that the employment of fire was intended to dispel any suggestion that God destroyed the Generation of the Flood simply to gain possession of their vast wealth:[59]

R. Eleazar said: 'It is written, אם לא נכחד קימנו, "Surely their wealth[60] is destroyed" [This implies that] God began by destroying their wealth so that they should not say, "He has need of our money!"'[61]

---

[55] See Ginzberg, *Legends*, vol. 5, p. 172, note 13.
[56] See *Tanhuma*, ed. Buber, 1, p. 36.
[57] Associating קימנו with קומה, 'height'.
[58] See further *Pirqei d'Rabbi Eliezer* chapter 22 (end) where the Antediluvians are depicted as boasting that on account of their great height, the waters of the flood would only reach their necks. Consequently, God destroyed them with boiling water. See also R. Johanan's exposition of Job 6:17 quoted on p. 39.
[59] See *Genesis Rabbah* 28:7, p. 266.
[60] For the basis of R. Eleazar's rendering of קימנו as wealth, compare his exposition of the expression יקום (Deuteronomy 11:6) in *BT Pesahim* 119a: 'This refers to a man's wealth which gives him standing (lit.: which stands him upon his feet)!'
[61] As R. Eleazer was active in the third century, it is highly probable that his comment here was directed against the notion current in Marcionite circles at that time, that the *Demiurgos* is desirous of worldly possessions (see *Clementine Homilies* 2, 48f; also Marmorstein, 'The Background to the Aggadah', *HUCA* vol. 6 (1929), p. 173f).

The notion of the Antediluvians' punishment by fire was extended to related forms of punishment, once again in conjunction with verses from Job. Thus R. Johnanan b. Nappaḥa declared on the basis of Job 6:17, that the Generation of the Flood were scalded to death:[62]

בחמו נדעכו ממקומם: What does בחמו mean? [It means] 'with hot water'.[63] R. Johanan said: 'Every drop of water which God brought down upon the [Antediluvians], He first heated in Gehinnom, and then brought it down upon them, as it is said, "Through His hot water they were annihilated out of their place."'[64]

In Babylonian sources, R. Ḥisda linked this tradition with the sexual crimes of the Antediluvians, implying that this mode of punishment was symbolic of the hot, seminal fluid with which they perpetrated their degenerate acts.[65] This notion is presupposed in a tannaitic source, a *baraita* of the School of R. Ishmael, where, on the basis of Job 12:5, the waters of the flood are described as 'harsh (i.e. hot and thick) like seminal fluid!'[66]

This motif was developed further by the *Amora*, R. Idi who,

---

[62] See *PT Sanhedrin* 10:3 (29b); *Leviticus Rabbah* 7:6 (p. 161); also *Genesis Rabbah* 28:9 (p. 267).

[63] Taking בחמו as בחמימיו, 'his hot waters'; see *BT Shabbat* 55a; *PT Avodah Zarah* 4:12 (44b); *Targum* on Job 6:17; also *Pirqei d'Rabbi Eliezer* chapter 22, and Luria's comment on the text.

[64] It is worthy of note that R. Johanan regarded חמי טבריה, 'the hot springs of Tiberias' – where he resided – as a remnant of the 'fountains of the mighty deep' referred to in Genesis 8:2 (see *BT Sanhedrin* 108a).

[65] See *BT Rosh Ha-Shanah* 12a:
By means of hot water (רותחין) they behaved corruptly and by means of hot water they were punished! By means of hot water they behaved corruptly – through sexual misconduct – and by means of hot water they were punished, for it is written here (Genesis 8:1), 'and the waters *cooled down* (וישכו – lit.: abated)' and it is written there (Esther 7:10), 'and the burning anger of the king *cooled down* (וחמת המלך שככה)'.
The wording of R. Ḥisda's statement here, is supported by MSS Munich and Florence to *BT Sanhedrin* 108a, *Yalqut Job* 910 and is confirmed by our extra-European source, *Midrash Ha-Gadol* to Genesis 8:1 (p. 175).

[66] See *BT Sanhedrin* 108b, and Rashi's comment on the text. Presumably רגל in the proof text, was taken as euphemism for the male membrum. Thus נכון למועדי רגל, might be rendered midrashically as 'prepared for those who err with the membrum'. Although in printed editions this comment is recorded anonymously, the reading תנא דבי ר' ישמעאל is to be found in MS Florence, *Yalqut Job* and *Midrash Ha-Gadol* to Genesis 8:1 (p. 175).

on the basis of Job 6:18, described how the Antediluvians' sexual abuses resulted in abnormal changes in their bodily functions:[67]

> R. Huna said in the name of R. Idi: 'The fate of the Generation of the Flood was not sealed until they wrote marriage contracts[68] to males and beasts! Consequently, flushes of heat came upon them like women, as it said, ילפתו ארחות דרכם (lit.: "the paths of their way do wind") – the expression ילפתו connotes a woman, as it said, ויחרד האיש וילפת והנה אשה (lit.: "The man trembled and turned himself, and behold a woman ... [Ruth 3:8]"). Similarly, ארחות connotes a woman, as it is said, אורח כנשים (lit.: "after the manner of women [Genesis 18:11]"); also דרכם connotes a woman, as it is said, כי דרך נשים לי (lit.: "for the manner of women is upon me [*ibid.*, 31:35]").'[69]

From the material we have cited thus far, which is by no means exhaustive, we see that rabbinic *Midrash* represents a climactic, rather than an initial phase in the ancient process of amplifying biblical narratives. The early rabbinic exegetes, however, did not simply develop or reformulate older traditions, they also authenticated them by providing them with a scriptural basis, though not necessarily in their original context. Thus, ancient legends relating to the story of the Flood were rooted in an extra-pentateuchal source, the Book of Job.

Moreover, this process must have been widely acknowledged. For the noteworthy feature of all the expositions cited in this chapter, both tannaitic and amoraic, is the total absence of any explanatory comment to justify the application of the verses quoted from to the Generation of the Flood. Evidently, the early aggadists expected their listeners to recognise the relevance of their quotations, relying upon an established and

---

[67] See *Tanhuma*, ed. Buber 1, p. 24; also the *Yelammedenu* fragment published by Ginzberg in *Ginzei Schechter*, vol. 1, p. 37; see further *Genesis Rabbah* 26:5 (p. 248) and *Leviticus Rabbah* 23:9 (p. 539).

[68] Reading גמיסיות = *gamos* = *gamikos*, so Theodor, *Genesis Rabbah* 26:5 (p. 248) and Margulies, *Leviticus Rabbah* 23:9 (p. 539).

[69] The exposition of the proof-text here is a good illustration of that most extrinsic form of midrashic interpretation discussed earlier in chapter 1, climatic exegesis (see pp. 4f). Since all three terms, דרכם, ארחות and ילפתו occur in the context, or climate of אשה, they are invested with this meaning, and taken as such in the context of Job 6:18.

well-known exegetical tradition. This assumption is supported by the extant *Targum* to Job which, in its original form, may have been produced in Roman Palestine.[70] Aggadic material preserved in such early *Targumim* is generally regarded as having gained wide currency in the talmudic period. It is significant, therefore, that the *Targum* to chapter 24 not only contains several recognisable allusions to the Antediluvians' offences and punishment,[71] but the translator has actually incorporated, into his rendering of verse 2, the operative phrase דרא דטובענא,[72] thus referring the passage as a whole to the Generation of the Flood.

Returning now to the homily with which we opened our discussions, where the anonymous preacher linked his description of the Antediluvians' deceitful practices with 24:11, we can assume that he relied upon his audience to recognise the relevance of his proemial verse for his chosen theme, because of a well-known and widely deployed tradition linking Job's utterances with the Generation of the Flood. As to the basis for this tradition, we can assume initially that Job's discourses on the conduct and conditions of the wicked contained in chapters 21 and 24, appealed to the early aggadists as a suitable scriptural source for amplifying the terse generalisations regarding the Antediluvians' corruption in Genesis.

However, we would suggest that the main factor which

---

[70] As is suggested by both Bacher ('Das Targum zu Hiob', *MGWJ* (1871), pp. 208ff) and Churgin (*Targum Ketuvim*, New York 1945, pp. 87ff). However, Komlosh and Weiss do not regard it as possible to pinpoint the date of the *Targum*'s composition, or assign it to a particular period (see Y. Komlosh, *The Bible in the Light of the Aramaic Translations* (Hebrew), Tel-Aviv 1973, pp. 76f; and R. Weiss, *The Aramaic Targum to Job* (Hebrew), Tel-Aviv 1979, pp. 70ff).

[71] See the *Targum*'s rendering to verse 20, 'The cruel ones who forget to love the poor are sweet feeding to the worm . . .'; and compare R. Aqiva's interpretation of this verse cited earlier, p. 42; also the rendering of verse 13, 'They were among those who rebelled against the *Torah*'. Similarly, the *Targum* to verse 24 in the *Antwerp Polyglot* (Biblia Regia 1569–72) adds the following aggadic amplification, which clearly echoes R. Ḥisda's comment on the Antediluvians' conduct and subsequent punishment quoted above (note 65):
. . . according to all that they did they were punished! They behaved corruptly through hot water (רתיחין), consequently they leaped about in hot water, and were punished!

[72] Although this phrase is not found in standard editions of the *Miqra'ot Gedolot*, it occurs in MSS and early printed editions.

influenced the development of this exegetical tradition, was the basic notion referred to above, that Moses wrote not only the *Torah*, but also the Book of Job. As the Pentateuch reveals so little regarding the circumstances which led to the Deluge, the early rabbinic exegetes sought this information specifically in the detailed descriptions of the archetypal wicked, recorded by the Law-giver himself.

CHAPTER 3

Traditional motifs in early rabbinic exegesis II: Job and Israel's early history as a nation

The special relationship between Job and the *Torah* in early rabbinic tradition is apparent particularly in the rabbis extensive use of the utterances of the book's principal characters in their homilies on Israel's experiences at the Exodus and in the wilderness. As will be seen from the material which follows, these themes clearly occupied a prominent place in the early rabbinic interpretation of the book as reflected in both talmudic-midrashic literature, as well as the *Targum* to Job. Moreover, the selection of verses was by no means random. Certain speeches of four of the characters in the book were evidently regarded as a commentary – either of a prophetic or of a contemporary nature – on events and incidents in Israel's early history, which provided the backcloth against which the drama of Job was enacted.

None the less, no explicitly formulated traditions have been preserved in our sources, comparable with those relating to the Generation of the Flood,[1] naming Job and his associates as 'expositors' of the events relating to the early history of the Israelite nation. However, the expressions employed in several sources to introduce proof-texts from Job, מפרשו איוב,[2] איוב

מפורש על ידי איוב,[4] אמר,[3] suggest the existence of such a tradition.[5]

THE SPEECHES OF JOB

Predictably, several speeches of Job himself have been associated with Exodus and Wilderness themes, notably that contained in chapter 28, which was interpreted already in tannaitic times, with reference to Moses himself. Moses' efforts to avoid death is a widely recurring theme in aggadic sources, to which we shall refer again subsequently. In the following passage, from *Midrash Tanna'im*,[6] two series of verses from chapter 28 are treated as a description of the Angel of Death's efforts to recover Moses' soul:

---

[3] See p. 54.

[4] This phrase is of particular interest, as it occurs in tannaitic sources. Two early *Tanna'im*, R. Joshua b. Ḥananiah and R. Eleazar Ḥisma, treated Exodus 17:8 as a רשום, a symbolic, or allegorical verse, representing a secondary meaning which has been expounded by Job in 8:11:

'Then came Amalek and fought with Israel in Rephidim (Exodus 17:8).' R. Joshua and R. Eleazar Hisma said: 'This verse is allegorical, and has been expounded by Job, as it is said, היגאה גמא בלא בצה, [which means] is it possible for the rush to grow without mire? ישגה אחו בלי מים, [which means] is it possible to have reed-grass without water? So it is impossible for Israel to exist without *Torah*! Because they departed from the words of the *Torah*, the enemy came upon them! For the enemy only comes as a result of sin and transgression, hence it is said, "Then came Amalek etc. . . ."'

See *Mekhilta Beshallaḥ, Amaleq* 1, p. 176, and the parallels cited there. While the reading ר' יהושע is supported by all MSS to the *Mekhilta*, and *Yalqut* 262, in *Mekhilta d'Rabbi Shimon b. Yoḥai* to Exodus 17:7 (p. 118) the reading is ר' יאשיהו, which is confirmed by the extra-European *Midrash Ha-Gadol* to Exodus 17:7 (ed. Margulies, p. 339). For the interpretation of רשום which we have adopted, see Lauterbach, 'The Ancient Jewish Allegorists in the Talmud and Midrash', *JQR* (NS) vol. 1 (1910–11), p. 300. Moreover, from the material quoted by Lauterbach (pp. 310 and 312) we see that the above homily presupposes to interpretations of the דורשי רשומות. Firstly, רפידים = רפיון ידים (*viz.* a slackening of the hands from the observance of the *Torah*) which was accepted by R. Joshua (see *BT Berakhot* 5b). Secondly, the well-known aggadic device, מים = תורה, which may have originated with the דורשי רשומות, if Lauterbach is correct in ascribing great antiquity to this early school of allegorists. We may also note the possibility that the two expressions גמא and אחו suggested a direct link between Job 8:11 and the early period of Israel's history, in which context both these expressions occur (see Genesis 41:18, and Exodus 3:3).

[5] See p. 59 for an explicitly formulated tradition linking a recurring expression in Elihu's speeches with a singular event in the wilderness.

[6] See ed. Hoffmann, pp. 224–5, and the parallels cited there.

Moses said to God: 'Lord of all Worlds, since You have decreed that I
must die, do not deliver me into the hand of the Angel of Death!' God
said to him: 'As you live, I Myself shall attend to you, and hide you
away!' God then showed him his seat [in the world to come] just as
He had done with Aaron his brother, and when he saw his throne in
the midst of the Garden of Eden, he was pacified. At that moment,
God said to the Angel of Death: 'Go, bring Moses' soul.' He went and
searched the entire world, but could not find him. He went to the sea
and said: 'Have you seen Moses?' It answered: 'From the day that he
brought Israel up from my midst, I have not seen him again!' He
went to the mountains and hills and said: 'Have you seen Moses?'
They answered: 'From the day that he received the *Torah* from
Mount Sinai, we have not seen him! Perhaps he is standing before
God and pleading that he might enter the Land of Israel.' He went to
the land of Israel and said: 'Perhaps Moses' soul is here?' It replied,
'It is not to be found in the land of the living (v. 13).' He went to the
Clouds of Glory and said: 'Perhaps Moses' soul is here?' They replied,
'It is hidden from the eyes of all the living (v. 21).' He went to the
Ministering Angels and said: 'Perhaps Moses' soul is here?' They
replied, 'It is concealed from the *flyers* of the heaven (*ibid.*)' – This
refers to the Ministering Angels, who are called 'flyers'.[7] He went to
the deep and said: 'Perhaps Moses' soul is here?' It answered, 'No!',
as it is said, 'The deep said: "It is not with me (v. 14)."'. He went to
the Nether World and Destruction and said: 'Have you seen Moses?'
They answered: 'We have heard report of him, but we have not seen
him', as it said, 'Destruction and Death say: "We have heard a
rumour thereof with our ears (v. 22)".' Abba used to offer the
following exposition in the name of R. Ishmael b. R. Yose:
'"Destruction and Death say: 'We have heard a rumour thereof with
our ears'"' – the Ministering Angels were standing in groups, praising
Moses' bier, saying, "He entereth into peace, they rest in their beds
(Isaiah 57:2)".' He [the Angel of Death] went to the Ministering
Angels and said: 'Have you seen Moses?' They answered: 'Go [ask]
the mortals!' He went to the mortals and asked: 'Have you seen
Moses?' They answered: 'God understandeth the way thereof, and
He knoweth the place thereof (v. 23) – He has hidden him away for
the life of the world to come and no creature has any knowledge of
him, as it is said, "But wisdom, where shall it be found?[8] ... (v. 12)".'

---

[7] Possibly this equation of עוף with מלאכי השרת is based on Isaiah 6:2, בשתים
יעופף.

[8] In the longer recension of this *Aggadah* in *Avot d'Rabbi Natan*, pp. 156–7, this verse is
presented as the funeral eulogy uttered by the Ministering Angels over Moses' bier.

A further two verses from this speech interpreted with reference to Moses, reflect a notion which is expressed in varying forms in our sources, God's miraculous manipulation of His voice. In a lengthy homily recorded in both editions of *Midrash Tanḥuma*,[9] 28:25–26 are cited as proof-texts in a description of God's special means of communication with Moses. Although, when addressing the prophet in the tent of assembly, God spoke in the thunderous voice He had employed at Sinai, He channelled it in such a way, that Moses alone could hear it:

... And whence do we know that He was speaking with the voice [He had employed at] the Giving of the Law? Because it says, '*The voice* of the Lord is powerful; *the voice* of the Lord is full of majesty. *The voice* of the Lord breaketh the cedars; (Psalm 29:4–5)'. And similarly it says, 'And when Moses went into the tent of meeting that He might speak with him, then he heard *the voice* speaking unto him ... (Numbers 7:89)' – the voice which he had heard at the Giving of the Law. And it was in this manner that [God] spoke every word and made every utterance [to Moses]. Perhaps, you might think that Israel could hear [God's] voice outside [the tent of assembly]. Therefore it says, 'then *he heard* the voice (*ibid.*)' – [indicating that] he alone could hear it! But, as God was speaking in a loud voice, how could they not hear it? Because God decreed that [His every] utterance should go forth directly to Moses, and God made a route for it, along which it might proceed without being heard on either side, until it reached Moses, as it is said, 'When He maketh a weight for the wind (28:25)' – implying that every utterance which issues forth from the mouth of God is carefully measured.[10] And thus it says further, ודרך להזיז קולות (v. 26),[11] which implies that God made a route for that voice to go forth directly to Moses alone. Thus it is said, 'And He called to Moses, and the Lord spoke *to him* (Leviticus 1:1)' – [This indicates] that it was audible to him alone, and to no other person.[12]

Possibly this tradition may have given rise to the practice among *Sephardim* of using this verse as a scriptural prologue to the memorial prayer recited for a sage.

[9] Ed. Buber, 3, p. 2; Old Version, *Wa-Yiqra* 1.

[10] The preacher has presumably taken רוח in the sense of רוח פיו, which occurs in Job 15:30.

[11] Lit.: 'and a way for the storm of thunders'. Evidently, the preacher has taken קולות in the sense of divine utterances, as it is traditionally interpreted in Exodus 20:15, 'And all the people perceived the thunder' (הקולות; see Rashi on this verse, and *Pirqei d'Rabbi Eliezer*, 41, end).

[12] The theme expounded here can be traced back to tannaitic times in association with a further verse from Job, 37:5, to which we shall refer again subsequently (see

The passage as a whole illustrates well the case for exegetical traditions, with which both the preacher and his audience were familiar. None of the proof-texts cited from Psalms and Job has any obvious bearing on the subject of the Giving of the Law, or God's method of communicating with Moses. Yet no explanation is offered to justify their application to these themes. Moreover, the verses from Psalm 29 are not simply treated as an allusion to the Giving of the Law, they are actually cited to substantiate the identification of the expression קול in another context, with the Voice of Sinai! This reflects a well-established tradition relating to the interpretation of Psalm 29 preserved in earliest rabbinic sources, which is to be discussed subsequently under its own heading.

The theme of God's discourse with Moses is reflected also in the interpretation of Job 28:27–28. These two verses are linked in our sources with several notions relating to the revelation at Sinai. The following passage, for example, describes God's own preparations for that event. Before addressing Himself to Moses, God first prepared his discourse, thus setting the example to be imitated by a mortal teacher:[13]

'Then did He see it and declare it'[14] – The Rabbis and R. Aḥa [offered differing interpretations for this verse]. The Rabbis said: 'Every utterance which God made to Moses, He would recite to Himself two times, and then say it to Moses! What is the scriptural basis for this? "Then did He see it and declare it" – [this indicates]

pp. 6of). Commenting on the same phrase, וידבר אליו in Numbers 7:89, Ben Azzai described God's special means of communicating with Moses in terms of a pipe, or tube reaching into his ear, thereby excluding even the ministering angels from His discourse with the prophet (see *Numbers Rabbah* 14:22; also *Sifrei Zutta* to Numbers 7:89, and the parallels cited by Horovitz, p. 254):
'And He spoke unto him' – exclusively, and not to the Ministering Angels who were present. Scripture indicates that the voice issued forth from the mouth of God in the form of a pipe [extending directly] into the ear of Moses, so that the angels standing in between could not hear it! Thus it is said, 'God showed them (reading יראם for ירעם) wonders with His voice' (Job 37:5). Hence [it is written], 'And He spoke unto him'.
13 See *Genesis Rabbah* 24:5, and the parallels cited by Theodor, p. 234.
14 Lit.: 'Then did He see it and declare it; He established it, yea, and searched it out. And unto man He said it.' The object presupposed in these verses, and with which Job 28:12ff deals, is חכמה which, in keeping with the well-known aggadic device, has been identified with *Torah*.

one – "He established it and also searched it out" – [also indicates] one, after which – "He said unto the man" – this refers to Moses.'[15] R. Aḥa said: '[He recited it to Himself] four times. "Then did He see it" – [indicates] one – "and declare it" – [indicates] one – "He established it" – [indicates] one – "and also searched it out" – [indicates] one, after which – "He said unto the man" – this refers to Moses.'[16]

There is evidence in our sources to suggest that Job's speech in chapter 12 was also associated in rabbinic tradition with Exodus and Wilderness themes.[17] The references in the latter part of this chapter to God's ability to dispense with princes, potentates and priests as He chooses, evidently suggested some association with the fate of Pharaoh and the Egyptians. This can be seen from the expositions of several verses from this chapter, notably 23–24, 'He increaseth (מַשְׂגִּיא) the nations and destroyeth them ... He taketh away the heart of the chiefs of the people of the land ...' In the following statement, these two verses are adduced to explain the neccesity of the ten plagues, when the first alone would have sufficed:[18]

... Was God not able to deliver Israel from the power of the Egyptians through the first plague? However, [the ten plagues were intended] to fulfil that which is said, 'He acts mightily towards the nations and so destroys them', and it is written, 'He taketh away the hearts of the chiefs of the people of the land.'

[15] Presumably the preacher has equated אָדָם = אִישׁ – מֹשֶׁה, on the basis of Numbers 12:3, 'Now the man (וְהָאִישׁ) Moses was very meek.' The reading זה משה is supported by MSS evidence (see Theodor, p. 234) and was known to Masnut, whose version of this *Aggadah* contains a lengthy addition, which, judging by its style and language, probably formed part of Masnut's midrashic *Vorlage* (see *Mayan Gannim*, ed. Buber, p. 90). However, in *Exodus Rabbah* 40:1, אָדָם is taken as an allusion to Israel on the basis of Ezekiel 34:31, 'And you My sheep, the sheep of My pasture, are men (אָדָם אַתֶּם)'. See also *Tanhuma*, ed. Buber, 2, p. 122; and the Old Version, *Va-Yaqhel* 4. For further interpretations of Job 28:27–28, see Appendix 2, pp. 179f.

[16] In *Exodus Rabbah*, as well as in both versions of the *Tanhuma* cited above, verse 28 is also applied to Miriam who, for her fear of God at the time of Pharaoh's wicked decree, was rewarded with Bezalel, who was filled with the spirit of חכמה.

[17] This is indicated already in the alternative *Targum* to verse 6, which introduces an allusion to the plagues brought upon Pharaoh: היך פרעה דאיתיה א-לוה עלוהי מחתא בידיה.

[18] See *Exodus Rabbah* 15:10. It is possible that the allusion to the plagues was found in verse 25, ימששו חשך ולא אור, which provides a verbal link with Exodus 10:21, וימש חשך.

The precise interpretation placed on verses 23–24 here is problematic. Our rendering presupposes that משגיא was treated as an internal *hiph'il*, hence, 'He acts mightily', – *viz.* through the plagues – in order to impress His power upon the Egyptians, a notion borne out by a further statement in the same context as this passage. It is more difficult, however, to determine how the anonymous aggadist understood verse 24, or how he related it to the theme of God's underlying motives in bringing the plagues upon the Egyptians. It is possible that his statement presupposes an exposition of verse 24 in connection with a well-known aggadic motif, by the *Amora*, R. Isaac, which has been preserved in a fragmentary *Midrash* from the *Genizah*.[19] According to R. Isaac, Job 12:24 alludes to Pharaoh's persistent obstinacy, which was not without purpose. While his initial hard-heartedness was of his own doing, it was God who subsequently made Pharaoh's retreat impossible, in order to display His wondrous power among the Egyptians:

R. Isaac said: 'It is written, "He taketh away the heart of the chiefs of the people of the land, and causeth them to wander in a wilderness where there is no way." You find that after God sent Moses to Pharaoh, he hardened his own heart, because you do not find in connection with the first five plagues, "And the Lord hardened the heart of Pharaoh (Exodus 9:12)". He hardened his own heart, as it is said, "And Pharaoh hardened his heart (*ibid.* 8:28)", "And Pharaoh turned and went into his house, neither did he lay even this to his heart (*ibid.* 7:23)". God said to him, "At first, you were hardening your own heart, from now on, I will add to your efforts!" Hence it is said, "For I have hardened his heart (*ibid.* 10:1)". And so God said to Moses, "And I know that the king of Egypt will not give you leave to go (*ibid.* 3:19)". Therefore He said, "And I will harden Pharaoh's heart, and I will multiply My signs and My wonders in the land of Egypt (*ibid.* 7:3)."'[20]

It is noteworthy that the application of Job 12:23 to the theme of the Egyptians' downfall can be traced back to tannaitic sources, where it occurs in connection with an aggadic

---

[19] See Mann, מדרש חדש על התורה ('A New *Midrash* on the *Torah*'), in *The Bible as Read and Preached in the Old Synagogue*, Cincinnati 1940, Hebrew Section pp. 216–17.

[20] The proem concludes in the text with Proverbs 16:4 which, as Mann observes (note 634) is out of place here, as it is the verse upon which the first *petihah* to this *seder* is based.

tradition which gained wide currency in talmudic times. The punishment wrought by God upon the deities of Egypt, as well as upon its population, is the subject of a number of legends.[21] However, according to an early tradition associated exclusively with 12:23, one idol, Baal Zaphon, was spared by God for a specific purpose, to delude Pharaoh. When he beheld the Israelites apparently helpless upon the shores of the Red Sea, before the sanctuary of Baal Zaphon, Pharaoh took it as an omen. He concluded that this idol, which had survived the fate of his other deities, was supporting his original intention to destroy the Israelites by water, and began to pay homage to it.[22] This, however, was merely a ruse, as the following passage reveals, to lure the Egyptians to their fate:[23]

Of all the objects of their veneration, Baal Zaphon remained in order to delude [the Egyptians into thinking that the idol] had saved itself, and concerning this it is said, 'He leadeth the nations astray[24] and destroyeth them etc. ...'[25]

A further theme relating to the Exodus which has been associated with Job's speech in chapter 12 concerns the part played by the elders at the time of the Redemption. Numerous panegyrics are to be found in our sources praising the nobility and godliness of these early leaders of the people, whom the rabbis of the talmudic period no doubt saw as their role-model.[26] In the following *petiḥah*, an anonymous aggadist has

---

[21] See *Targum Pseudo-Jonathan* to Exodus 12:12; *Exodus Rabbah* 15:15; *BT Sukkah* 29b; *Tanhuma*, ed. Buber, 5, p. 32.

[22] See *Mekhilta Beshallaḥ, Va-Yeḥi* 2, p. 91; also *Leqah Tov* to Exodus 10:10, ed. Buber, p. 45.

[23] See *Mekhilta Bo, Pisha* 13, p. 43; also *Beshallaḥ, Va-Yeḥi* 1, p. 84; *Mekhilta d'Rabbi Shimon b. Yoḥai*, pp. 28 and 48; *Exodus Rabbah* 15:15; also *Targum Pseudo-Jonathan* (and Rashi) to Exodus 14:2.

[24] Presumably the *Tanna* has taken משגיא as משגה, *hiph'il* of שגה ‖ שגא, 'to go astray' (see Job 12:16).

[25] It is possible that the allusion here to Baal Zaphon is contained once again in verse 25, ימשש חשך, חשך being closely linked in rabbinic tradition with צפון, the north. See, for example, *Numbers Rabbah* 2:10 and 3:12. צפון משם חשך יוצא לעולם.

[26] See *Exodus* 3:8 and the parallels cited there; also *Numbers Rabbah* 15:17; *Tanhuma*, ed. Buber, 2, p. 16, and 3, p. 58; Old Version, *Shemot* 29, *Shemini* 11, *be-Ha'alotekha* 13.

employed 12:12 as his proemial verse to elaborate on the theme
of the elders' role in securing Israel's faith in God:[27]

'And Moses called for all the elders of Israel, and said unto them:
"Draw out, and take you lambs according to your families, and
slaughter the paschal lamb (Exodus 12:21)." ' Thus it is written,
'With the aged is wisdom, and with length of days understanding.'
Why did the elders deserve to be involved in Israel's redemption?
When God revealed Himself to Moses in the bush, He said to him,
'Go, gather the elders of Israel ... (*ibid.* 3:16)' When Moses came,
immediately, 'Moses and Aaron went and gathered all the elders of
the children of Israel (*ibid.* 4:29)', [after which] it says, 'And the
people believed; (*ibid.* verse 31)'. God said: 'Behold I will repay the
elders because they made Israel believe in My name!' When Moses
said, 'The God of your fathers hath sent me unto you (*ibid.* 3:13)',
had the elders not accepted Moses' words, then all Israel would not
have accepted [them]. But the elders accepted them first, and drew
all of Israel after them, and made them believe in God's name.
[Therefore,] God said, 'I will also do them honour, and they will be
instrumental in Israel's redemption, since the Israelites will slaughter
their paschal offerings under the aegis of the elders.' Thus it is said,
'And Moses called to all the elders of Israel etc ...' Therefore,
Scripture praises them, [with the words,] 'With the aged is wisdom
etc. ...'[28]

The remaining passage, which indicates some association
between Job's speech in chapter 12 and events in early Israelite
history, reflects a well-known and widely recurring theme in
aggadic literature, the gentiles' refusal to accept the *Torah*
before it was offered to Israel. According to a tradition found in
older sources only in *Genesis Rabbah* 53:9,[29] those gentiles who,
as a result of their suckling at the breasts of the matriarch,
Sarah, had been granted dominion in this world, were

---

[27] See *Exodus Rabbah* 16:1.
[28] It is probable that the aggadist has interpreted the continuation of Exodus 12:21 as
a two-fold injunction, ויקחו לכם was addressed to the elders that they themselves
should accept Moses' words, משכו implying that they should 'draw' the rest of
Israel in their wake. Einhorn, in his commentary to the text, suggests the preacher's
comments here presuppose Job 12:11, הלא אזן מלין תבחן וחך אכל יטעם לו:
'Because [their] ears tested [and accepted Moses'] words, they caused Israel to taste
(יטעם = יטעים) אכל' (= the paschal lamb, on the basis of Exodus 12:8, 'and they
shall eat (ואכלו) the flesh').
[29] For the many sources in which this tradition occurs, see Ginzberg, *Legends*, vol. 6,
pp. 30–1, note 181.

deprived of this distinction because of their alienation from God at Sinai:[30]

The Rabbis and R. Aḥa [held differing views]. The Rabbis said: 'Anyone who came [to suckle] for the sake of Heaven, became a God-fearer'. R. Aḥa said: 'Even one who did not come for the sake of Heaven, was granted dominion in this world. But when they separated themselves at Sinai and did not receive the Torah, that dominion was taken away from them, as it is said, "He looseneth the bond of kings ..."'[31]

THE SPEECHES OF ELIPHAZ

Although the material to be quoted here is not as extensive as that relating to the speeches of Job, none the less, it is of special interest and significance. While the aggadic interpretation of Eliphaz's utterances with reference to Exodus and Wilderness themes is limited almost entirely to his two speeches in chapters 5 and 15, it does support our initial observation that certain sections of the Book of Job were evidently regarded as a commentary – either of a contemporary, or prophetic nature – on Israel's early history.

A considerable portion of chapter 5 has been interpreted with reference to a whole range of subjects, commencing with the Exodus and the downfall of the Egyptians, the war with the Amalekites, the giving of the Law, Balaam and the Midianites, Og and Sihon, the Canaanites – a veritable résumé of all the events in the early history of the nation from their redemption to the time of their arrival in the Holy Land. Moreover, the source for this lengthy exposition is an unusual one, the *Targum* to Job. This *Targum* – at least in its present form – is not especially rich in aggadic content,[32] consequently the numerous allusions to the above-mentioned themes, which have been

---

[30] For parallels, see Theodor, pp. 564f.

[31] Although this verse is not found in printed editions, it appears in MSS London, Paris, Munich, Vatican, Stuttgart, Oxford 1 and 2.

[32] Bacher (see above p. 40, note 70) who assigns this *Targum* to the period of Roman rule in Palestine, maintains that its aggadic content was more extensive. In its current form, however, allusions to the period of the Exodus and the wilderness, apart from chapter 5, are virtually limited to the following: 7:12; 12:6 (version B); 14:19; 15:29; 34:20; 38:23.

incorporated into its rendering of chapter 5, are all the more remarkable. It is also interesting to note that the translator has portrayed Eliphaz as speaking of the events immediately surrounding the Redemption in the past tense, while the hazards of the wilderness, Balaam, Og, Sihon, etc, are referred to as future events. It is possible that he was simply adhering to the tenses of the verbs in the Masoretic Text. On the other hand, it is conceivable that he was influenced by the notion referred to earlier, that Job's trial and his discussions with his friends actually occurred while Israel was proceeding across the Red Sea towards Sinai. Therefore, the translator has treated the latter part of Eliphaz's speech in this chapter as prophecy:

12) He set at nought the plans of the Egyptians, who cleverly devised to do evil to Israel, but their hands did not perform the counsel of their wisdom.

13) He ensnares the wise men of Pharaoh in their wisdom, and the counsel of his trickster astrologers, He brings down upon them.[33]

14) They meet with darkness in the daytime, and grope at noon-day as in the night.[34]

15) And He delivered His people from the slaughter of their mouth, and from the hand of a powerful king, He delivered a luckless people.

19) He will deliver you in six troubles, even in the seventh He will not allow evil near to you.

20) In the famine of Egypt, He delivered you from death,[35] and from the slaughter of the sword in the war with Amalek.

21) From the damaging tongue of Balaam, you will hide between the

---

[33] Midrashic sources preserve an exposition of this verse relating to quite a different theme from that reflected in the *Targum*. According to an anonymous aggadist, verse 13 refers to the predicament of Moses when challenged by the people to bring forth water from a rock other than that indicated by God (see *Tanhuma*, ed. Buber, 4, p. 120; Old Version, *Ḥuqqat* 9; *Numbers Rabbah* 19:9 and Einhorn's comment on the text). Compare also the midrashic interpretation of Exodus 18:11, אֲשֶׁר זָדוּ עֲלֵיהֶם, in *Targums Onqelos* and *Pseudo-Jonathan*; *BT Sotah* 11a; *Mekhilta Yitro*, *Massekhta d'Amaleq* 1, p. 195, and the parallels cited there.

[34] It is probably this verse in particular which provided the link between this passage and the Egyptians (see above, note 18).

[35] The precise allusion here is doubtful. It may simply be a reference to the dearth of food created by the plagues.

clouds of glory,[36] and you shall not fear the injury of the Midianites when it comes.

22) You will laugh at the destruction of Sihon and the famine of the wilderness, and you shall not be afraid of the soldiers of Og, who is likened to a wild beast of the earth.[37]

23) For your covenant will be with the tablets of stone, which were given with great publicity in open country;[38] moreover, the Canaanites, who are compared to wild beasts, have made peace with you.

The above rendering of the *Targum* is unusual in a further respect. Although we may usually assume that material which was incorporated into a *Targum* gained wide currency in talmudic times, in the entire corpus of talmudic-midrashic literature, we find no parallels either for the passage as a whole or for the renderings of the individual verses. However, this does not exclude the possibility that the translator had before him a single source, rather than a number of *Midrashim* upon which he based his exegesis.[39] Our sources actually preserve a midrashic excerpt of this type, containing an exposition of a whole series of consecutive verses from Eliphaz's speech in chapter 15, relating to a specific personality, Korah:[40]

Job said: 'And he hath dwelt in desolate cities, in houses which no man would inhabit, which were ready to become heaps. He shall not be rich, nor shall his substance continue, neither shall their produce bend to the earth. He shall not depart out of darkness; the flame shall dry up his branches, and by the breath of his mouth shall he go away. Let him not trust in vanity, deceiving himself; for vanity shall be his

---

[36] Once again the allusion here is obscure. The notion that the clouds protected and cared for Israel on various occasions occurs widely in our sources (see for example Ginzberg, *Legends*, vol. 6, p. 6, note 35; pp. 22f, note 136; p. 26, note 153; p. 52, note 270; p. 71, note 365). However, there appears to be no parallel for the notion expressed here, that the clouds protected Israel also on the occasion of Balaam's attempt to curse them.

[37] The targumist is once again alluding to aggadic traditions for which we can find no trace in existing sources.

[38] For the great publicity surrounding the Giving of the Law, see *Mekhilta Yitro, Ba-Ḥodesh*, 1, pp. 205–6, and the parallels cited ad loc; see also Ginzberg, *Legends*, vol. 6, p. 32, note 185.

[39] See also Appendix 2, pp. 181f, for further expositions of 5:22ff.

[40] See *Numbers Rabbah* 18:15. The association of this passage with Korah is probably based on verse 34, 'For the company of the godless shall be desolate, and fire shall consume the tents of bribery', which was linked with Numbers 16:26 and 35.

recompense. It shall be accomplished before his time, and his branch shall not be leafy. He shall shake off his unripe grape as a vine, and shall cast his flower as the olive. For the company of the godless shall be desolate, and fire shall consume the tents of bribery (vv. 28–34).'

'He hath dwelt in desolate cities, in houses which no man would inhabit, which were ready to become heaps' – this was Korah, who was the controller[41] of Pharaoh's household, and the keys of his treasuries were in his hand. God said to him, 'What benefit will you derive [from your office]? You will not continue to hold sway over [these treasures]!', as it is said, 'He hath dwelt in desolate cities, in houses which they would not [continue] to dwell, אשר התעתדו לגלים'[42] – For whom were they intended? For those who were to be 'exiled', [namely], Israel who were to be 'exiled' from Egypt. As for Korah, 'He shall not be rich, neither shall his substance continue – [implying that] even after his death it would not endure (as he would have no heirs)[43] – 'neither shall their produce bend to the earth'. לא יסור מני חשך, [means that] he is not to depart from darkness. יונקתו תיבש שלהבת[44] – Our rabbis said that when Korah's wife descended into Gehinnom, she extinguished it.[45] 'And he departs with his breath in his mouth (*viz.* unable to speak)' – so that he should not say, 'Samuel is destined to be my descendant, and on his account I should be spared!'[46] None the less, he shall depart with the breath of

---

[41] *Viz.* KATHOLIKOS, 'financial officer', 'controller', compare *Exodus Rabbah* 37:1. Apart from an allusion in *PT Sanhedrin* 10:1, 27d, to Pharaoh's treasures having been revealed to Korah, the tradition recorded here has no parallels in older sources. However, see the material cited by Ginzberg, *Legends*, vol. 6, p. 99, note 560, which refers to Korah's great wealth, a notion which presumably gained wide currency, as it was incorporated into *Targum Pseudo-Jonathan* to Numbers 16:19. It is interesting to note further that this tradition which locates Korah within Pharaoh's retinue, coincides exactly with the view that this was the historical setting for Job, who was also a member of Pharaoh's פמליא (see p. 25, particularly note 12). This may have influenced the aggadic treatment of Eliphaz's speech as a contemporary account of Korah's activities and fate.

[42] Lit.: 'which were ready to become heaps'. However, the preacher has taken גלים as גולים, hence 'exiles'.

[43] See Luria's (רד'ל) commentary to the text, where he offers this interpretation of אינו קם, but suggests the alternative that the phrase might refer to Korah himself who will not 'rise up' with the resurrection of the dead.

[44] Lit.: 'The flame shall dry up his branches.' Probably יונקתו (*qal*) has been taken with the force of the *hiph'il*, מינקת, a feature of the Palestinian dialect of Hebrew, hence she who suckled his children, his wife (compare, for example, *Mishnah Bava Qama* 6:1, הכונס צאן לדיר, for המכניס, 'one who gathers sheep into a fold').

[45] Taking כיבת as the Neo-Hebrew equivalent of the biblical כבתה (see Einhorn on the text).

[46] On Samuel as the descendant of Korah, see *Numbers Rabbah* 18:8; *Tanhuma*, ed. Buber, 4, p. 89; Old Version, *Qorah* 5.

his mouth. אל יאמן בשוא נתעה[47] – God cried out to the two hundred and fifty men who had joined him in his dispute: 'Have no faith [in him], he has gone astray.' 'Let no one believe [him for] he errs after vanity. The column of smoke [from his incense] will be in vain.'[48] בלא יומו תמלא [means] even before his time to die has arrived, he kills himself! 'As a vine he shaketh off בסרו' – this refers to his wife[49] – 'and shall cast off his flower as an olive' – this refers to his children.[50] Why so? 'For the company of the godless shall be desolate, and fire shall consume the tent of bribery.' [Thus it is written,] 'And a fire came from the Lord . . . (Numbers 16:35)'

There is also some evidence to suggest that Eliphaz's speech in chapter 4 was similarly associated in early rabbinic tradition with Israel's experiences at the Exodus and in the wilderness. Once again, several proof-texts from this chapter have been applied to a single theme, the giving of the Law. The first passage, which occurs anonymously in a tannaitic source, contains an exposition of verses 15 and 16 in connection with a curious notion, which is not found elsewhere in aggadic literature. As a result of the awesome experience of the revelation at Sinai, the Israelites' hair stood on end. However, the significant feature of the passage is that, without any word of explanation, the anonymous *Tanna* has taken Eliphaz's personal encounter with the Divine Presence described in these verses, as a direct allusion to the revelation at Sinai, reflecting,

[47] Lit.: 'Let him not trust in vanity deceiving himself.' For this emendation, see Luria's commentary to the text.
[48] This rendering is based on the assumption that the preacher has equated the expression תמורה with the denominative verb תמר, 'to rise up in a straight column', referring particularly to the smoke of incense (see *Tosephta Yoma* 2:6, ed. Zuckermandel, p. 184; also Jastrow, s.v. תמר, p. 1678). As such, this rendering presupposes the tradition that Korah persisted in offering the incense despite Moses' warning of the fatal consequences of his action. Korah deceived himself that his life would not be forfeited because of his illustrious progeny (see *Exodus Rabbah* 18:8, and the parallel cited above from *Tanhuma*, which are clearly presupposed by the exposition of the verses in our source).
[49] Presumably בסרו has been equated with בשרו, 'his flesh', hence 'his wife', on the basis of Genesis 2:23, 'This is now the bone of my bones, *and flesh of my flesh*; she shall be called Woman etc'.
[50] For the imagery of נצה, 'a blossom' as children, compare פרח, used metaphorically to connote a young man, as in פרחי כהונה, 'priestly youths' (see *Mishnah Middot* 1:8).

no doubt, the early tradition which locates Job's discussions with his friends against the backdrop of these events:[51]

'They sacrificed unto demons, no-gods, Gods that they knew not, new gods that came up of late, לא שערום אבותיכם[52] (Deuteronomy 32:17)': [This means that your fathers' hair did not stand on end before them,] as it had done at Mount Sinai, as it is said, 'Then a spirit passed before my face, [that made the hair of my flesh to stand up.][53] It stood still, but I could not discern the appearance thereof; a form was before mine eyes; I heard a still voice . . .'

In the second passage, which contains a homily elaborating on the relationship between the Decalogue and the ensuing legal code (Exodus 21:1ff) Job 4:21 is adduced to support the notion that the punishments prescribed in *Seder Mishpatim*, were instituted to ensure Israel's obedience to the injunctions embodied in the Decalogue:[54]

'Now these are the ordinances which thou shalt set before them (Exodus 21:1)': [It is written,] 'And it came to pass on the third day, when it was morning (*ibid.* 19:16)' – [this implies that] in the morning, the Law (i.e. the principles of the Law) was given,[55] while in the evening, the 'judgements' (the punishments and penalties for infringing the Law) were given. Thus it is said, מבקר לערב יכתו מבלי משים לנצח יאבדו, 'They shall be punished [for their infringement of that which was given] in the morning, [on the basis of that which was given] in the evening; for without penalties, they would perish in perpetuity (through breaking the Law).'[56] It may be com-

---

51 See *Avot d'Rabbi Natan* Version B, chapter 38, p. 101. We have emended the text extensively on the basis of the *Sifrei* to Deuteronomy 32:17, *pisqa* 318, p. 364; see also Rashi to this verse.

52 Lit.: 'which your fathers dreaded not'.

53 We have included the continuation of verse 15, which is clearly required by the text as it contains the allusion to the raising of the hair, but, as is frequently the case in midrashic literature, has been omitted.

54 See *Exodus Rabbah* 30:11.

55 Compare, however, Jastrow's rendering of this phrase (s.v. משפט, p. 857): 'In the morning the Law (*viz.* religious principles) was given, and in the evening the civil law.' This rendering is open to question, as no support can be found in our sources for the notion that civil legislation was instituted merely to ensure the performance of the religious injunctions.

56 The allusion to the Torah in this passage is provided by the immediate context of the next verse, 'They die and that without חכמה'. The rendering of משים as 'judgements' is a further example of climatic exegesis, which can be traced back to tannaitic sources, see p. 174.

pared to two who entered the arena for combat,[57] the one a professional, the other an amateur. Why was the amateur beaten? Because he had no one to train him! Thus God stood on Sinai, dealing with the dispensing of justice, as it is said, 'My hand laid on justice (Deuteronomy 32:41)'.[58]

We may note in conclusion, that these two homilies – like the two lengthier expositions relating to verses from chapters 5 and 15 – are without parallel in the entire corpus of talmudic-midrashic literature. Yet this association between Eliphaz's utterances and Israel's early history as a nation, was evidently acknowledged by both preachers and their audiences in talmudic times, as no word of explanation is offered to justify this midrashic treatment of the text. We would assume, therefore, that these isolated expositions are excerpts, or the fragmentary remains of a more comprehensive midrashic commentary on Eliphaz's utterances, relating them to Exodus and Wilderness themes, which was current in early times.

THE SPEECHES OF ELIHU

The evidence for an established association between Elihu's speeches and Israel's early history, is more explicit than for any other character in the Book of Job. For this enigmatic figure, who is the subject of several strange and unparalleled traditions in both rabbinic and non-rabbinic sources,[59] is distinguished further by a tradition associating him with a singular event:[60]

---

[57] This is the rendering offered by Jastrow (s.v. מוקמא, p. 747). Following the *Arukh*, Katz in his commentary to the text (*Matnot Kehunah*) takes מוקמא as 'work', מוקמא being the stand upon which the workmen presumably operate. Hence, 'It may be compared to two men who embark upon a job, a skilled and an unskilled labourer.'

[58] Possibly the notion expressed here that the legislative code contained in *Seder Mishpatim* was presented in the afternoon of the same day as the giving of the Decalogue, may be derived simply from the view that this code is the supplement of the Decalogue, and therefore, the natural corollary of the Ten Commandments both in time and content (see *Mekhilta Mishpatim* 1, p. 246, and the parallels cited there).

[59] See p. 161, note 34.

[60] See *Genesis Rabbah* 26:7, p. 255.

R. Joḥanan said: 'Wherever the expression אור occurs in the speeches of Elihu, it alludes to rain-fall.'[61] R. Hoshaiah Rabbah said: '*It alludes to the Giving of the Law.*'

The notion expressed here by R. Hoshaiah, as with other traditions relating to Elihu, is an isolated one, unsupported by any exegetical examples.[62] None the less, its implications for those expositions of Elihu's utterances which have been preserved in our sources, are important. For R. Hoshaiah's statement is not simply a further example of the well-known midrashic device equating אור with תורה, as is suggested by printed editions of *Genesis Rabbah*.[63] In taking אור as an allusion to מתן תורה – a reading supported by all manuscripts – R. Hoshaiah has invested אור in the context of Elihu's speeches with an historical significance. No basis for this exegetical device is to be found in talmudic-midrashic literature. Consequently, we can only assume that R. Hoshaiah's comment presupposes an extensive interpretation of Elihu's speeches with reference to the Exodus and the Wilderness, in which context, אור – the aggadic epithet for *Torah* – figured as an allusion to the events at Sinai.

This assumption is not entirely without support, as is to be seen from the midrashic treatment of verses from chapter 33. However, before proceeding to consider this material, there are several initial observations to be made regarding Elihu's speech in chapters 36–7, where the expression אור actually occurs.[64] It is possible that certain expressions and ideas in this speech appealed to the early exegetes as allusions to the events at Sinai, particularly the term הגה in 37:2, 'Hear attentively the noise of His voice (קולו) and the sound (הגה) that goeth

---

[61] For further comment on this exegetical motif, see below, Appendix 2, אור = Rain, pp. 182f.

[62] We do find the expression אור in 37:21 (לא ראו אור) interpreted as an allusion to the *Torah* by the *Amora*, R. Joseph (see *BT Ta'anit* 7b; also *Targum B* to this verse). However, no reference is made in this source to the historical event of the Giving of the Law, as is implied in R. Hoshaiah's dictum.

[63] Which add a proof-text from Proverbs 6:23, כי נר מצוה ותורה אור. This verse is not found in any of the MSS cited by Theodor (p. 255) and was in all probability introduced erroneously (see Theodor's comment).

[64] See 36:30 and 32; 37:3, 11, 15, and 21.

out of His mouth.' The connection between הגה, in both its nominal and verbal forms, and the *Torah*, is the subject of a detailed and exhaustive study.[65] For our purposes, it is sufficient to note that הגה in this verse is actually interpreted in our sources as דברי תורה.[66]

It is also possible that the expression קול in this verse was identified specifically with the awesome voice of the revelation, explicitly mentioned in Exodus 19:19, 'Moses was speaking and God was answering him with a voice (בקול)'. This was certainly the case with Job 37:5, 'God thundered marvellously with His voice (בקולו)', which was regarded as an allusion to a theme mentioned earlier in connection with Job's speeches,[67] God's miraculous manipulation of His voice at Sinai. According to an anonymous aggadist, this verse describes the ventriloquist-like effect God produced with His voice on Sinai, projecting it to all four points of the compass, as well as to the heavens and to the earth:[68]

ירעם א־ל בקולו נפלאות: What does [the expression] ירעם mean? When God gave the *Torah* at Sinai, He showed Israel wonders of wonders with His voice![69] In what way? God was speaking, and His

---

[65] See N. Wieder, *The Judean Scrolls and Karaism*, London 1962, pp. 215ff.

[66] See *Genesis Rabbah* 49:2 and 64:4 (pp. 501 and 704): Now [the expression] הגה connotes words of *Torah*, just as you say, '[This book of the Law shall not depart from thy mouth,] but thou shalt meditate therein (והגית בו) day and night.'

[67] See above, pp. 46f.

[68] See *Exodus Rabbah* 5:9; also *Tanhuma*, ed. Buber, 2, p. 13; Old Version, *Shemot* 25. On the notion that God's voice was heard from all four points of the compass, see *Sifrei Deuteronomy* 314 and 343, pp. 356 and 395, and the sources cited there.

[69] Like Ben Azzai quoted earlier (note 12) the unknown author of this statement has read ירעם ('He thundereth') as יראם ('He showed them'). This same midrashic device is presupposed in the following passage, which deals with the summoning of Moses and Aaron at the beginning of their mission. God's voice went forth on a dual transmission, reaching both Moses in Midian and Aaron in Egypt, yet it was heard by no other living being (see *Tanhuma*, ed. Buber, 2, p. 14; Old Version, *Shemot* 26; also *Exodus Rabbah* 5:9):

'God showed them wonders with His voice' – When did God show them wonders with His voice? At the time when He sent Moses on His mission to redeem Israel, he was in Midian, afraid because he had fled before Pharaoh lest he slay him, as it is said, 'And Moses fled from before Pharaoh etc. (Exodus 2:15)'. When the Divine word was revealed to him in Midian, and he was told that he should return to Egypt – as it is said, 'And the Lord said to Moses in Midian; Go, return to Egypt!' (*ibid.* 4:19) – at that time the Divine word was divided into two voices, assuming a double character (דיו פרצופין = *DIPROSOPOS*, lit. 'double-faced') so that Moses heard in Midian, 'Go, return to Egypt!', while Aaron heard in Egypt,

voice went forth and traversed the whole world. Israel, hearing the voice coming to them from the south, were running to the south to receive the voice. Then from the south it changed to the north, and they were running to the north. Then from the north it changed to the east, and they were running to the east. Then from the east it changed to the west, and they were running to the west. Then from the west it changed, [coming] to them from the heavens, and they were lifting up their eyes, but it turned earthwards, and they were looking down at the ground, as it is said, 'Out of the heavens, He made thee hear His voice, that He might instruct thee; [and upon earth He made thee see His great fire; and thou didst hear His words out of the midst of the fire] (Deuteronomy 4:36).' [Consequently,] the Israelites were saying to one another, 'Where is the *Torah*[70] to be found? (Job 28:12)'.

More substantial evidence has been preserved to suggest that the exposition of chapter 36 with reference to events at the Exodus and in the wilderness, was more extensive. It is clear from our sources that verse 22 of this chapter in particular was regarded as a comment by Elihu on these events. The following exposition of this verse is particularly significant as it alludes to the giving of the Law, God's role on this occasion being contrasted with the manifestation of His prowess at the Red Sea:[71]

Come and see that the attributes of God are not like those of mortal man! A mortal king is not able to be a warrior and, [at the same time], a scribe and teacher of children. But it is not so with God. Yesterday, at the sea [He appeared] as a warrior, as it is said, 'The Lord is a man of war (Exodus 15:3)', and it says, 'He stirreth up the sea with His power, and by His understanding He smiteth through Rahab (Job 26:12).'[72] Yet, today, at the giving of the Law, He came

'Go, meet Moses in the Wilderness! (*ibid.* 4:27)' However, any one between the two did not hear a thing. Hence [it is written], 'God showed them wonders with His voice.'

[70] Equating the scriptural expression חכמה with *Torah*, see p. 82.

[71] See *Exodus Rabbah* 28:5.

[72] The inclusion of Job 26:12 – which deals with God's victory over the sea (*viz.* Rahab, see p. 155) – in a context relating to the drowning of the Egyptians, is unusual. However, this may reflect a tendency in biblical sources, whereby God's victory over the Egyptians at the Red Sea was equated with, and superseded the older notion of God's victorious battle against the sea at the time of creation (see particularly S. E. Lowenstamm, *The Tradition of the Exodus and its Development*, Jerusalem 1965, pp. 108ff).

down and taught Torah to His children, and so it says, 'Behold God does loftily in His power, who is a teacher like unto Him?'[73]

Our sources preserve two further interpretations of this same verse relating to the one theme, God's treatment of Pharaoh and the Egyptians. We have already encountered the well-known tradition of God's purposely hardening Pharaoh's heart in order to bring upon him adequate retribution.[74] The following two passages reflect a different motif in the rabbinic treatment of this topic, that Pharaoh was, in reality, granted ample opportunity to repent and thereby avert the horror of the plagues. Presumably, this motif has a polemical or apologetic colouring, and is a reaction to the criticism in Gnostic circles of God's conduct towards sinners. The Generation of the Flood, the Tower-builders, the Sodomites as well as the Egyptians, were all regarded as victims of Divine injustice and maltreatment.[75] In the following passage, an anonymous teacher, in his exposition of verse 22, has employed the same homiletical device as in the previous passage, which occurs frequently in statements of this nature, stressing the total superiority of God's qualities over those of mere mortals:[76]

'And thou shalt say unto him: "The Lord God of the Hebrews etc . . . Thus saith the Lord: 'In this thou shalt know that I am the Lord – behold, I will smite with the rod that is in my hand upon the waters which are in the river, and they shall be turned to blood' (Exodus 7:16–17)."' Thus it is written, 'Behold God is supreme in His power [so that none can deliver from His hand]; therefore, who like Him instructs [His creatures to repent and so avert their fate]?'[77] Normally, when a human being wishes to inflict some harm upon his foe, he does so suddenly, before his foe realises it! However, God gave due

---

[73] Or, 'Behold God exalteth by His power etc...(AV)' Probably the preacher has taken the biblical ישגיב (*hiph'il*) with the meaning of post-biblical ישגב (*pi'el*) 'to overpower', hence, 'God overpowers in His strength'; compare *BT Temurah* 16a: שלא ישגבני יצר הרע מלשנות ('so that the evil inclination should not have power over me [preventing me] from studying'). In connection with this homily, compare also the maxim, 'Either soldier or scribe!' (אי סייפא לא ספרא אי ספרא לא סייפא; *BT Avodah Zarah* 17b).

[74] See p. 49.

[75] See Marmorstein, 'The Background to the Aggadah', *HUCA* vol. 6 (1929), p. 159.

[76] See *Exodus Rabbah* 9:9; also *Tanhuma*, ed. Buber, 2, p. 33.

[77] This interpretation of clause B is recorded explicitly in *Tanhuma* (see also Rashi on the verse).

warning to Pharaoh with every plague, that he might thereby do repentance. Hence it is written, 'In this thou shalt know that I am the Lord etc. . . .', 'behold, I will smite all thy borders with frogs (Exodus 7:27)', '[Now, therefore,] send, hasten in thy cattle . . . (*ibid.* 9:19)'.

We have suggested that in both this and the preceding interpretation of 36:22, ישגיב was treated as internal *hiph'il*. In the following proem, however, the later *Amora*, R. Berechiah, has invested this verb with a transitive meaning, God strengthens those who perform His will, and instructs sinners in the ways of penitence:[78]

'And the Lord said unto Moses: "Rise up early in the morning etc. . . . (9:13)".' Thus it is written, הן א-ל ישגיב בכחו מי כמוהו מורה. R. Berechiah said: הן means "one", thus in Greek they call one *hen*.[79] [Therefore, our verse] implies that our God is unique, since ישגיב בכחו, He fortifies the strength of the righteous to do His will. ומי כמוהו מורה, [implies] that He indicates the way to repentance. Thus you find with Moses that God strengthened him to undertake His mission, and to carry out His commands. Moreover, He was directing the wicked Pharaoh to do repentance, since He did not wish to send a plague before He had admonished him to repent. Thus it is written, "Rise up early in the morning and stand before Pharaoh." He imbued Moses with strength to rise up early and to stand before Pharaoh, to whom He indicated the way to do repentance, as it is written, "and thou shalt say unto him etc. . . ."'

God's treatment of the Egyptians is reflected in the exposition of a further verse from this chapter, preserved in a tannaitic source. According to an anonymous *Tanna*, the expression וינער in Exodus 14:27 alludes to the youthful angels into whose hands the Egyptians were delivered for punishment, as is indicated in Job 36:14, תמות בנער נפשם. As with all the examples cited thus far, the preacher offers no basis for the application of his proof-text to his theme. Presumably, he was aware of an established association between the context of

---

[78] See *Exodus Rabbah* 12:1; also *Pesiqta d'Rav Kahana* 24, ed. Buber, p. 158b (ed. Mandelbaum, p. 354).
[79] Compare *Targum* to this verse: הא בלחודוהי א-להא תקיף. R. Berechiah appears to have favoured this interpretation of הן, as he resorts to it elsewhere (see *Pesiqta d'Rav Kahana* 9, p. 77b (ed. Mandelbaum, p. 156) on Isaiah 41:24, see also Buber's comment on the text.

his quotation, and the events of the Exodus, which he evidently expected his audience to recognise:[80]

ויער יי את מצרים [means] that God delivered into the hands of young angels and cruel angels, as it is said, 'therefore, a cruel angel shall be sent against him (Proverbs 17:11)',[81] and it says, 'Their soul shall die through the agency of the youthful ones.'

One further verse from chapter 36 was employed as the basis of another homily relating to a wilderness-theme, Israel's encounter with the Midianites. We referred earlier to the widely recurring motif of Moses' unwillingness to accept his death.[82] His final acquiescence was procured, according to the tannaitic source quoted above, by God's assurance that he would not fall into the clutches of the Angel of Death. According to the following source, however, Moses was willing to surrender his life when he saw the defeat and annihilation of the Midianites:[83]

'Avenge the Children of Israel of the Midianites (Numbers 31:2)': The verse states, לא יגרע מצדיק עיניו (36:7 – lit.: 'He withdraweth not His eyes from the righteous'). What does this verse mean? [It means that] God does not withhold from the righteous what he wishes to see with his eyes. This teaches [us] that Moses was longing to see vengeance on the Midianites before he died, and was concerning him that it was said, 'The righteous shall rejoice when he

---

80 See *Mekhilta Behallah, Va-Yeḥi* 6, p. 111; also, p. 67. See also the opposing view that God rejected the help of the angels, and did battle with the Egyptians alone, *Pesiqta Rabbati* 21, ed. Friedmann, p. 104; *Avot d'Rabbi Natan* Version A, chapter 27, p. 83; *Numbers Rabbah* 8:3. On the suffering of the Egyptians at the time of their death, see also *Mekhilta Beshallaḥ, Shirta* 6, p. 138, and *Mekhilta d'Rabbi Shimon b Yoḥai*, p. 87, where Job 41:23 is cited in support of the notion that the souls of the Egyptians were trapped within their bodies, as though within 'skin bottles securely tied, neither admitting nor releasing air!'

81 The preacher may have been familiar with an exegetical tradition linking this verse and its context specifically with the punishment of the Egyptians, for which we have not yet found any further evidence. Alternatively, he may have regarded it as a comment on God's treatment of the wicked in general, as we find it in a further tannaitic source, *Sifrei* to Deuteronomy 34:5, *pisqa* 357 and the parallels cited by Finkelstein, p. 428.

82 See above, pp. 44f.

83 See *Tanhuma*, ed. Buber, 4, p. 159; Old Version, *Mattot* 4; *Numbers Rabbah* 22:5. This passage presupposes a longer account cited from the lost *Midrash Yelammedenu* in the *Yalqut* (*Mattot* 785) which depicts Moses as ultimately accepting his fate, so long as he might see subjugation of the Midianites before his death. See also *Sifrei* to Numbers 31:2, *pisqa* 157, p. 209.

seeth the vengeance (Psalm 58:11)'. 'The righteous shall rejoice' –
this refers to Moses – 'when he seeth the vengeance' – [that is] the
vengeance of Midian – 'he shall wash his feet in the blood of the
wicked' – this refers to Balaam.

As we indicated above, more substantial evidence has been
preserved in our sources for the traditional interpretation of
Elihu's speech in chapter 33 with reference to events at the
Exodus and in the wilderness. Several series of verses from this
chapter have been related to notable incidents in the pentateuchal narrative. In view of R. Hoshiah's statement quoted
earlier, linking Elihu specifically with מתן תורה, it is noteworthy that one of these series, verses 22–4, was treated as a
comment on the tragic aftermath of the revelation at Sinai, the
making of the Golden Calf. On perpetrating this sacrilegious
act, the Children of Israel were condemned before God by the
angels. Had not Moses intervened, reminding God of His
covenant with the patriarchs, they would have been consigned
to perdition:[84]

'Yea, his soul draweth near unto the pit, and his life to the destroyers
(v. 22)' – [Elihu] speaks here about Israel at the time when they
made the Golden Calf. The angels came and were accusing them at
that time, as Moses himself said, 'For I was in dread of *Anger* and
Wrath (Deuteronomy 9:19)'.[85] Immediately, Moses arose at that
time, girded up his loins in prayer, and was pleading in Israel's
defence, seeking mercy [for them] from God, as Job explicitly states,
'If there be for him a מלאך, an intercessor ... (v. 23)' – the term
מלאך connotes Moses, as it is said, 'And He sent a מלאך and
brought us forth from Egypt (Numbers 20:16)'. How did he plead
their cause for mercy? He said to God: 'Lord of all worlds, why doth
Thy wrath wax hot against Thy people? (Exodus 32:11)'. 'Then He is

---

[84] See *Pesiqta Rabbati* 10, p. 38b.

[85] The preacher alludes here to a notion which occurs widely in our sources, the
enmity of the angels either towards Moses, or towards Israel at the time of the giving
of the Law (see *BT Nedarim* 32a; *Pesiqta Rabbati* 10, p. 37b; *Sifra* [*Baraita d'Rabbi
Ishmael*] p. 3a end; *Tanhuma*, ed. Buber, 5, p. 51; *Midrash Psalms* to 7:6, pp. 65–6;
Exodus Rabbah 44:3; *Pirqei d'Rabbi Eliezer* 46. It is noteworthy that this notion was
associated in particular with a verse from Job, 26:9; see *Exodus Rabbah* 42:2, and
41:7; *Tanhuma*, ed. Buber, 2, p. 113 (see Buber's comments); *BT Shabbat* 88b; *BT
Sukkah* 5a. See further Altmann's observations regarding the possibility of some
association between this motif and the similar tradition relating to Adam ('The
Rabbinic Adam Legends', *JQR* vol. 35 (1944–5), p. 371).

gracious unto him, and saith, "Deliver him from going down to the pit, I have found a ransom (v. 24).'" How so? Moses said to Him: 'Lord of all worlds, I know that they deserve to die, You have told me so, "He that sacrificeth unto the gods shall be utterly destroyed (Exodus 22:19)." However, I beseech You, deliver them from the Angels of Destruction, be mindful of the merit of their fathers! "Remember Abraham, Isaac and Israel Thy servants to whom Thou didst swear by Thine own self ... (*ibid.* 32:13)"'.[86]

The exposition of one of this series of verses with reference to Israel's early history, can be traced back to tannaitic sources. According to R. Tarphon, verse 24 sheds light on the phrase דק ככפר על הארץ in Exodus 16:14, which refers to God's presentation of the manna to Israel. It is interesting to note that this early *Tanna* offers no explanation for the application of his proof-text, which suggests once again, that he already recognised a link between its context and his chosen theme:[87]

R. Tarphon said: 'The Manna came down upon the [outstretched] palms [of God].[88] ["As hoar-frost (ככפר) on the ground (Exodus 16:14)"] – God, as it were, stretched forth His hands and took the prayers of our patriarchs who were lying in the dust, and brought down the Manna like dew for Israel, as it is said, "And He was gracious unto them (*viz.* Israel) and said: 'Deliver them from

---

86 We may note further, that Elihu's words in 34:24, are also associated with an aspect of the unfortunate incident of the Golden Calf, the heroic death of the original group of seventy elders on account of their opposition to the making of this idol; see *Tanhuma*, ed. Buber, 4, p. 58, and the parallels cited there.

87 See *Mekhilta Beshallaḥ, Va-Yassa* 3, p. 166; also *Mekhilta d'Rabbi Shimon b. Yoḥai*, p. 110.

88 This rendering is based on Jastrow (see p. 31, s.v. אופסים) who gives the singular of אופסים as אפס = פס. Consequently, R. Tarphon may have based his *aggadah* on the expression מחספס in Exodus 16:14, which he has treated as a *Notarikon* for פס מחוסה, 'covered by a palm'. Löw, however, suggests that אופסים is a corruption of איסקופים, 'a threshold', which occurs in *Sifrei Numbers* 11:9, 89, p. 90 (see 'Lexikalische Mizellen' in *Festschrift zum Siebzigsten Gebürtstage David Hoffmanns*, Berlin 1914, pp. 119–20). Although there is some external evidence to support Löw's emendation (see the MSS of *Midrash Ha-Gadol* cited by Epstein in *Mekhilta d'Rabbi Shimon b. Yoḥai* p. 110, which read איסקופים = סעיפים) it cannot be accepted without serious reservations. Firstly, we can find no midrashic basis for equating איסקופים with מחספס in Exodus 16:14, to which R. Tarphon's exegetical comment relates. Secondly, the reading אופסים has some manuscript support which cannot be disregarded. MSS Oxford and Munich read אוספיים, which is merely a metathesis for אופסים, rather than a corruption of איסקופים. This reading is also preserved in a Genizah fragment of the *Mekhilta* (see Ginzberg, *Legends*, vol. 6, p. 17, note 101).

descending into the pit [for want of food] for I have found כפר' (*viz.* the patriarchs)."'[89]

The second series of verses from this same chapter are applied in the following homily to a personality with whom Elihu is actually identified in rabbinic sources, Balaam.[90] According to the anonymous preacher, a sinner, like Balaam, is not informed of the dreadful consequences of his evil ways. Once his fate has overtaken him, Satan reveals to him the cause of his downfall:[91]

'And God came to Balaam at night (Numbers 22:20)': Scripture states, 'In a dream, in a vision of the night, when deep sleep falleth upon men, in slumberings upon the bed; then He openeth the ears of men, and by their chastisement sealeth the decree, that men may put away their purpose, and that He may hide pride from man (33:15–17).' What does this last phrase mean? God conceals from a man that his way is going to destroy him totally, and bring him to the pit of destruction! For when a man goes to commit a sin, Satan dances before him until he completes the offence. Once he has destroyed him, he returns and informs him, as it is said, He goeth after her straightway ... Till an arrow strike through his liver; [as a bird hasteneth to the snare – and knoweth not that it is at the cost of his life] (Proverbs 7:22–23)'. Thus God concealed from Balaam [his fate] until he went and destroyed himself. Once he had departed from his glory, destroyed himself, and realised the position he was in, he began to pray for his soul, 'Let my soul die the death of the righteous (Numbers 23:10).'[92]

---

[89] We may assume initially that R. Tarphon, like the anonymous preacher in the excerpt from *Pesiqta Rabbati* cited above, identified כפר in Job 33:24 with the patriarchs. This in turn, provided him with the basis for his interpretation of ככפור in Exodus 16:14. However, he probably saw the allusion to the prayers of the patriarchs in the phrase, ותעל שכבת הטל, as did R. Eleazar of Modi'in (see *Mekhilta Beshallaḥ*, Va-Yasa 3, p. 165). Thus he may have rendered the verse as, 'Behold, there was upon the face of the wilderness Manna covered by the hand [of God (*viz* מחוסה פס = מחספס)], Manna according to כפור, the merit of the patriarchs.'

[90] See above, p. 25.

[91] See *Tanhuma*, ed. Buber, 4, p. 137 and the parallels cited there.

[92] The application of 33:15–17 to Balaam warrants some closer consideration, as it may not be based purely on a verbal association with Numbers 22:20. Elihu's words in verse 15 bear an obvious resemblance to Eliphaz's statement in 4:12–13, 'Now a word was secretly brought to me, and mine ear received a whisper thereof. In the thoughts from the visions of the night, when deep sleep falleth on men.' These two verses occur frequently in our sources as the scriptural basis for a description of

In the remaining passage to be quoted in this context, verses
28 and 29 are related to the theme of Moses' initial unwillingness to accept God's commission to return to Egypt and to
confront Pharaoh. God did not summon Aaron to share the
distinction of bearing His word to Pharaoh, until Moses had
refused His bidding on three occasions:[93]

'[He redeemeth his soul from going into the pit, and his life beholdeth
the light.] Lo, all these things doth God work, twice, yea thrice, with
a man.' Three times does God wait for a man [to submit to His will],
if he repents [after the third occasion] all is well, if not, He imposes
upon him [the consequences of his] initial refusals! Thus you find that
when God said to Moses, 'Come now therefore, and I will send thee
unto Pharaoh (Exodus 3:10)', he answered initially, 'Behold, they
will not believe me (*ibid.* 4:1).' Subsequently, he said, 'I am not a
man of words (v. 10).' Thereafter he said, 'Send by the hand of him
whom thou wilt send (v. 13)'. This constitutes the three occasions
[when God tolerated his refusals]. When he did not retract, but said,
'The Children of Israel have not hearkened to me, how then shall
Pharaoh hear me? (*ibid.* 6:12)', the divine word was addressed to
Aaron as well as to [Moses], thus it is written, 'And the Lord spoke to
Moses *and to Aaron* (v. 13)'.

God's method of communication with pagan prophets (see *Genesis Rabbah* 52:5, and
the parallels cited by Theodor, p. 544; also *Tanhuma*, ed. Buber, 1, p. 177). Urbach
suggests that this description – a version of which we have included below – was not
purely academic, but alluded to the pagans, Christians, and particularly Gnostics
who laid claim to prophecy and the prophetic experience during the talmudic
period. The biblical prototype selected by the Rabbis to represent these latter-day
prophets, Urbach suggests further, was Balaam (see דרשות חז"ל על נביאי אומות
העולם ועל פרשת בלעם, *Tarbitz*, vol. 25 (1955–6), pp. 278f). It is interesting to note that in the following passage, which casts Balaam in the role of the
representative of the pagan prophets, the words of both Eliphaz and Elihu are cited
to indicate God's purely nocturnal association with them (see *Numbers Rabbah* 20:12;
also *Tanhuma*, ed. Buber, 4, p. 137, and the Old Version, *Balaq* 8, on the basis of
which the text here is emended):

> Why did [God] reveal Himself to Balaam by night? Because he was not fit to
> [receive] the Holy Spirit save by night (so *Tanhuma*, ed. Buber) because with all
> pagan prophets, [God] communicates only by night. Thus Eliphaz says, 'Now a
> word was secretly brought to me, and mine ear received a whisper thereof. In
> thoughts from the visions of the night, when sleep falleth upon men (Job
> 4:12–13)'; and thus Elihu says, 'In a dream, in a vision of the night, when deep
> sleep falleth upon men [in slumberings upon the bed] (Job 33:15).'

93 See *Exodus Rabbah* 7:2, where only 33:29 is cited; however, the preceding verse is
clearly presupposed by the anonymous preacher. On Job 33:29, see further *BT
Yoma* 86b; also *Tosephta Yoma* 5(4):13, ed. Zukermandel, p. 191.

THE SPEECHES OF ZOPHAR

Although Zophar's speeches are limited to two chapters, 11 and 20, there is none the less, some evidence in our sources to suggest that the former of these was linked in early rabbinic tradition with a specific theme, the Giving of the Law. As we have seen from the material cited above, this motif was associated with the name of Elihu, and is also discernible in the aggadic exegesis of one of Eliphaz's speeches.[94] The passages which follow suggest that Zophar's speech in chapter 11 was regarded as his contribution to the discussion among his companions relating to this auspicious event. In all probability, the basis for the association of this chapter with the theme of מתן תורה, may have been provided by the term חכמה (= תורה)[95] which occurs in verse 6: 'And that He would tell the secrets of wisdom (חכמה), that sound wisdom is manifold. Know therefore that God exacteth of thee less than thine iniquity deserveth'.

In the following homily, this verse is expounded in connection with an unusual notion which is without parallel in talmudic-midrashic literature. When Moses ascended Mount Sinai to receive the second set of stone tablets, these contained not only the written code, but also the Oral Law.[96] This view is clearly incompatible with the well-known concept that the תורה שבעל פה was purposely preserved in its oral form so that it might remain the exclusive possession of the nation of Israel:[97]

---

[94] See pp. 56ff on Eliphaz's speech in chapter 4.
[95] For a more extensive comment on this well-known and widely recurring aggadic device, see p. 82.
[96] See *Exodus Rabbah* 46:1.
[97] Thus the Oral Law was perceived to be the means by which the true Israel might be distinguished from false claimants; see *Exodus Rabbah* 47:1 and the parallels cited there; also *Tanhuma*, ed. Buber, 1, p. 88, and the parallels cited there; *PT Pe'ah* 2:6, 17a; and *Numbers Rabbah* 14:10. In connection with the view that the two tablets of stone contained more than the Decalogue, see the statement of Ḥananiah the nephew of R. Joshua (*PT Sheqalim* 6:1, 49d): 'Between each and every word were the details and letters of the *Torah*.' The parallel passage in *Numbers Rabbah* 13:16, reads: 'The sections and details of the *Torah* were written on the tablets [of stone].' See further, *Canticles Rabbah* to 5:14; also Philo, *De Decalogo* 29, for the view that the Decalogue contains the kernel of the entire *Torah*.

'And the Lord said to Moses: "Hew for thyself etc. (34:1)"'. Thus it is
written, ויגד לך תעלמות חכמה כי כפלים לתושיה ודע כי ישה
לך א־לוה מעונך: Moses began to be troubled by the breaking of the
tablets, but God said to him, 'Do not be troubled about the first
tablets, since they contained only the Ten Commandments. On the
second tablets which I am going to give you, there will be laws,
Midrash and *Aggadot*. Thus it is written, "And He imparted to you
the secrets of the *Torah*, for the *Torah*[98] is two-fold." Moreover, you
are given the glad tidings that I have forgiven your sin, as it is said,
"And know that God has forgiven you your iniquity".'[99]

Verse 9 of this same chapter occurs as the scriptural basis for
one of the solutions offered in our sources for the problem
presented by God's choice of the barren, arid wilderness as the
location for the Revelation.[100] According to an anonymous
teacher, the geographic extensiveness of the wilderness was
intended to symbolise the character of the Law which, in
Zophar's words, is without bounds:[101] 'Why was the *Torah*
given in the Wilderness? ... Just as the Wilderness is boundless,
so the words of the *Torah* are boundless! As it is said, "The
measure thereof is longer than the earth"'.

One further verse from chapter 11 has been employed as the
basis of a homily containing both well-known and unusual
aggadic elements relating to the events at Sinai, and their
implications for Israel's deliverance from Egypt. Clause B of
verse 11, וירא עון ולא יתבונן, has been taken as Zophar's

98 On the equation of תושיה with תורה, see *Pirqei d'Rabbi Eliezer* 3 on Proverbs 8:14
('Counsel is mine and sound wisdom (תושיה)'). Moreover, the anonymous
preacher probably saw in the term ויגד an allusion to oral information apart from
the Written Law, which God communicated to Israel. In medieval sources, הגדה
occurs with the meaning of קבלה (see Maimonides, *Hilkhot Mamrim* 1:2, and his
commentary to *Mishnah Sanhedrin* 11:2). There is also some evidence to suggest that
הגדה was employed in the sense of 'oral tradition' already in talmudic times, see
Leviticus Rabbah 18:2 (p. 402) אמר ר' סימון: מסורת אגדה היא; see also the MSS
cited by Margulies, where the reading אגדה alone occurs.
99 Which presupposes that the preacher took וישה as וישא. Alternatively, he may
have associated this expression with נשה, 'to forget' (see Deuteronomy 32:18, צור
ילדך תשי) hence, 'He has made you forget your iniquity.'
100 See *Numbers Rabbah* 19:26; *Tanhuma*, ed. Buber, 4, pp. 7 and 128; Old Version
Ḥuqqat 21; *BT Eruvin* 54a; see further the sources cited in the next note, also
Ginzberg, *Legends*, vol. 6, p. 32, note 185.
101 See *Pesiqta d'Rav Kahana* 12, p. 107a (ed. Mandelbaum, p. 219); *New Midrash on the
Torah*, Mann, *The Bible as Read and Preached*, p. 244.

formulation of the well-known principle, instrumental in the redemption from Egypt, 'God only judges a man in his current situation [and not in the light of his future conduct].'[102] Had God judged Israel at the Exodus in the light of the events at Sinai, which He could foresee, then their deliverance would not have taken place. The homily is of further interest, as the preacher offers an unusual explanation for the phenomenon of Israel's worship of the Golden Calf:[103]

'And the Lord said: "I have surely seen (ראה ראיתי) the affliction of My people (Exodus 3:7)."' Thus it is written, 'He knows men of falsehood, [but He foresees iniquity, yet does not take it into consideration]'.[104] God knew the people who would in future commit an act of 'falsehood' and be slain on account of it,[105] but 'He foresees iniquity, yet does not take it into account.' ... Thus when Israel was in Egypt, God saw what they would do in the future! Hence it is written, 'And the Lord said: "I have surely seen ..."'. [The verse does not employ only the one expression] ראיתי, but ראה ראיתי, [a dual expression, implying that] God said to him, 'Moses, you can foresee only one thing, I can foresee two! You can foresee them coming to Sinai and receiving My *Torah* and I can foresee them receiving my *Torah*, this [is implied in the expression] ראה. However, [the expression] ראיתי alludes to [My] foreseeing the making of the Golden Calf, concerning which it is said, "I have seen (ראיתי) this people (*ibid.* 32:9)." Moreover, when I will come to Sinai to give them the *Torah*, I will descend in My *quadriga*[106] and they will reflect upon it[107] and detach one of [the creatures drawing it] and thereby provoke Me to anger. None the less, I do not judge

---

[102] See further *PT Rosh Ha-Shanah* 1:3, 57a.

[103] See *Exodus Rabbah* 3:2; also *Tanhuma*, Old Version, *Shemot* 20.

[104] Lit.: 'For He knoweth base men; and when He seeth iniquity, will He not then consider it?'

[105] Evidently the preacher has taken מתי as the construct of מתים, hence 'dead', or 'slain'. It is also possible that the expression שוא has been taken as an allusion to idolatry on the basis of Hosea 12:12, 'If Gilead be given to iniquity becoming altogether vanity (שוא) in Gilgal they sacrifice unto bullocks.' See also Jonah 2:9.

[106] אני יורד בטטראמולי שלי; the hybrid expression *TETRAMOULI* is not recorded in Greek dictionaries; see M. Jastrow, *A Dictionary of the Targumim, the Talmud Babli and Yerushalmi, and the Midrashic Literature*, London/New York 1903, p. 528, also Levy, *Wörterbuch* 2, *Nachtrage*, p. 209.

[107] See further *Exodus Rabbah* 43:8, also 30:7, and Einhorn's observations on the text. See also the account of the origin of the Golden Calf recorded in *Midrash Shir-Shirim* 1, ed. Grunhut, pp. 13a-b, which does suggest some association with the *Merkavah*.

them on the basis of deeds yet to be performed, but on the basis [of their] present situation.'

Although the material cited here is limited, it shares the same significant feature of all the homilies and expositions cited thus far. In every case, the early preachers have selected their proemial and proof-texts from the speeches of Job and his companions, and applied them to Exodus and Wilderness themes, without offering any basis for their choice. They – and, presumably, their audiences – readily acknowledged the relevance of Job, a work ascribed to Moses himself, as a source of supplementary information relating to major events of Israel's early history. We would conclude, therefore, that our extant sources have preserved only the fragmentary remains of a major trend in the early, traditional exegesis of the Book of Job.

MOSES AND JOB'S BOLD SPEECH

An unusual but interesting manifestation of the tradition of the Mosaic authorship of Job is the attribution to Moses of one or two of Job's most audacious utterances. This occurs already in a tannaitic source, the *Sifrei* to Numbers 27:12,[108] where an anonymous teacher amplifies Moses' utterances in Deuteronomy 3:24 with the following declaration:

The characteristics of the Omnipresent are not like those of humans! It is a human characteristic for [a judge] who is senior to his colleague to overrule him,[109] but who can prevent You [from doing what You wish]? Thus it says, 'He is alone [in judging His world], therefore who can dispute with Him, [as His soul desires so He does]'.[110]

108 See *pisqa* 134, p. 180.
109 From the parallel passage in the *Sifrei* to Deuteronomy 3:24 (*pisqa* 27) it is clear that the allusion is to the judicial procedures of Roman magistrates (see Finkelstein's comments, pp. 43f).
110 The anonymous teacher here has evidently understood the verse as did Pappos, who caused R. Aqiva much consternation by his rendering of 23:13 (see *Mekhilta Beshallaḥ, Va-Yeḥi* 6, p. 112):

Pappos expounded [the verse] והוא באחד ומי ישיבנו ונפשו אותה ויעש, as, 'He alone judges all the inhabitants of the world, and there is no one to contradict His words!' R. Aqiva said: 'Enough, Pappos!' He retorted: 'How then would you expound [the verse] והוא באחד ומי ישיבנו?!' He said to him: '[It means that] one may not contradict the words of Him who spoke and the world came into being, for He judges everyone in truth and in justice!'

Possibly the most daring of Job's assertions, for which he is sharply criticised in our sources, is contained in 9:22, 'It is all one – therefore I say: He destroyeth the innocent and the wicked!' Yet in the following homily, which relates to a theme discussed earlier, Moses' desperate efforts to avoid the inevitability of his death,[111] these words are attributed to Moses:[112]

'All things come alike to all; there is one event to the righteous and to the wicked (Ecclesiastes 9:2)' – Moses said to God: 'Lord of all worlds, all are equal before You, "He destroyeth the innocent and the wicked!" The spies provoked You to anger through [their] evil report of the land, while I have served Your children for forty years in the wilderness. Yet they and I share the same fate! ...

'The spies spoke slander [concerning the Land of Israel], "[The land through which we have passed to spy it out,] is a land that consumeth the inhabitants thereof (Numbers 13:32)". I did not see it, yet I praised it to Your children and said, "For the Lord thy God bringeth thee into a good land etc. ... (Deuteronomy 8:7)". Now let me see if it conforms with my description or with theirs! As it is said, "Let me go over, I pray Thee, and see the good land ... (*ibid.* 3:25)"'. [God] said to him: 'For thou shalt not go over [this Jordan] (*ibid.* v. 27)'. [Moses] said to Him, 'He destroyeth the innocent and the wicked!'

In its original context, Job 17:9, 'Let the righteous holdeth on his way' (ויאחז צדיק דרכו) is normally construed as Job's expression of confidence in the fortitude of the righteous. In the following homily, however, an anonymous preacher has interpreted the verse as Moses' bold attempt to assuage God's anger, by commanding Him[113] to remember His characteristic virtue of forgiveness, by which He is known to His creatures:[114]

'Let the Righteous One hold fast to His way!' – When the spies provoked God, Moses said: 'Lord of the Universe, Hold fast to Your way! Hold fast to Your characteristic virtue! Because all the righteous ones have held fast to their characteristic virtues. Abraham held fast to the covenant of circumcision, Isaac to prayer, Jacob to truth, [as it is said], "Thou bestowest truth upon Jacob (Micah 7:20)", Joseph to

---

[111] See above, pp. 44f.
[112] See *Tanhuma*, ed. Buber, 5, pp. 8–9, also p. 7; and *Yalqut Va-Ethanan* 811.
[113] On Moses' ability to command God, see below, Appendix 2, pp. 183ff.
[114] This homily is quoted in *Yalqut Job* 907, apparently from the lost *Yelammedenu*.

piety, [as it is said,] "And He inclined unto him on account of his piety (Genesis 39:21)",[115] Moses to humility, [as it is said,] "And the man Moses was exceedingly humble (Numbers 12:3)", Aaron to peace, [as it is said], "My covenant was with him of life and peace (Malachi 2:5)", Phineas to zealousness, [as it is said], "... in that he was zealous with My zealousness (Numbers 25:2)". You also hold fast to Your characteristic virtue!' 'And what is My characteristic virtue?' – God asked. Moses replied: 'A merciful and gracious God, hence it is said, "And now, I pray Thee, let the power of the Lord be great, [according as Thou hast spoken saying: 'The Lord is slow to anger and plenteous in loving-kindness, forgiving iniquity and transgression'] (*ibid.* 14:17–18)"'.

The theme of Moses' boldness of speech when communicating with God, which features already in the biblical narrative,[116] is part of a much wider motif in early rabbinic and non-rabbinic literature, involving a number of biblical personalities. Although this motif requires a much more comprehensive analysis than is permitted by the scope of this chapter, we can at least note here some of the basic details.[117] Philo is apparently the earliest writer to deal with this subject at length.[118] He elaborates upon the theme of bold speech in a lengthy homily which, J. Amir suspects, was based on contemporary Palestinian sources.[119] In conjunction with Abraham's contentious words in Genesis 15:3, Philo develops the notion that the friend of God – as typified by the patriarch and Moses – may speak in an audacious manner which true friendship (= אהבה) permits, as long as it is controlled by an awareness of God's awesomeness (= יראה).[120] Apart from the parallels in tannaitic sources[121] for service of God based on a

---

[115] The preacher here may be alluding to the piety displayed by Joseph in resisting the overtures of Potiphar's wife even in prison (see *Genesis Rabbah* 87:10, p. 1075 and the parallels cited there).

[116] See, for example, Exodus 5:22–23 and Numbers 11:22.

[117] On the theme of boldness in communicating with God, see below, Appendix 2, pp. 185f.

[118] See *Quis Haeres Sit* IV, 19ff.

[119] 'Philo's Homilies in Love and Fear and their Relationship to Palestinian Midrashim', *Zion* vol. 30 (1965), pp. 47–60.

[120] See particularly VI, 28ff.

[121] For a review of the relevant material, see my article, 'Understanding Rabbinic Midrash', *L'Eylah* no. 21 (Spring 1986), pp. 55–6.

synthesis of love and fear, which Philo advocates, there are more significant traces of the concept which he develops in rabbinic literature. Firstly, in connection with the incident of Moses striking the rock (Numbers 20:8ff) which resulted in his being condemned to die, an anonymous preacher observed:

It may be compared to a king who had a friend (אוהב) who behaved presumptuously (מגיס) towards the king in private [uttering] harsh words, but the king was not angered by him. On one occasion he behaved presumptuously [towards the king] in the presence of [his] legions, and he condemned him to death![122]

The implications of this parable require little clarification. Moses' audacious utterances were tolerated by God, because he was an אוהב, a friend, from whom such familiarity was acceptable.[123] It is conceivable, therefore, that Job's bold utterances were ascribed to Moses, not only because of his acknowledged authorship of their source. On the lips of Moses, these otherwise unpalatable statements, could be regarded as an acceptable expression of the Law-giver's especial relationship with God.

THE VOICE OF GOD IN JOB AND PSALM 29

We noted above that allusions to God's voice in verses from both Job and Psalm 29 were treated as a reference to the revelation at Sinai, without any explanation being offered

---

[122] See *Tanhuma*, ed. Buber, 4, p. 121; Old Version, *Ḥuqqat* 10; *Numbers Rabbah* 19:10. See also p. 184 below, where R. Joshua b. Ḥananiah employs the same imagery of the friend of the king, who can give him orders which he obeys.

[123] This notion is implied in a tannaitic source, which has been the subject of much debate because of the unique statement which it contains. Commenting on the maxim of Antigonus of Sokho in *Avot* 1:3, an unknown teacher declares service of God out of love to be inferior to that which is motivated by fear. The significant factor for our discussion is his characterisation of the עושה מאהבה:

It may be compared to a man who performs the will of his master, but his heart is over-bold (לבו גס) in so doing, or to a man who performs the will of his father, but his heart is over-bold in so doing!

See *Avot d'Rabbi Natan* Version B, 10, p. 26; see Schechter's observations in note 10; also L. Finkelstein, *Mavo Le-Massekhtot Avot ve-Avot d'Rabbi Natan*, New York 1950, pp. 32ff; E. E. Urbach, *The Sages: Their Opinions and Beliefs* (trans. Israel Abrahams), Jerusalem 1975, p. 403; and A. Büchler, *Studies in Sin and Atonement*, Oxford 1928, p. 159. Our rendering of the key phrase לבו גס, is based on *BT Ketubot* 12a (see also 28a) where R. Judah b. Illai records the original practice in Judaea to allow the groom to be alone with his bride before entering the nuptial chamber,

regarding the basis for this identification.[124] We may observe initially that, in the case of Psalm 29, this reflects an exegetical motif which is to be found in talmudic-midrashic literature, in the *Targum*, and is echoed in the liturgical usage of this psalm. Moreover, it can be illustrated exclusively from tannaitic sources, which suggests that this motif was well established at an early period.

The *Sifrei* to Numbers 6:26[125] records the following anonymous comment on the concluding term of the priestly benediction: 'שלום here refers to the Torah, as it is said, "The Lord will give strength unto His people, the Lord will bless His people with peace (Psalm 29:11)".' The midrashic device employed here is a common one, climatic exegesis. This, as we indicated above,[126] permits a scriptural term or expression to be invested with the meaning of the context, or 'climate' in which it occurs, and is then taken in that meaning in another context. However, our unknown aggadist's use of this device here exhibits an unusual feature. Neither the proof-text he cites to establish the identification of שלום with תורה, nor the context from which it is taken, contains any reference to the *Torah*. That the expression עוז in verse 11 is an allusion to the *Torah* is a well-known exegetical tradition, which is reflected in tannaitic and amoraic sources, as well as in the *Targum*.[127] However, on what was this tradition based?

This question may be answered initially by a cursory review of the aggadic treatment of Psalm 29 in tannaitic sources. In the *Mekhilta d'R. Ishmael, Yitro, Ba-Hodesh* 5,[128] verses 3–9 are cited to confirm that the earth itself quaked at God's utterance

---

כדי שיהא לבו גס בה, 'in order that he might become bold (*viz.* intimate, familiar) towards her'. See further, *Mishnah Qiddushin* 7:4, Lifschitz's comment on the text (*Tipheret Yisrael*, note 17).

[124] See pp. 46f.   [125] *Pisqa* 42, p. 46.   [126] See pp. 4f.

[127] See, for example, *Mekhilta Beshallah, Shirta* 3, p. 126, on the expression עוז in Exodus 15:2, which is equated with *Torah* on the basis of Psalm 29:11, and 99:3; also *Shirta* 9, p. 146, where נהלת בעזך (15:13) is identified with *Torah* on the basis of Psalm 29:11; *Exodus Rabbah* 27:4, where this same verse is used to identify עז as *Torah* in I Samuel 2:10, ויתן עז למלכו; *Tanhuma*, ed. Buber, 5, p. 55, where הודעת בעמים עזך (Psalm 77:15) is taken as an allusion to *Torah* on the basis of 29:11; finally see the *Targum* on this verse.

[128] See pp. 220–1.

of the opening words of the Decalogue. Verse 4 is quoted in
Ba-ḥodesh 1,[129] to attest to the audibility of the Divine voice at
Sinai. This verse appears again in *Ba-ḥodesh* 9,[130] as the proof-
text cited by R. Aqiva to support his interpretation of Exodus
20:18, that the multitude gathered at Sinai, actually saw the
words of the Decalogue emanating in a fiery form from the
mouth of God. In the same passage, verse 7 appears in support
of the notion that the voice of God was miraculously modu-
lated to accommodate the hearing capacity of every individual
present at Sinai. Finally, in *Yitro, Amaleq* 1,[131] we find verses
9–11 as the basis for the tradition – recorded here in the name
of R. Eleazar of Modi'in – regarding the terror of the pagan
nations at the time of the revelation at Sinai, and their subsequent consultation with Balaam.

We see, therefore, that nine of the eleven verses of Psalm 29
were treated as references to the events at the time of the
revelation at Sinai. Yet in none of the sources cited is any
explanation offered for this treatment of the psalm. The early
aggadists evidently expected their audiences to recognise the
source of their quotations as a '*Torah*-psalm', an extra-
pentateuchal account of the giving of the Law, which could be
quoted in connection with this event without further comment.
The basis for this midrashic characterisation of Psalm 29 is not
difficult to perceive. In all probability, the recurring phrase
קול יי presented an obvious link with the key sentence describing God's dialogue with Moses at Sinai, 'Moses spoke and the
Lord answered him by a voice (בקול – Exodus 19:19)'. Consequently, Psalm 29, with its graphic portrayal of the awesome
power of God's voice, came to be regarded as the classical
description of its manifestation at Sinai.[132] Similarly, the refer-

---

[129] See p. 205.   [130] See p. 235.   [131] See p. 188.

[132] While this tradition is not explicitly formulated anywhere in our sources, at least
one tannaitic source records the view that Psalm 29 is the extra-pentateuchal
source which defines the nature of God's voice referred to in the *Torah* (see *Sifra* to
Leviticus 1:1, 2:10, ed. Weiss, p. 4a, and compare the homily cited above, p. 46,
based on Psalm 29:4–5 and Job 28:25–26, with which the following exposition has
obvious affinities):

'[And the Lord called unto Moses, and spoke unto him] out of the tent of
meeting...' – This teaches that the voice [of God] was cut off, and did not issue
forth beyond the tent of meeting. You might think that it was lowered! Therefore

ences to God's thunderous voice in Job, a work attributed to Moses himself, recording an incident which occurred within his own generation,[133] were likewise treated as allusions to the same crucial event in Israel's early history.

While this may provide the background for the widely accepted interpretation of Psalm 29:11 as an allusion to the Law, it does not offer a basis for the actual identification of עוז in this verse with תורה. It is interesting to note, therefore, that according to a further tannaitic source, this was based on climatic exegesis, involving a verse from Job. The *Sifrei* to Deuteronomy 33:2,[134] preserves a parallel account of the tradition cited earlier, regarding the pagan nations' consultation with Balaam, which concludes as follows:

They said to [Balaam]: 'What is this voice?' He replied: 'The Lord is giving His people עוז (*viz.* the *Torah*)', for עוז connotes the *Torah*, as it is said, עמו עוז ותושיה, 'With Him is strength and *Torah* (Job 12:16)'.[135]

It is possible, however, that this motif of עוז = תורה was influenced initially by the poetic description of the Philistines' capture of the Ark of the Covenant and its contents from Shiloh, in Psalm 78:61, 'And He delivered His strength (עוזו) into captivity',[136] which in turn echoes the imagery of Psalm 132:8,[137] 'Arise, O Lord, unto Thy resting-place; Thou and the ark of Thy strength (עוזך)'.

---

it says, '[And when Moses went into the tent of meeting that He might speak with him,] then he heard the Voice [speaking unto him...]' (Numbers 7:89). Scripture need not have said '*the* Voice', why then does it say '*the* Voice'? [This implies that it was] the Voice defined in the Hagiographa. How so? [As it says in Psalm 29,] 'The voice of the Lord is powerful, the voice of the Lord is full of majesty. The voice of the Lord breaketh the cedars; yea, the Lord breaketh in pieces the cedars of Lebanon... The voice of the Lord heweth out flames of fire... (vv. 4–5 and 7)'.

[133] See above, pp. 24ff.   [134] See *Pisqa* 343, p. 398.

[135] For the equation of תושיה with *Torah*, see above, p. 70, note 98. It should be noted, however, that the context in Job 12 deals with the subject of חכמה, *viz.* *Torah*.

[136] An interpretation that may have gained wide currency, as it has been incorporated into the *Targum* to this verse.

[137] Again, see the *Targum* to this verse, and compare Solomon's prayer in II Chronicles 6:41.

CHAPTER 4

Popular legends and traditions 1: the archetypal sage

Exegetical traditions of the type discussed in the preceding two chapters – further examples of which will be cited subsequently – may represent only one aspect of a more extensive corpus of popular knowledge upon which the early preachers relied in their selection of proemial verses. A further factor, which does not appear to have been considered hitherto, is the store of legends and traditions which abound in aggadic sources. Many of these are of great antiquity, as can be seen from the material relating to the Generation of the Flood cited above. Rabbinic *Midrash*, as we observed earlier, is to be regarded only as the latest phase in the process of the amplification of biblical narratives, which has its origins in the Bible itself.[1] Moreover, it reached a highly developed form long before the beginning of the Christian Era, as is suggested by such works as Jubilees, and the more recently discovered Genesis Apocryphon.[2] It is highly probable that such traditions were being popularised at an early period, (a) through the weekly homilies, which have provided much of the material for our extant midrashic works; and particularly (b) through the medium of the *Targum*, the

---

[1] For the relevant literature on this subject, see I. L. Seeligman, 'Voraussetzungen der Midraschexegese', *VTSup* 1 (1953), pp. 150ff; G. Vermes, *Scripture and Tradition in Judaism*, Leiden 1973, p. 4, and note 6; also p. 7 and note 2.

[2] The high antiquity of numerous traditions found in rabbinic literature has long been acknowledged, and is indicated by the examples we have quoted in connection with the Generation of the Flood in chapter 2. However, it is far better illustrated by Ginzberg's masterly presentation of the vast range of material culled from virtually every relevant source, in his indispensable reference work, *The Legends of the Jews*. On the antiquity of the *Genesis Apocryphon*, see N. Avigad and Y. Yadin, *A Genesis Apocryphon, a Scroll from the Wilderness of Judæa*, Jerusalem 1956, p. 38; see also Vermes, *Scripture and Tradition in Judaism*, Leiden 1973, p. 96, note 2.

paraphrastic translation of the weekly scriptural lections, which amplified both the narrative and legal sections of the Pentateuch, as can be seen from our extant *Targumim*.[3] In due course, this continuous and widespread practice of publicly expounding the Scriptures in the ancient synagogues,[4] gave rise to a considerable corpus of popular knowledge, not only of the contents of the biblical text, but also of the numerous traditions and legends with which it was embellished.

This corpus of assumed popular knowledge, we would suggest, played an important role in establishing a rapport between the early preachers and their audiences. Relying on his congregation's familiarity with well-known traditions, the preacher could challenge their perceptiveness by selecting a text, not for its obvious verbal or thematic link with the pericope, but because of its more subtle allusion to a popular tradition associated with the principal character, or main event in the morning's lection. To illustrate this, we have taken a series of proems relating to a major biblical figure, Abraham, who was the subject of numerous popular stories and legends, many of which have their origins in high antiquity.

The compiler of *Genesis Rabbah*[5] opens his midrashic commentary to Genesis 12:1ff (= *Seder* 10 of the Triennial Cycle)[6] which describes Abraham's departure from Haran and his arrival in Canaan, with six proems based on the following verses:

1) Psalm 45:11–12 (R. Isaac Nappaḥa)
2) Canticles 1:3 (R. Berechiah)
3) Canticles 8:8–10 (R. Berechiah)

---

[3] The antiquity of the paraphrastic, or free, *Targumim*, as opposed to the more literal translations, is generally accepted by scholars, although not without dissent. For a review of this discussion and the relevant literature, see Y. Komlosh, *The Bible in the Light of Aramaic Translations* (Hebrew), Tel Aviv 1973, pp. 21–2, also p. 38, note 124, and p. 40; see further Vermes, *Scripture and Tradition*, pp. 2ff.

[4] The classical sources which relate to the public 'Reading/Teaching' of the Law in ancient times, are well known, and have been adequately reviewed by K. Kohler in his article 'Reading from the Law', in *JE* vol. 7 (New York/London 1925), pp. 647f.

[5] See chapter 39:1–6, pp. 365–8.

[6] Our numbering of the *Sedarim* follows the list published by A. Büchler from the Cairo Genizah; see *JQR* (OS) vol. 6, pp. 39–42; also J. Mann, *The Bible as Read and Preached in the Old Synagogue*, vol. 1, Cincinnati 1940, pp. 561ff.

4) Ecclesiastes 7:19 (anonymous)
5) Jeremiah 51:9 (R. Azariah)
6) Psalm 45:8 (R. Azariah in the name of R. Aḥa)[7]

The majority of these texts appear, once again, to support Heinemann's contention regarding the element of surprise in the selection of proemial verses, particularly the implied designation of Abraham as a 'daughter' (Psalm 45:11) or 'little sister' (Canticles 8:8)! None the less, it is possible to show, at least in connection with five of the six proems, that the preacher has selected his text because it contains one or more elements which he expected his audience to recognise as an allusion to some aspect of the patriarch's life or character in popular tradition. We begin with the anonymous proem based on Ecclesiastes 7:19.

'Wisdom (חכמה) is a stronghold to the wise (חכם) more than ten rulers that are in a city.' – This alludes to Abraham, [to whom God said:] 'Of the ten generations from Noah to Abraham, I did not communicate with anyone save with you.' [Hence,] 'And the Lord said to Abraham: "[Get thee out etc. ....]".'

While the preacher has linked the 'ten rulers' of his proemial verse with the ten generations from Noah to Abraham, he offers no explanation or basis for the less obvious identification of Abraham with the חכם referred to in the text. We may note, however, that this identification is by no means limited to this one source. *Genesis Rabbah* 44:2 (p. 425) preserves two proems relating to Abraham's vision and promise of progeny in Genesis 15:1 (= *Seder* 12) based respectively on Proverbs 14:16, 'A *wise man* feareth, and departeth from evil' and 3:7, 'Be not *wise* in thine own eyes, fear the Lord and depart from evil.' In both cases, the scriptural epithet חכם is applied to Abraham without any explanation. Similarly, in an anonymous proem connected with Genesis 20:1 (= *Seder* 17) recorded in 52:3 (p. 542) Proverbs 10:8, 'The *wise* in heart will receive commandments', is expounded with reference to the patriarch, without any indication of the basis for its application. Finally, the compiler of *Midrash Ha-Gadol* (p. 211) records a further

[7] On a lectionary cycle from the Hagiographa, see Appendix 3, pp. 187f.

proem relating to *Seder* 10, based on 2:14–16, 'The *wise man*, his eyes are in his head . . .', where, once again the epithet חכם is equated with Abraham, without any explanatory comment. These examples represent only part of the relevant material. However, they are sufficient to indicate the existence of an exegetical motif identifying the biblical epithet חכם with Abraham, which the early preachers evidently expected their audiences to recognise. Yet the expression חכם never occurs as a scriptural epithet for Abraham, unlike נאמן and ירא, which provided preachers with an easily recognisable verbal link in their selection of proemial verses. We would suggest, therefore, that the application of the term חכם to Abraham was based upon a broader background of popular tradition relating both to the activities of the patriarch, and to the specific meaning of the biblical epithet.

As is well known, the identification of חכמה – particularly in the Wisdom Literature – with תורה, and correspondingly, the equation of חכם with תלמיד חכם, is a widely recurring exegetical motif in rabbinic sources.[8] In addition, there is a well-established tradition associated with Genesis 26:5[9] – which has its origins in high antiquity – that Abraham studied and observed the minutiae of the *Torah*[10] centuries before the revelation at Sinai. He emerges in rabbinic *Aggadah* as a judge,[11] the head of a *Yeshivah*, whose teachings were disseminated by his scholarly attendant, Eliezer.[12] He is portrayed, therefore, as an archetypal חכם, a *Torah*-sage, an imagery which, presumably, was familiar to both preachers and audiences alike. This allowed the early aggadists to apply both

---

[8] See, for example, *Sifrei Deuteronomy*, *pisqa* 1, pp. 3–4 on Proverbs 9:8, and *pisqa* 48, p. 111, on Job 12:12; *BT Eruvin* 64b on Proverbs 12:18; *BT Rosh Ha-Shanah* 17a on Job 37:24; *BT Sotah* 21a on Job 28:12; *Ecclesiastes Rabbah* to 2:3 and 13 (the statement of R. Meir); *Midrash Mishlei* to 2:10, 5:1 and 9:10.

[9] In addition to the material cited in this chapter, see *Genesis Rabbah* 64:4, pp. 703f, and the parallels cited there. Philo may also have understood this verse as a reference to Abraham's observance of the Law before the revelation at Sinai, see *De Abrahamo* viii, 46.

[10] On the antiquity of the tradition regarding the patriarchs' observance of the *Torah*, see the sources cited by Ginzberg, *Legends*, vol. 5, p. 259, note 275.

[11] See *Avot d'Rabbi Natan* Version A, 33, p. 94.

[12] See *BT Yoma* 28a; see further Ginzberg, *Legends*, vol. 5, p. 260, note 277.

proemial and proof-texts containing the key term חכם – or a synonymous expression[13] – to Abraham, relying upon their listeners' collaboration in recognising the relevance of their quotations.

Viewing our original proem in *Genesis Rabbah* 39, in the light of this tradition of Abraham as the archetypal *Torah*-sage, we now have a midrashic basis for the application of the epithet חכם to Abraham. Similarly, we can assume, in the light of the exegetical traditions cited above, that חכמה in the proemial verse was taken as the wisdom of the *Torah*, which proved to be stronghold to Abraham, the חכם. None the less, the proem has been preserved only in a truncated form and there is no indication of the way in which the preacher developed his theme, or demonstrated the significance of his imagery for the pericope.

We may note, however, that the anonymous aggadist, in stressing Abraham's superiority over the generations which preceded him, was alluding to a well-known theme which occurs already in *Mishnah Avot* 5:2, 'There were ten generations from Noah to Abraham, to make known how long-suffering God is, seeing that all those generations continued to provoke Him until Abraham came, and received the reward they might all have earned!'. In *Avot d'Rabbi Natan*,[14] this statement is amplified, indicating the nature both of the wicked generations' provocation and of Abraham's singular merit:

'There were ten generations from Noah to Abraham' – what purpose did they serve for man-kind? It was to show how those generations were [consistently] provoking God, and that not a single one of them

---

[13] See *Midrash Ha-Gadol* to Genesis 15:9 (pp. 253–54) where Proverbs 10:19, 'In the multitude of words there wanteth not transgression; but he that refraineth his lips is wise (משכיל)', is applied to Abraham in connection with a theme which closely resembles that developed in the two proems from *Genesis Rabbah* 44, cited below pp. 85f, Abraham harbouring doubts regarding his possession of the land. The passage – the source for which is unknown – is an interesting one, as it clearly contradicts the view expressed in *Genesis Rabbah* 44:14 (p. 435) to Genesis 15:7, (also cited in *Midrash Ha-Gadol*, see p. 253) that Abraham was in no way questioning the validity of God's promise, but merely sought to know why he merited it.

For the identification of מבין with Abraham, see our reference on p. 94, to the homily from the *New Midrash on the Torah*, based on Proverbs 28:2.

[14] Version A, 33, pp. 93–4.

would walk in His ways, until Abraham our father came and walked in the ways of God, as it is said, 'Because Abraham hearkened to My voice, and kept My charge, My commandments, My statutes and *My laws* (Genesis 26:5)'. The singular תורה is not used here, but תורות, the plural.[15] Yet how did he know of them? This indicates that God conditioned father Abraham's two kidneys to act like two sages, and they were instructing him and counselling him, and teaching Wisdom (*viz. Torah*) all night, as it is said, 'I will bless the Lord who has counselled me, even by night my kidneys have instructed me (Psalm 16:7)'.[16]

According to this early source, therefore, Abraham's superiority over the 'ten generations' was due to his continuous acquisition of חכמה, the wisdom of the תורה. As to the

---

[15] The anonymous teacher is evidently alluding here to the interpretation of תורתי found in amoraic sources (see *BT Yoma* 28a): '[The expression תורתי implies two Laws,] the one the Written Law, the other the Oral Law.' See further, the proem in *Tanhuma*, ed. Buber, I, pp. 71–2, where the theme of Abraham's observance of 'all the Laws' (כל התורות) is developed in conjunction with Proverbs 2:7, 'He layeth up sound wisdom (תושיה) for the upright (לישרים).' On ישר as an epithet for Abraham, see p. 129, and on the identification of תושיה with תורה, see above, p. 70, note 98).

[16] This imagery, together with its proof-text, Psalm 16:7, is recorded in older sources in the name of R. Aqiva's pupil, R. Shimon b. Yoḥai (see *Genesis Rabbah* 61:1 and the parallels cited by Theodor, p. 657; also the excerpt from the lost *Yelammedenu* published by Wertheimer, *Batei Midrashot*, vol. I, p. 153). In all these sources, the proof-text is cited without any indication of its relevance specifically for Abraham, which raises the question, was Psalm 16 – like other psalms discussed in these chapters – regarded as an 'Abrahamic' psalm? In support of this, we may note the following. In a statement ascribed to R. Shimon b. Yoḥai in *Pirqei d'Rabbi Eliezer* 24 (see also *Yalqut Psalms* 667) verse 6, 'The lines are fallen unto me in pleasant places; yea, I have a goodly heritage', is cited as God's expression of delight at Abraham and his family being assigned to Him by lot, at the time of the Separation of the Tongues. Of particular significance, however, is the passage recorded in *Bereshit Rabbati* to Genesis 23:16 (ed. Albeck, p. 99) where the opening verses of this psalm are presented as a dialogue between David and God. The former asks why he is given no credit for his acknowledgement of God. In reply, God cites the exemplary character of Abraham (implied in verse 3, 'As for the holy that are in the earth') who acknowledged God, *and observed his Torah even before the revelation at Sinai* (citing Genesis 26:5). This is followed by a catalogue of Abraham's major trials, the departure from Haran, the journey to Egypt, the abduction of Sarah, her death, and Abraham's acceptance of the need to purchase a plot to bury her, despite the Divine promise that the whole land had been assigned to him. Although it appears only in a late midrashic commentary, its language, style and content, suggest that the passage has evidently been taken from earlier sources. In addition to those already cited by Albeck (p. 99), we may note the striking parallel with *Jubilees* 19:8ff, where the burial of Sarah is portrayed as Abraham's climactic trial (see further my observations below, pp. 127f). It is possible, therefore, that the compiler

connection between this aggadic notion and *Seder* 10, with which it is linked in *Genesis Rabbah* 39, this is indicated in the halakhic exordium to this *seder* in *Tanḥuma* (ed. Buber, 1, pp. 57–8). To illustrate the notion that the scrupulous observance of the Law merits a great reward – a phrase which recalls *Avot* 5:2 – Abraham is cited for his meticulous compliance with the minutiae of the *Torah*, which necessitated his departure from his idolatrous environment:

> You find that one who is meticulous in the observance of the precepts of the Law receives a great reward. So Abraham was meticulous in the observance of precepts. R. Aha said in the name of R. Alexandri, and R. Shemuel b. Nahamani in the name of R. Yonathan: In Abraham's house they observed even the regulations relating to preparations for the Sabbath on a festival which immediately precedes it! As it is said, 'Because Abraham hearkened to My voice, and kept my charge, My statutes and My *Torot* (Genesis 26:5)'. But, surely, there is only one *Torah*?! [However, the plural here implies] that he was meticulous in the observance of each and every precept in the *Torah*.' God said to him, 'You are meticulous in the observance of My precepts, yet you dwell among idolaters, depart from among them!' Whence do we know this? From that which we have read in the lection, 'And God said to Abraham: "Get thee out etc. ..."''.

We see, therefore, that the anonymous author of the truncated proem recorded in *Genesis Rabbah* 39, evidently expected his audience to be familiar with a complex of aggadic traditions relating to Abraham. Primarily, that he was a חכם, a *Torah*-sage, who enjoyed pre-eminence over the preceding generations as a result of his knowledge of חכמה, *Torah*-wisdom. This ultimately precipitated his removal to the more conducive environment of the Holy Land.

A similar observation may be made regarding the proem based on Proverbs 14:16, referred to earlier, relating to *Seder* 12 (= Genesis 15:1ff). This proem is so terse, it does not even appear as a separate entity in printed editions of *Genesis Rabbah*:[17]

of *Bereshit Rabbati*, R. Moshe Ha-Darshan, has preserved a significant element of the traditional interpretation of this psalm, relating it to the personality and qualities of the patriarch.

[17] See 44:2, p. 425.

'חכם ירא וסר מרע' – חכם את וסר מרע, "ירא" – 'אל תירא
אברם'

Theodor, whose reconstruction of the text is cited here, suggested that the fuller version of this proem has been preserved
in *Tanḥuma* (ed. Buber, 1, p. 75) where Proverbs 14:16 is
expounded with reference to Abraham's fear of Shem (=
Malkizedek) whose four royal descendants he had slain in
battle, a theme which occurs subsequently in *Genesis Rabbah*
44:7. However, as Theodor himself concedes, this would
require the deletion of the pronoun את in our text, where the
proemial verse is construed as being addressed to Abraham,
and not descriptive of him, as in the *Tanḥuma* version. Consequently, we would offer an alternative interpretation of this
obscure passage in the light of its own context. In *Genesis
Rabbah* 44:2, this proem is coupled with a more elaborate
petiḥah based on a further verse from Proverbs, 3:7, which
contains strikingly similar terminology to 14:16. It deals with a
well-known theme from the *seder*, Abraham's despondency at
his lack of an heir:

'Be not wise in thine own eyes; fear the Lord and depart from evil.' –
[which means,] be not wise in that which your own eyes observe (*viz.*
in the stars) so that you say, 'I shall have progeny!', or, 'I shall not
have progeny!' – 'Fear the Lord [and depart from evil (*viz.* the
portents of the stars)]'.[18] [Hence, God said,] 'Fear not, Abraham, I
am thy shield!'

This proem anticipates an important motif in the aggadic
interpretation of Genesis 15, as recorded in *Genesis Rabbah* 44
and parallel sources, which is based on a tradition of great
antiquity, that Abraham was a master of astrological lore.[19] By
means of his astrological skills, he divined that he would not
have progeny, which, according to R. Ishmael b. Isaac, might

---

[18] See the comment on the text by Samuel Jaffe (*Yepheh To'ar*) in the standard (Vilna)
      edition.
[19] For evidence of this tradition in early pre-Christian sources, see the review of the
      relevant material by Vermes, *Scripture and Tradition*, pp. 80–1. With regard to
      rabbinic literature, apart from the material cited in this chapter, see particularly
      the statement of the early *Tanna*, R. Eleazar of Modi'in in *BT Bava Batra* 16b, that
      Abraham was consulted on astrology by all the kings of the orient and the occident;
      also Ginzberg, *Legends*, vol. 5, p. 227, note 108.

be inferred from his complaint in Genesis 15:3, 'Behold, to me
Thou hast given no seed!': 'Astral influences [Abraham
claimed] determine my fate,[20] decreeing that Abram shall not
have progeny!'[21]

For the early rabbinic exegetes, God's response to this claim
was implied in verse 5, 'And He brought him outside (החוצה)
and said: "Look now toward heaven etc. . . ."' According to R.
Johanan b. Nappaḥa, this phrase indicated that God actually
elevated Abraham above the vault of the heavens.[22] Alternatively, God's action was intended to impress upon Abraham
that he was no longer an astrologer, but a prophet.[23] The
fourth century aggadist, R. Levi, expounded the verse in even
more graphic terms, depicting God as encouraging Abraham
to take advantage of his elevated position, and trample the
stars beneath his sandal: 'Only one who is situated beneath the
stars *need fear them*, but you, who are above them, tread on
them!'[24]

A more elaborate version of Abraham's dialogue with God
regarding his astral fate is recorded in *Exodus Rabbah* 38:6, in
the name of the early *Amora*, R. Ḥizkiyah b. Ḥiyya:

When God said to Abraham, 'Get thee out of thy country [. . . and I
will make of thee a great nation, and make thy name great; and be
thou a blessing.]', he said to God: 'Lord of the Universe, what benefit
is there for me in all these blessings, seeing that I am to quit this world
without children?' God said to Abraham: 'You already know that
you are not going to have progeny?' 'Lord of the Universe – he
replied – I have observed this in my stars that I am not to have
progeny!' 'You fear the [portents of the] stars?' – He retorted – 'As
you live, just as it is impossible for a man to count the stars, so it will
be impossible to count your descendants!'

---

[20] Or 'my birth-planet compels me! (המזל דוחקני)'. Einhorn suggests that this
exposition is based upon the superfluous expression הן in Genesis 15:3, which has
been taken as an allusion to the heavens on the basis of Deuteronomy 10:14, . . .
הן ליי א-להיך השמים, thus 'The heavens [indicate] that to me you are not giving
seed!'

[21] See 44:10, pp. 432; also *BT Shabbat* 156a, *Nedarim* 32a, and particularly *Tanhuma*,
Old Version, *Shophetim* 11 and *Aggadat Bereshit* 37, p. 73.

[22] See *Genesis Rabbah* 44:12, pp. 432f and the parallels cited there by Theodor.

[23] *Genesis Rabbah* 44:12, p. 433.

[24] *Genesis Rabbah* 44:12, p. 434.

While the elements contained in this version are substantially the same as those found in *Genesis Rabbah* and its parallels, God's dismissal of astrology is connected here with His injunction to Abraham to quit his homeland. This is found also in the writings of Philo, who, as Ginzberg has noted, describes God's command to Abraham to forsake the 'Chaldaean science', in language strikingly similar to that employed in rabbinic sources.[25] Moreover, Philo provides us with a further element in this complex of aggadic traditions, which has special significance for the obscure proem in *Genesis Rabbah* 44:2. Philo, like the rabbinic exegetes, attaches considerable importance to the patriarch's change of name from Abram to Abraham.[26] The former, Philo asserts, signified one who was an astrologer and meteorologist, while the latter indicated that the patriarch was a *sage* (= *sophos* = חכם).[27]

If we now view our original proem against the background of this highly developed complex of *aggadot*, it is possible to offer an exposition of the text as it stands, anticipating the traditional exegesis of the *seder* which it introduces:

'A sage feareth, and departeth from evil' – You are a sage, and [therefore] one who departs from the evil (*viz.* of astrology)! You fear [the portents of the stars]? 'Fear not Abram, [I am thy shield]!'

In *Genesis Rabbah* 44:2, therefore, we have a couplet of proems, dealing with a common theme, based on similar verses which, presumably, were selected on account of the allusive term חכם. It is interesting to note further that the popular tradition of Abraham as a *Torah*-sage, to which this term alludes, is reflected in the aggadic exposition of the immediate context of these two proemial verses in Proverbs 3 and 14. Thus in conjunction with the main pentateuchal source for the tradition of Abraham's total knowledge of the *Torah*, Genesis 26:5, R. Levi cites Proverbs 14:14 to support his explanation

25 See *De Abrahamo*, xv, 68–71 and Ginzberg, *Legends*, vol. 5, p. 227, note 108.
26 *De Abrahamo*, xviii, 81; see also Ginzberg, *Legends*, vol. 5, pp. 232–3, note 122.
27 *De Abrahamo*, xviii, 82–3.

for Abraham's possession of this knowledge long before the revelation at Sinai:[28]

... Behold, it is written in connection with Abraham, '... and he kept My charge, [My commandments, My statutes and My laws]'. Whence did Abraham learn *Torah*? ... R. Levi said: 'He learned it from himself, as it is said, מדרכיו ישבע סוג לב ומעליו איש טוב "The dissembler in heart shall have his fill from his own ways, while *the man* (= Abraham) shall be satisfied with *Torah* from himself."'[29]

Similarly, in an aggadic exposition of Proverbs 3:8, cited in the *Yalqut* from the lost *Midrash Yelammedenu*, Lot's salvation from the destruction of Sodom is presented as a direct result of Abraham's constant application to the study of the *Torah*:[30]

רפאות תהי לשרך – [For לשרך, read] לשארך, [hence,] 'Be thou a source of healing to *thy relative*.'[31] A man's merits benefit himself and his relatives. Thus, through the merits of Abraham, who was toiling in the study of the *Torah*, Lot, his brother, was saved from Sodom.

The association of Proverbs 3:8 with Abraham is indicated further in a context, which provides an interesting parallel for the couplet of proems cited earlier, relating to Genesis 15:1. *Genesis Rabbah* 57, which contains the midrashic commentary to Genesis 22:20ff, opens with a similar couplet of proems, based on verses from the same chapters in Proverbs, 3 and 14, dealing with a closely related theme in rabbinic *aggadah*, the birth of Rebekah. The communication of this event is portrayed in *Genesis Rabbah*, in terms which clearly recall the circumstances preceding Isaac's birth, described in Genesis 15. Abraham is beset by the gravest misgivings following the *Aqedah*, that Isaac might have died childless. Therefore, God assures him that

---

[28] See *Genesis Rabbah* 95:3, p. 1189; also *Numbers Rabbah* 14:2 and the *Yelammedenu* fragment cited earlier in note 16.

[29] R. Levi has presumably identified the expression איש with Abraham, on the basis of Genesis 20:7, 'Restore the wife of the man (האיש) for he is a prophet', an exegetical device which occurs in a number of sources. See, for example, *Leviticus Rabbah* 36:6, pp. 851–2 (on Hosea 2:12); *Pesiqta d'Rav Kahana* 18, p. 134a (on Psalm 4:3); also *Midrash Psalms* to 1:1, p. 12. Similarly, he identified טוב in his proof-text with *Torah* on the basis of Proverbs 4:2, as in *BT Berakhot* 5a: Now טוב connotes *Torah*, as it is said, 'For I have given you a good doctrine (לקח טוב) forsake not my *Torah*'.

[30] See *Yalqut Proverbs* 932.

[31] Taking שאר in the sense of kin, as in Leviticus 18:6, 'None of you shall approach to any that is near of kin to him (אל כל שאר בשרו) to uncover their nakedness ...'

Isaac's intended partner had been born. The similarity thus created in the *Midrash* between these two events, was, in all probability, suggested by the biblical text itself. The opening words of Genesis 15:1 and 22:20, are virtually identical, **ויהי אחרי הדברים האלה; אחר הדברים האלה**, and are subjected to the same midrashic treatment in *Genesis Rabbah*. It is noteworthy, therefore, that these corresponding phrases are also linked homiletically through proemial verses selected from the same two chapters in Proverbs:[32]

'And it came to pass after these things that it was told to Abraham saying: "Behold, Milcah, she also hath born children [unto thy brother, Nahor]"': **חיי בשרים לב מרפא** (14:30)[33] – [this implies] that while he was standing on Mount Moriah, he received the glad tidings that his son's partner had been born. [Hence,] 'Behold, Milcah, she also hath born etc. . . .'

רפאות תהי לשרך ושקוי לעצמותיך (3:8)[34] : R. Berekhiah in the name of R. Isaac: [God said,] 'If you are a healer,[35] then be so for your own!' What is the scriptural basis for this? 'Thou art a healer, therefore, be so to thine own kin.'[36] [Thus,] while he was standing on Mt Moriah, he received the glad tidings that his son's partner had been born. [Hence,] 'Behold, Milcah, she also hath born etc. . . .'[37]

---

[32] See 57:1–2, pp. 612–13.

[33] Lit.: 'A tranquil heart is the life of the flesh.' However, the anonymous preacher has taken **בשר** – a synonym for **שאר** – in the sense of kin, hence, 'The life of relatives is healing to the heart.' This is the suggestion of Samuel Jaffe, and is preferable to that of Einhorn and Luria, who equate **בשר** with **בשורה**. It is further possible that the preacher associated **חיי** with the post-biblical expression **חיה**, 'a woman in confinement'. Thus the verse may be rendered midrashically as, 'The confinement of relatives is healing to the [troubled] mind.'

[34] Lit.: 'It shall be health to thy navel, and marrow to thy bones.'

[35] The preacher has apparently taken **רפאות** as a *Notarikon* for **רופא את** (see Theodor's comment).

[36] In this context, both Luria and Jaffe have noted the interpretation of **לשרך** as **לשארך** found in the excerpt from the *Yelammedenu*. Moreover, the latter suggests that an allusion to Isaac's future partner is contained in the expression **עצמותיך**, **עצם** connoting a woman – or marital partner – on the basis of Genesis 2:23, 'And the man said: "This is now *bone of my bone* and flesh of my flesh, she shall be called Woman . . ."'

[37] As Theodor has noted, R. Isaac's exposition here presupposes an aggadic tradition recorded in an excerpt from the lost *Yelammedenu* recorded in *Yalqut Balaq* 766, which describes Abraham's reservations while on Mount Moriah, on receiving the Divine promise 'and in thy seed shall all the nations of the earth be blessed (Genesis 22:18)':

> Abraham was harbouring doubts saying: 'Others are to be blessed on account of my merit, yet is not Milcah my relative, my wife's sister (equating Iscah in

We may note in conclusion, that other verses from Proverbs 3 were associated with Abraham in our sources. Verse 4 occurs as the basis of a complex proem relating to Genesis 18:17 (= *Seder* 15a) which concludes with the following, main exposition:[38]

'So shalt thou find favour in the sight of אלהים and man' – this refers to Abraham, who was favoured by both men and angels,[39] as it is said, 'Hear us, my lord, thou art a mighty prince among us (Genesis 23:5)'.[40] This [indicates that he was favoured] by men. Whence do we know that [he was similarly favoured] by God and the angels? As it is said, '[And the Lord said:] "Shall I conceal from Abraham that which I am about to do? (*ibid.* 18:17)"'.[41]

The early *payyetan*, Yannai, was apparently familiar with an aggadic interpretation of a further verse from Proverbs 3, in connection with Abraham, as can be seen from the opening of his *Qedushta*, for *Seder* 7 (= Genesis 12:1ff = Mann, *Seder* 10).[42] Following his usual practice, Yannai incorporates a number of aggadic elements into his composition, which are to be found in extant proems relating to this *seder* and subsequently cites the relevant proemial verses, concluding with Proverbs 3:6,

Genesis 11:29, with Sarah; see Ginzberg, *Legends*, vol. 5, p. 214, note 38) in need of a Divine visitation?!' Whereupon [he was informed], 'Milcah, she also hath borne children etc ...' Scripture does not simply state, 'Milcah hath borne children', but [stresses] 'she also' (גם הוא) [indicating] that just as Sarah was barren and was [ultimately] visited [by God], so Milcah was barren and was [ultimately] visited [by God].

Apparently, R. Isaac in his proem to Genesis 22:20, expounded Proverbs 3:8 as God's response to Abraham's doubts regarding the fortunes of his own family, 'You are a healer, therefore, be so to your own kin!'

[38] See *Tanhuma*, ed. Buber, 1, pp. 88–9.
[39] This interpretation of the expression אלהים gained wide currency in talmudic times, as is indicated from its inclusion in early *Targumim*; see, for example, the *Targum* to I Samuel 28:13, Psalms 82:6 and 86:8.
[40] See *Genesis Rabbah* 41:3 (and the parallels cited by Theodor, p. 410) where the adoration of Abraham by all the nations of the world is described in conjunction with this verse.
[41] The preacher may simply have taken God's readiness to confide in Abraham as evidence of His especial affection for him. However, it is equally possible that his comment presupposes an amplification of this verse, which may have been widely current during the talmudic period, as it is to be found in the fragmentary *Targum* to Genesis 18:17: 'Am I to conceal from Abraham *My friend* (אוהבי = רחמי) that which I am doing?' On the antiquity of this rendering, see below, p. 153, note 24.
[42] See M. Zulay, *Piyyutei Yannai*, Berlin 1938, p. 17.

'In all thy ways acknowledge Him and He will direct thy ways.'
We have, therefore, a series of verses (4, 6, 7 and 8) from
Proverbs 3, which were associated midrashically with
Abraham in our sources. It is unlikely that this is merely
coincidence. Nor can we seek an explanation for this phenomenon in a conjectured lectionary cycle of hagiographic texts
corresponding to the *sedarim* and *haphtarot*, in which a selection
from Proverbs 3 figured as one of the readings, since each of
these verses is cited in conjunction with different *sedarim* in
Genesis. Yet in none of the passages quoted above does the
preacher offer any explanation for the selection of his text or its
relevance for Abraham. This leads us to conclude that the
sources cited above, may reflect an exegetical tradition which
linked the opening section of Proverbs 3 – a chapter extolling
the virtues and pursuit of תורה/חכמה, with Abraham, the
archetypal *Torah*-sage.[43]

As we indicated earlier, the evidence for this tradition, and
its influence on the selection of proemial and proof-texts, is
more extensive. The following is only a brief description of the
remaining sources collected by the writer thus far:

(a) In a proem recorded in *Genesis Rabbah* 52:3 (p. 542f) the
epithet חכם לב, in Proverbs 10:8, is identified with
Abraham, who perceived that he could no longer practise
hospitality after the destruction of the cities of the plain.
Therefore, he decamped to Gerar.

(b) In *Midrash Ha-Gadol* to Genesis 19:1 (p. 316) Proverbs
13:20, 'He that walketh with wise men shall be wise', is
applied to Lot, who, having been reared by Abraham,
acquired some of his hospitable practices.[44]

---

[43] The one verse from this series, for which we have not yet found an aggadic
exposition relating it to Abraham is verse 5. None the less, this verse may have been
regarded as relevant to the patriarch. According to a tradition formulated already
in tannaitic times, Abraham is the patriarchal prototype for the whole-hearted love
for God enjoined in Deuteronomy 6:5, 'And thou shalt love the Lord thy God with
all thy heart . . .', a tradition which may have its origins in high antiquity (see
pp. 148f, and particularly p. 149, note 13. It is conceivable that the early rabbinic
exegetes saw an allusion to this in verse 5, 'Trust the Lord *with all thy heart*', thus
linking the passage as a whole with Abraham.

[44] We may note further that in *Exodus Rabbah* 1:1 (also *Tanhuma*, Old Version, *Shemot*
1) Abraham's failure to discipline Ishmael is cited to illustrate 13:24, 'He that

(c) In *Ecclesiastes Rabbah* to chapter 10, verse 2, 'A wise man's understanding is at his right hand; but a fool's understanding is at his left', is taken to indicate the contrast between the character of Abraham and that of Lot, as manifested in their choice of territory in Canaan.[45]

(d) Again in *Ecclesiastes Rabbah* to chapter 2, verses 14 and 15, 'The wise man, his eyes are in his head; but the fool walketh in darkness. And I also perceived that one event happeneth to them all ...', are taken to represent Abraham's complaint that he must share the same fate as Nimrod, both in terms of royal status and death. Therefore, Abraham demands to know why he should 'surrender his soul for the sanctification of God's name', more than Nimrod! Consequently, God responds with verse 16, כי אין זכרון לחכם עם כסיל לעולם (*viz.* 'the fool shall not enjoy the same memorial as the sage').[46]

(e) Abraham and Nimrod are contrasted once again in *Ecclesiastes Rabbah*, in connection with 4:13–14, 'Better is a poor wise child (ילד מסכן וחכם) than an old and foolish king, who knoweth not how to receive admonition any more ...', which are taken to imply that Abraham's rise to kingship would signal the eclipse of Nimrod.[47]

(f) In *Midrash Ha-Gadol* to Genesis 18:1 (p. 289) Proverbs 11:30, 'The fruit of the righteous is a tree of life; and he that is wise winneth souls', is cited to support one of the views

---

spareth his rod hateth his son', while clause B, 'but he that loveth him chasteneth him betimes', is taken as a reference to Abraham's educating Isaac in the *Torah*.

[45] See also *Midrash Ha-Gadol* to Genesis 13:29, p. 229.

[46] See also *Midrash Ha-Gadol* to Genesis 12:1 (and the parallels cited by Margulies, pp. 211–12) where this appears as a proem to *Seder* 10.

[47] The text is clearly defective, and should be emended as follows:
'Better is a poor and wise child (verse 13)' – this alludes to Abraham – 'than an old and foolish king' – this alludes to Nimrod. ['For out of prison he came to be king (verse 14)', as it is said, אל עמק שוה הוא עמק המלך (lit.: 'at the vale of Shaveh, the same is the king's vale'; 14:17)]. What does אל עמק שוה mean? [It implies] that there they reached agreement, cut down cedars, and made for him a great platform, sat him there on high and were praising him etc. ...
The inclusion of verse 14 here is clearly required by the sense of the passage, which speaks of Abraham's ultimate elevation to kingship. Moreover, we can assume that the preacher took בית הסורים, 'house of prisoners' (= האסורים, so LXX) as an allusion to Abraham's incarceration by Nimrod; see Ginzberg, *Legends*, vol. 5, p. 212, note 28. On Abraham's elevation to kingship, see p. 106.

offered for God's specific choice of the Oaks of Mamre, to manifest His Divine Presence to Abraham, 'to inform you that, just as a tree, when it is pruned, it produces fruit, so with Abraham, once he was circumcised, he was worthy to have issue'.[48]

(g) The homily for *Seder* 11 (= Genesis 14:1ff) in the *New Midrash on the Torah* published by Mann,[49] opens with a proem based on Proverbs 28:2, which contains the synonymous expression מבין[50] 'For the transgression of a land many are the princes thereof; but by a man of understanding and knowledge established order shall long continue.' The 'man of understanding and knowledge' is identified with Abraham, who from his own heart, deduced knowledge of the *Torah* and observed it, even before it was given at Sinai.[51]

(h) We may note in conclusion, that the scriptural epithet חכם – or חכמה – was extended also to the immediate members of the patriarch's family. Thus in a homily relating to *Seder* 25 (= Genesis 25:19ff) in which the three patriarchs are portrayed as three successive generations of בני תורה, the epithet בן חכם in Proverbs 10:1, is predicated of Isaac.[52] Similarly, Yannai was apparently familiar with a proem to *Seder* 10 in his lectionary cycle (= *Seder* 13 = Genesis 16:1ff)[53] based on Proverbs 14:1, חכמות נשים בנתה ביתה, in which the female sage alluded to in the proemial verse is identified with Sarah.[54]

---

[48] On the midrashic exposition of Proverbs 11:30, see below, Appendix 3, pp. 188f.

[49] *The Bible as Read*, vol. 1, pp. 156–7.   [50] See p. 83.

[51] For a further exposition of Proverbs 28:2 with reference to Abraham, see *Yalqut Mishlei* 961.

[52] See *Tanhuma*, ed. Buber, 1, p. 124.   [53] See Zulay, *Piyyutei Yannai*, p. 28.

[54] The verbal link with proemial verse is clearly contained in the second verse of the *seder*, אולי אבנה ממנה. The theme of Sarah's childlessness and her wise conduct to redress the situation, is taken up in final strophe of the opening *piyyut*:

כחכמות נשים פעלה לו \ להצדיק כי לא ילדה לו

'Like the wisest of women, she acted toward him, to rectify [the fact that] she had not borne him a child.'

CHAPTER 5

Popular legends and traditions II: the archetypal priest-king

Turning once again to our original collection of proems in *Genesis Rabbah* 39, we see that the first and the last are based on verses from the same psalm, 45:8 and 11–12:

'Now the Lord said to Abraham: Get thee out etc': R. Isaac opened [with the following proemial verse], 'Hearken O daughter, and consider, and incline thine ear; forget also thine own people and thy father's house [So shall the king desire thy beauty; for he is thy lord, and do homage unto him.]'. R. Isaac said: 'It may be compared to one who was travelling from place to place, and saw a castle ablaze. "Is it possible – he said – that the castle is without a controller?!" The controller of the castle looked forth and said to him, "I am the controller of the castle!" Thus, because Abraham was asking, "Is it possible that the world is without a controller?!" – God looked forth and said to him, "I am the controller, the Lord of all the world!"[1] ויתאו המלך יפיך [which means, "The King desires] to beautify you[2] in the world". "For He is thy Lord, and do homage unto Him" – Hence [the opening words of the *seder*,] "And the Lord said to Abraham: Get thee out etc. ...."'

R. Azariah in the name of R. Aḥa opened [with the following proemial verse]: 'אהבת צדק ותשנא רשע על כן משחך א־להים א־להיך שמן ששון מחבריך.[3] R. Azariah in the name of R. Aḥa expounded the verse in connection with our father Abraham. 'When

---

[1] The imagery of the burning castle is intended to represent the world which, figuratively speaking, had been set ablaze by the wickedness of the sinners. This is implied in the phrase מוקדי עולם (Isaiah 33:14; lit. 'everlasting burnings') which was taken midrashically as an epithet for the wicked incendiaries who, 'if given the opportunity, would set the world ablaze' (see *Genesis Rabbah* 48:6, p. 481).

[2] Taking יפיך as an objective rather than a subjective genitive, 'the beautification of you'.

[3] Lit.: 'Thou lovest righteousness and hatest wickedness; therefore God, thy God, hath anointed thee with the oil of gladness above thy fellows.'

our father Abraham arose to seek mercy for the Sodomites, what is
written there? "That be far from Thee to do after this manner etc. ...
(Genesis 18:25)".' R. Aḥa said: '[Abraham declared:] "You swore
that You would not bring a flood upon the world, why do you
cunningly evade Your oath?! You will not bring a flood of water but a
flood of fire, yet if You do so, you will not escape the consequences of
Your oath!"'
R. Levi said, '[Abraham declared:] "The Judge of all the earth
cannot execute strict justice![4] If You want the world [to exist] there
cannot be strict justice! If, however, You want the latter, You cannot
have the former! You wish to seize the rope at both ends, You want
the world and You want strict justice, yet if You will not be a little
indulgent, then the world cannot exist!" God said to him: "Abraham,
אהבת צדק ותשנא רשע' – Thou lovest justification and hatest
condemnation,[5] therefore, God thy God hath anointed thee with the
oil of gladness above thy fellows.' – From Noah until you there were
ten generations, yet I spoke with none of them save with you."
[Hence the opening words of the *seder*] "Now the Lord said to
Abraham etc. ...."'

Taken on its own, R. Isaac's choice of proemial verses would
appear to support fully Heinemann's thesis regarding the
element of surprise in the selection of such texts. One might,
therefore, reasonably assume that R. Isaac's listeners were left
wondering how he would apply the imagery of the young bride
to the patriarch Abraham. However, as we observed earlier,
the selection of proemial verses from the same psalm by two
Amora'im, cannot be dismissed as mere coincidence. On the
contrary, a review of the aggadic treatment of Psalm 45 as a
whole in our sources, reveals a more basic factor which probably influenced both preachers on their choice of texts.

Verse 3 is expounded as a proemial verse in a *petiḥah* to
 Genesis 24:1 (= *Seder* 20)[6] with reference to Abraham's
 being praised among both the celestial and terrestrial
 beings.
Verses 3–4 form the basis of a *petiḥah* to Genesis 17:1 (= *Seder*

---

[4] Taking the rhetorical question as an affirmative statement.
[5] This rendering of צדק and רשע with their legalistic connotations is explicitly stated
in the parallel passage (*Leviticus Rabbah* 10:1, p. 197): אהבת צדק [means] you love
to justify My creatures; ותשנא רשע, [means] you hate to condemn them.'
[6] See *Genesis Rabbah* 59:5, p. 633.

14)[7] and are expounded with reference to Abraham's superiority over all the descendants of Adam, his encounter with Malchizedek and the necessity for him to be circumcised before embarking on his mission to disseminate the knowledge of God among mankind.

Verse 8 not only occurs as a proemial verse in our *petiḥah*, it also forms the basis of a lengthy proem relating to the same *seder*, preserved in a *Genizah* fragment published by Mann,[8] which elaborates upon the well-known traditions of Abraham's treatment of his father's customers who came to purchase idols and his reflection on the nature of the true God.

Verse 9 occurs in a significant context in *Tanḥuma Va-Yera*[9] where it is cited to substantiate the application of a further verse to Abraham. An unknown aggadist took Canticles 4:6, 'I will get me to the mountain of *myrrh*', as a reference to Abraham on the basis of '*Myrrh* and aloes and cassia are all thy garments.'

Verse 10 is cited in *Genesis Rabbah* 45:1[10] as the basis for the tradition that both Pharaoh and Abimelech gave their daughters to be hand-maidens in Abraham's household.

Verse 13 is interpreted in *Genesis Rabbah* 43:1[11] with reference to Abraham's harassment of the four kings and Malchizedek's tribute on his return from battle (Genesis 14:13ff).

Finally, *verse 17* ('Instead of thy fathers shall be thy sons') is treated in *Tanḥuma Toledot*[12] as an allusion to Isaac acquiring the qualities of his father Abraham.

The most significant statement in our sources, however, is preserved in the passage in *Tanḥuma Va-Yera* referred to earlier: 'With reference to whom did the Sons of Korah utter this psalm? *With reference to Abraham!*'

In the light of this review – and particularly the last statement – we can assume that the selection of proemial verses from

[7] See *Tanḥuma*, ed. Buber, 1, pp. 78–9.
[8] *The Bible as Read and Preached*, vol. 1, Hebrew Section, pp. 59–60.
[9] Ed. Buber, vol. 1, p. 85.   [10] See p. 448.   [11] See p. 420.
[12] Ed. Buber, vol. 1, p. 130.

Psalm 45 by both R. Isaac and R. Aḥa, was neither coincidental nor arbitrary. Both these *Amora'im*, we would suggest, were relying on an established tradition that the source for their proemial texts was an 'Abrahamic' psalm, composed with reference to the patriarch, alluding to, or amplifying details of his life and personality recorded in Genesis.

What was the basis for this tradition? Once again, we cannot look for an answer to a conjectured lectionary cycle of readings from the Hagiographa, in which Psalm 45 might have featured as the corresponding lection for *Seder* 10, as verses from the psalm occur in proems connected with two further *sedarim*, 14 and 20. In order to explain this phenomenon, in our view, it is necessary to examine more comprehensively the aggadic exegesis of Psalm 45 in both rabbinic and non-rabbinic sources. For in addition to its association with Abraham, we find a further three, independent and well developed motifs in the midrashic exposition of this psalm, relating to,

a) The Messianic King
b) Moses
c) The *Torah* and its sages

THE MESSIANIC KING

The messianic interpretation of Psalm 45 reflects a general tendency in early Jewish exegesis, which has its parallel in Christian tradition, to treat descriptions of the idealised monarch in the Psalter, as prophetic predictions relating to the Messianic King.[13] In rabbinic sources, this interpretation is preserved primarily in the *Targum* to Psalm 45, which suggests that it gained wide currency at an early period. The Aramaic translator presents the entire psalm as a prophecy uttered by the Korahites[14] taking the address to the prince in verses 3–10, as a panegyric to the Messianic King. This exegetical motif

---

[13] See, for example, *Targum* to Psalms 21 and 72; Hebrews 1:8–9 (relating to Psalm 45:7–8); see also Mowinckel, *The Psalms in Israel's Worship*, Oxford 1982, vol. 1, p. 49; see further R'daq's (R. David Qimḥi) commentary to Psalm 45 where he reviews and severely criticises its christological interpretation, although he accepts the messianic character of the psalm.

[14] On the prophetic gift of the sons of Korah, see below, note 19.

occurs rarely in midrashic literature, notably in tannaitic sources. In the *Sifrei* to Deuteronomy 1:10,[15] verse 1 appears as one of the seven proof-texts cited by R. Shimon b. Yoḥai to describe the countenance of the righteous in the hereafter. Similarly, in the *Mekhilta d'Rabbi Ishmael*[16] R. Eliezer the son of R. Jose the Galilean cites verse 17 as the scriptural source for the notion that every member of the House of Israel in the messianic era, will have children of the calibre of those who participated in the Exodus.

MOSES

The main source for this exegetical motif is the comparatively late *Midrash Psalms*[17] the compiler of which, has presumably drawn his material from earlier sources. The panegyric to the prince (verses 3–10) is interpreted with reference to Moses and his contemporaries, commencing with the sons of Korah, the composers of the psalm.[18] Because their conduct was 'more comely' than that of their father, they merited the gifts of psalm-composition and prophecy.[19] The text continues,

'Gird thy sword upon thy thigh, O mighty one (v. 4)' – this refers to Moses who merited the *Torah*, which is likened to a sword[20] – 'And in thy majesty prosper, ride on, (v. 5)' – [this alludes to] his having ridden upon a cloud and ascended to the heavens. Why was this so? 'On account of the truth and meekness and righteousness (*ibid.*)' which was in him, as it is said, 'Now the man Moses was very meek

---

15 *Pisqa* 10, ed. Finkelstein, p. 18.
16 *Yitro, Bahodesh*, 2, pp. 208–9. This reflects the well-known and highly developed motif in rabbinic sources, which has its counterpart in Christian and sectarian traditions, to draw parallels between the First Redemption (גאולה ראשונה) led by Moses and the Final Redemption (גאולה אחרונה) in the messianic age.
17 Ed. Buber, 45, p. 271.
18 See *Targum* to verse 1; also Ginzberg, *Legends*, vol. 6, p. 105, note 590.
19 The tradition relating to their prophetic gift is apparently an early one, found already in *Seder Olam Rabbah* 20, ed. Ratner, p. 83. See further *Midrash Psalms*, 45, p. 271; also to Psalm 46, p. 272.
20 See *Tanḥuma*, ed. Buber, 1, p. 19, where the expression חרב in Genesis 3:24 is identified with *Torah* on the basis of Psalm 149:6: חרב connotes *Torah*, as it is said, 'and a two-edged sword (חרב פיפיות) in their hand' (see further *Yalqut Bereishit* 34, end). This presupposes the interpretation of פיפיות by the *Tanna*, R. Judah b. Ilai, as an allusion to the 'two Laws, the Written Law and the Oral Law' (see *Pesiqta d'Rav Kahana* 12, p. 102b, ed. Mandelbaum, p. 207, which is the text cited here).

(Numbers 12:3).' 'Thine arrows are sharp – the peoples fall under thee – [they sink] into the heart of the king's enemies (v. 6)' – [this alludes to the wars] he waged against Amalek, Sihon and Og. 'Thy throne, O God, is for ever and ever (v. 7)'[21] – [this alludes to that] which is said, 'The hand upon the throne of the Lord (Exodus 17:16)'. 'Thou hast loved righteousness (v. 8)' – as it is said, 'He executed the righteousness of the Lord (Deuteronomy 33:21)'. 'Therefore God, thy God, hath anointed thee (v. 8)' – this refers to Aaron etc. ...

An interesting interpretation of verse 2 is found in a fragment of the lost *Midrash Yelammedenu*, preserved in the *Yalqut*. According to an anonymous aggadist, the words רחש לבי דבר טוב, although uttered by David, express the sentiments of the sons of Korah. Confronted with the dilemma of giving due respect to Moses, or honouring their father at the time of the revolt, they chose to show deference to Moses, since 'they planned to do penitence'.[22]

In *Tanḥuma Ki-Tissa*[23] the words 'Thou art fairer than the children of men' in verse 2, are applied directly to Moses, whose achievements surpassed those of ordinary mortals. While God first kills a man before consigning him to the grave, Moses could bring Korah and his followers down to the nether world alive and was able to thwart the Divine decree to destroy the Israelites.[24]

The interpretation of the psalm with reference to Moses, was not limited only to its opening ten verses. In *Tanḥuma b'Midbar* (Old Version) 3,[25] verse 14, 'All glorious is the king's daughter within the palace', is cited in conjunction with the notion that once the Sanctuary was erected, God preferred to communicate with Moses within its precincts, rather than in the open, as he had done hitherto.[26]

---

[21] So *Targum* to this verse (also *AV* and *RV*).

[22] See *Yalqut Qoraḥ* 752. As is frequently the case in midrashic literature, only the first part of the relevant verse is cited. It is highly probable that verse 2 in its entirety was regarded as expressing the sentiments of the sons of Korah. Consequently, the continuation of the verse, אמר אני מעשי למלך, may have been taken as the declaration of their resolve to honour Moses, the king.

[23] Old Version, *Ki-Tissa* 17.

[24] See the comments of Chanoch Zundel b. Yoseph (*Etz Yoseph*) on the text.

[25] See also *Numbers Rabbah* 1:3.

[26] See the continuation of the passage, where משבצות זהב is identified with Aaron, on the basis of Exodus 28:13, ועשית משבצות זהב.

Similarly, verse 15 occurs as the basis of a proem in *Exodus Rabbah* 52:1, relating to the erection of the sanctuary. We offer a translation of the full text here, as its treatment of imagery of the proemial verse is of special significance for our overall discussion, and will be evaluated subsequently:

'And they brought the Tabernacle unto Moses (Exodus 39:33)': R. Tanhum bar Abba opened [with the following proemial verse]: לרקמות תובל למלך וגו'‎[27] – What does לרקמות connote? It connotes the Tabernacle, which was embroidered, as it is written, "and of the weaver in colours (רוקם) in blue etc.... (*ibid.* 35:35)". Hence [it is designated as] רקמות. What does תובל למלך imply? [It implies that it was brought to] Moses, who was called a king, as it is written, "And he (= Moses) was a king in Jeshurun,[28] when the heads of the people were gathered, all the tribes of Israel together (Deuteronomy 33:5)." אחריה בתולות[29] – this alludes to Israel, who are called "virgins", as it is written, "A garden shut up is my sister, my bride; a spring shut up, a fountain sealed (Canticles 4:12)."[30] רעותיה – [Israel is so called] since they are the friends of God, as it is said, "For my brethren and companions' (רעי) sakes, I will now say: 'Peace be within thee (Psalm 122:8).'"[31] מובאות לך [alludes to the fact that] on the day that the Tabernacle was completed, they brought it to Moses. Hence [the opening words of the *seder*], "And they brought the Tabernacle to Moses".'

THE *TORAH* AND ITS SAGES

A trace of this exegetical motif, to which we have already referred above, is preserved in at least one tannaitic source, the

---

[27] Lit.: 'She shall be led unto the king on richly woven stuff'

[28] This interpretation of the verse is apparently based on the assumption that Moses, who is mentioned in the preceding verse ('Moses commanded us a Law ...') is also the subject of the verb ויהי at the beginning of verse 5. This, apparently, is also the rendering of *Targum Pseudo-Jonathan* to the verse. See further *Exodus Rabbah* 2:6 (end); *Leviticus Rabbah* 31:4 and 32:2 (pp. 719, 721 and 740), and particularly Naḥmanides' comments to Deuteronomy 33:5.

[29] Lit.: 'the virgins in her train', omitting רעותיה at this point in the text, as it forms the basis of a separate comment.

[30] R. Tanḥuma here presupposes the traditional interpretation of this verse, found frequently in our sources, which treats גן נעול as a symbolism for a virgin; see *Leviticus Rabbah* 32:5, and the sources cited by Margulies, pp. 745f.

[31] The preacher presupposes God to be the speaker here; compare *Ecclesiastes Rabbah* 4:8; *Tanḥuma* Old Version, *Yitro* 4, and *Behar* 1; ed. Buber, 3, p. 104.

Sifrei to Deuteronomy 6:7,[32] where verse 6, 'Thine arrows are sharp – the peoples fall under thee – [they sink] into the heart of the king's enemies', is cited among a collection of verses from the Hagiographa, to illustrate the merit of clarity and sharpness in *Torah* learning. No indication is offered in this source regarding either the relevance of these verses or the manner of their application, which suggests that these were acknowledged already at an early period.

However, our main example for this motif[33] is an exposition of verses 5–6 reported in the name of R. Eleazar b. Pedath, an leading Palestinian scholar of the third century CE, in *BT Shabbat* 63a:

When two sages sharpen each other's halakhic acumen, God grants them success, as it is said, וֹהדרך צלח, do not read הדרך, but חדדך.[34] Moreover, they also achieve greatness, as it is said, רכב.[35] You may think [that this would still be the case] even if it were not for the sake [of the *Torah*, but for personal advantage], therefore it says, על דבר אמת, 'for a true cause'. [Similarly] you might think [that

---

[32] *Pisqa* 34, p. 60.

[33] That there was a more extensive exposition of Psalm 45 with reference to the *Torah* and its sages in talmudic times, is suggested by Rashi, who adopted this motif as the basis of his interpretation of this psalm, apparently employing material from both known and unknown sources. We may note in particular his comment on the expression ששנים in the psalm-heading which, presumably, has been taken from an unidentified source (however, see the sources cited by I. Maarsen, *Parshandatha: The Commentary of Rashi on the Prophets and the Hagiographa*, Part 3: *Psalms*, Jerusalem 1936, p. 43):
> They composed this psalm in honour of the *Torah*-sages, who are gentle (lit.: soft) and comely like lilies, and who are filled with the sap of good deeds like lilies!

[34] Hence, 'Succeed in your acumen (lit.: sharpening)!' Samuel Edels (*MaHarSha*) in his commentary to the text, suggests that this unusual midrashic rendering of the term וֹהדרך stems initially from the fact that it occurs twice in succession, at the end of verse 4 and at the beginning of verse 5. Consequently, in midrashic terms, וֹהדרך on the second occasion is superfluous, and might be exploited by the preacher for his own aggadic purposes. It is interesting to note that in *BT Menahot* 88b, verse 5 is applied – apparently with the same meaning – to R. Jeremiah, who reports R. Eleazer's statement in our source. Because of his well-reasoned response to a query regarding the replenishing of the oil in the lamp of the Sanctuary which had been extinguished, R. Zeriqa, another of R. Eleazar's disciples, praises him with the words וֹהדרך צלח רכב (the reading ר' זריקא is supported by MS Munich; however, *Shittah Mequbbetzet*, records the reading, ר זירא).

[35] The basis for this equation of רכב with גדולה is obscure. Edels offers the plausible suggestion that it is based upon the scriptural usage of רכב to connote greatness or elevation in rank, as in the case of Joseph and Mordechai (see Genesis 41:43 and Esther 6:11; also Deuteronomy 32:13).

this would be the case] even if one became presumptuous! Therefore it says, וענוה צדק, '[with] humility and righteousness'. If they act in this way, then they will merit the *Torah*, which was given by the right hand [of God], as it is said, ותורך נוראות ימינך.[36]

We noted above, in connection with the Abrahamic interpretation of the psalm, that this motif was so well established, that an aggadist could cite a verse from Psalm 45 to substantiate his application of a further verse from a different context, to Abraham.[37] It is interesting to note, therefore, that a similar phenomenon occurs also in conjunction with its treatment as a *Torah* psalm. In order to substantiate his analogy of *Torah* with oil, an anonymous aggadist cites a verse from Psalm 45, without any indication of the relevance of his quotation for his theme. Evidently this motif was sufficiently well established, to render any explanatory comment unnecessary:[38]

And whence do we know that the words of the *Torah* are compared to oil? As it is said, 'Therefore God, thy God has anointed thee with the oil of gladness above thy fellows (v. 8).'[39]

---

[36] The precise meaning of this statement and more specifically, the interpretation of its proof-text is not at all clear. Edels suggests that *Torah* in this context is to be taken in the sense of *Hora'ah*, teaching the Law, or formulating halakhic decisions. Hence, they will merit the status of a *Moreh Hora'ah*, one who has achieved the level of authoritative learning enabling him to give halakhic rulings. He also notes that the allusion to *Torah* in the proof-text is contained in the expression ימינך, which recalls Deuteronomy 33:2, 'At His *right hand* was a fiery law unto them.' While this suggestion is plausible, it is nonetheless difficult to determine how R. Eleazar would have interpreted the phrase as a whole. We may note that Rashi, who was obviously familiar with our talmudic source, treats verses 4–5 in his commentary to Psalm 45 (ed. Maarsen, p. 43) as an exhortation to the *Torah*-sage to gird on his sword for the battle of *Torah* and to give his rulings in accordance with its truth. However, Rashi renders the final clause as, 'It (= the *Torah*) shall teach you [the strategy of war] so that your right hand [may perform] wondrous things', which sheds no further light on our problem.

[37] See above, p. 97.

[38] See *Midrash Ha-Gadol* to Exodus 19:14, ed. Margulies, p. 386; also *Mishnat R. Eliezer* Chapter 13, ed. H. G. Enelow, p. 256.

[39] On the analogy of the *Torah* with oil, see *Canticles Rabbah* 1:3, לריח שמניך טובים, the verse on which the second proem in *Genesis Rabbah* 39 is based:

The Rabbis said: '[The plural שמניך implies that] there are two Laws, the Written and the Oral Law.' R. Yudan said: '[The continuation of the verse] "Thy name is oil poured forth", [implies] that Your name (reading שמך for שמן, see Strashun (*R'Shash*) on the text) is aggrandised by every one who is occupied with the oil of the *Torah*.'

This exegetical motif is presupposed in a further three contexts. Firstly, in *BT Rosh Ha-Shanah* 4a, where Rav's exposition of the rare term שגל as כלבתא, 'a bitch', is seen as problematic for the traditional interpretation of Psalm 45, where this term occurs in verse 10, 'At thy right hand doth stand the שגל (lit.: queen, consort) in gold of Ophir':

If שגל means 'a bitch', [this raises the question,] what glad tidings does the prophet announce to Israel [through these words]? This is the import of his words. As a reward for the being as precious to Israel as a bitch is to idolaters (*viz.* for carnal purposes)[40] you merit the gold of Ophir.

Secondly, in *BT Hagigah* 15b, where R. Ḥanina suggests that verse 11, 'Hearken, O daughter and consider and incline thine ear', may have been R. Meir's scriptural sanction for learning *Torah* from the apostate, Elisha b. Abuya.[41] Finally, there is the highly significant passage in *BT Shabbat* 63a, which has already been discussed above, in connection with the issue of traditional interpretation and plain meaning.[42] R. Kahana, as we saw earlier, challenged the suggestion that R. Eliezer's view that weapons were an adornment which might be carried – or worn – on the Sabbath, was based on Psalm 45:4, since the verse 'was written with reference to the words of the *Torah*'. In reply to this, Mar the son of R. Huna, asserted that 'a verse does not lose its plain meaning'.

Despite their differing points of view, as we observed above, both these *Amora'im* evidently accepted the context from which the quotation was taken, as a *Torah* psalm. For them it was an established tradition. However, both were equally aware of the plain meaning of the Hebrew text. It was this awareness of plain meaning on the part of the early rabbinic exegetes which, we would argue, was crucial for the entire midrashic process. As we observed above, the plain meaning of a passage – or even a single term – established the parameters within which the midrashic process was obliged to function. No meaning could

---

[40] See Rashi's comment on the text.
[41] According to Rashi, the key-phrases in the verse are to be rendered as: '. . . incline thine ear [to learn] and forget thy people (i.e. disregard their conduct)'.
[42] See pp. 8ff.

be attached to a scriptural expression unless it could be supported – however tenuously – by a parallel usage elsewhere in the Scriptures.[43]

It is in this context that we must view the midrashic exegesis of Psalm 45 in rabbinic sources, which present us with four disparate, and apparently arbitrary, interpretations of the same biblical passage. Since the text of the psalm is their only common denominator, does it contain some predeterminative factor which influenced all four exegetical motifs? While the early rabbinic exegetes may not have been familiar with the categorisation of royal psalms, we can assume that they were aware that Psalm 45 deals with a royal personage. It can hardly be coincidental, therefore, that all four personalities with whom the psalm is associated, are regarded as kings in rabbinic tradition, in either real or metaphorical terms.

The most obvious of these is the Messiah, the final redeemer and representative of Israel's royal line. However, the first redeemer, Moses is also depicted in rabbinic sources as the first to exercise the functions of a monarch in ancient Israel,[44] a tradition which is clearly reflected in the exposition of verse 15 cited above.[45] Similarly, the sages themselves were designated as kings,[46] a tradition which may already be presupposed by

---

[43] See pp. 4f.

[44] For the sources relating to this early and widely recurring tradition, see Ginzberg, *Legends*, vol. 6, p. 28, note 170.

[45] See p. 101.

[46] In addition to the well-known maxim, מאן מלכי? רבנן!, 'Who are kings? The Rabbis!', see *BT Gittin* 62a:

> ... He (G'niba) said to [R. Huna and R. Ḥisda]: 'Peace be upon you, O kings, peace be upon you, O kings!' They said to him: 'Whence do you know that the rabbis are called kings?' He said to them: '[From that] which is written, "By me kings reign (Proverbs 8:15)"'.

The speaker in Proverbs 8 is of course חכמה, which is traditionally identified with *Torah*, as we have already observed (see above, p. 82). See also Rashi's comment on 45:2 (ed. Maarsen, p. 43) which is based presumably on older sources:

> 'I say: "My work is concerning a king."' – This song which I have composed and compiled, I utter to one who is worthy to be a king, as it is said, 'By me kings reign'.

See further the epithet accorded to Moses on the basis of Isaiah 19:4, in *Tanḥuma* Old Version, *B'midbar* 3: 'And a strong king shall rule over them (= the Egyptians)' – this alludes to Moses, who was the *king of Torah* (מלכה של תורה) which is called עז, as it is said, 'the Lord will give strength (עז) to His people (psalm 29:11; see pp. 76ff).

the passage from the *Sifrei* cited earlier, where Psalm 45:6 is adduced to illustrate the need for sharpness and clarity in learning.[47] Finally, Abraham, the founding father of the Israelite nation, is portrayed as a king in very early sources, and emerges in rabbinic tradition as the source for kingship in Israel.[48]

Thus a royal psalm was associated with a variety of royal personages in rabbinic tradition. Because of this link between the plain meaning of the psalm, and the various themes with which it was midrashically associated, the early exegetes drew their proemial and proof-texts from it, without offering any explanation for the appropriateness or relevance of their scriptural source. We may perhaps speculate that the earliest of the four exegetical motifs is the messianic interpretation, which comes closest to the plain meaning of the psalm. When this was adopted and adapted by the early Church, the reaction in rabbinic circles may have been to remove the psalm from its eschatalogical setting and to historicise it, referring it to personalities traditionally regarded as kings. Alternatively, it was treated as an allegory, alluding to the spiritual rulers of the Jewish people.

However, apart from the significance of the plain meaning of a text for determining the various forms of its interpretation, we must emphasise the other factor which emerges from this analysis of the midrashic treatment of Psalm 45, the role played by tradition. There is hardly more explicit scriptural evidence for the kingship of Abraham or Moses than there is for that of the *Torah* sages. Their royalty existed only in that corpus of popular tradition, to which we referred earlier, which was widely acknowledged by congregations in the ancient synagogues and was freely exploited by the early exegetes in their expositions of the biblical text. This can be demonstrated further by the midrashic treatment of another royal psalm, 110. Once again, there is evidence in our sources for three

---

[47] See above, p. 102.
[48] In addition to the material cited in this chapter (pp. 121ff), see Ginzberg, *Legends*, vol. 5, p. 216, note 46.

independent motifs in the early exegesis of this psalm: a) Davidic, b) messianic and c) Abrahamic.

The Davidic motif

Although the association with David is suggested by the heading of the psalm, there is scant evidence for the Davidic motif in midrashic sources.[49] None the less, it may have gained wide currency in talmudic times as it is clearly reflected in the *Targum*. The Aramaic translator has treated the psalm as a whole as an account by David of God's address to him, when granting him sovereignty over Israel in perpetuity. We would note in particular, the *Targum*'s rendering of two verses which occupied a special place in the early exegesis of Psalm 110, 1 and 4:

By David; a psalm. The Lord promised me by His word to appoint me master over all Israel. But He said to me, 'Sit and wait until Saul of the Tribe of Benjamin dies, for one sovereignty cannot function in conjunction with another, and afterwards I shall set your enemies as a foot-stool for your foot!'
'The Lord has sworn and will not retract that you are appointed a master[50] in the world to come, on account of the merit that you [will] have been a righteous king.'[51]

---

49 See particularly *Midrash Psalms* 110, pp. 466–7, which develops the same theme as the *Targum* to verse 1 and provides us with the basis for its rendering of שֵׁב as 'wait': שֵׁב [here] means 'wait', as it is said, שְׁבוּ נָא בָזֶה (Numbers 22:9) which we translate as 'wait' (see *Targum Onqelos* to this verse). See also *Tanna d'Bei Eliyahu* 18, ed. Friedmann, p. 94, where verse 4 is taken as an assurance by God to David that his throne will be secure, despite attempts to overthrow him.
50 This rendering of כֹּהֵן as רַבָּא gained wide currency in talmudic times through the medium of the *Targumim*; see, for example, *Targum Onqelos* and *Targum Pseudo-Jonathan* to Exodus 18:1; also the material cited on p. 121, in connection with Abraham. The basis for this rendering may be the act of anointing by which both kings and priests were consecrated and which was perceived as conferring greatness upon them. Thus *Targum Onqelos* renders Leviticus 7:35, זֹאת מִשְׁחַת אַהֲרֹן, as דָּא רַבּוּת אַהֲרֹן (see also *Targum Pseudo-Jonathan* to this verse). Similarly, the *Targum* to Zechariah 4:14, renders שְׁנֵי בְנֵי הַיִּצְהָר – which is taken midrashically as an allusion to a high priest and a king (see below, pp. 109ff) – as בְּנֵי רַבְרְבַיָּא. See also Rashi to psalm 45:8 (ed. Maarsen, p. 44): 'The imagery of anointing with oil after the manner of kings is applicable to any expression of greatness.' Compare also his comment to Genesis 31:13.
51 Taking מַלְכִּי צֶדֶק as מֶלֶךְ צֶדֶק, as in Hebrews 7:2 (see also below, note 71).

The Messianic motif

The messianic interpretation of Psalm 110 was evidently in vogue at a very early period. It was adopted and adapted by the Church, figuring prominently in New Testament writings. This applies particularly to the two key verses, 1 and 4, which are taken respectively to refer to the Messiah's place at the right hand of God, and to the high priesthood of Jesus, a subject to which we will return subsequently.[52]

This exegetical motif is equally well represented in rabbinic sources. The *Amora*, R. Hama, took verse 1 as the invitation which will be extended to the Messiah to sit at the right hand of God – as in Christian sources – while Abraham will be seated at His left. As this apparent demotion discomforts Abraham, God appeases him with the thought that 'the Lord is at thy right hand (verse 5)', implying that, in effect, God will be sitting at his right hand.[53]

In a quotation from the lost *Midrash Yelammedenu*,[54] verse 2 is cited as the proof-text for the notion that the rod which the Messiah will receive in the hereafter, and which he will employ to assert his dominion over the nations, is the staff of Jacob. This was handed down via Judah, Moses, Aaron and David, to every successive monarch, until its concealment at the time of the destruction of the Temple.[55]

Verse 2 also occurs in an interesting context in *Genesis Rabbah* 85:9,[56] where it is cited as the proof-text to substantiate the interpretation of Judah's rod in Genesis 38:18, as an allusion to the King Messiah. This was based, presumably, on a form of climatic exegesis. Although there is no overt reference to the

---

[52] See, however, Mark 12:36, 14:62 and 16:19; Luke 20:42; Acts 2:34; I Corinthians 15:25; Hebrews 1:13, 5:5ff, 7:17 and 21, and 10:13. It is interesting to note that the Church Fathers, Tertullian and Justin Martyr, assert that the Jews interpret Psalm 110 with reference to Hezekiah (see Ginzberg, *Legends*, vol. 6, p. 366, note 70). While there is no trace of this exegetical motif in rabbinic sources, we do find the notion that Hezekiah was originally destined to be the Messiah (see Bar Qappara's statement in connection with Isaiah 9:6, in *BT Sanhedrin* 94a). It may have been in this context that Psalm 110 was linked with Hezekiah.

[53] See *Midrash Psalms* 18, p. 157.   [54] In *Yalqut Psalms* 869.

[55] See also *Yalqut Ḥuqqat* 763, and *Numbers Rabbah* 18:23.

[56] P. 1043.

Messiah in Psalm 110, since it was treated midrashically as a messianic psalm, the term מטה could be invested with the connotation of the Messiah, and taken with this meaning in another context.[57]

The second of the two key verses in this psalm, verse 4, is cited in a messianic context in a tannaitic source, *Avot d'Rabbi Natan*, which calls for closer evaluation.[58] Commenting on the imagery employed in 4:14, שני בני היצהר, 'The two anointed ones who stand by the Lord of the whole earth', an anonymous teacher observes:

This refers to Aaron (*viz.* the high-priestly scion of Aaron[59]) and to the Messiah. Yet I do not know which of them is the more beloved [in the eyes of God]. However, since it is stated [in Psalm 110:4] נשבע יי ולא ינחם אתה כהן לעולם על דברתי מלכי צדק,[60] you may infer that the King Messiah is more beloved than the Priest of Righteousness.[61]

The obvious difficulty arising from this passage is what interpretation did the anonymous teacher place upon his proof-text? Evidently, he – or the redactor – expected his audience to be familiar with some well-known exposition of Zechariah 4:14 relating to his theme, which required no further elaboration. Several of the standard commentators to *Avot d'Rabbi Natan*[62] suggest that אתה כהן לעולם was taken as a declaration to the messianic King, on the basis of the traditional identification of כהן with שר, a prince or ruler. However, this does not allow for the element of comparison between the Messiah and the Righteous Priest which the text

---

57 As is the case with Psalm 29:11, which is frequently cited to support the identification of the expression עז with *Torah*, although there is no reference to it in the psalm (see above, pp. 76ff). See further *Leviticus Rabbah* 24:4 (p. 556) where verse 2 is cited as a proof-text by R. Levi to support his inclusion of strength among the benefits which will emanate from Zion in the hereafter.

58 Version A, chapter 34, p. 100.

59 See L. Ginzberg, *An Unknown Jewish Sect* (trans. R. Marcus, H. L. Ginzberg, Z. Gotthold and A. Hertzberg) New York 1976, p. 240.

60 Lit.: 'The Lord hath sworn and will not repent: Thou art a priest for ever after the manner of Malchizedek.'

61 For a detailed discussion on this messianic figure in talmudic-midrashic sources and early *piyyut*, see Ginzberg, *An Unknown Jewish Sect*, pp. 239ff.

62 See, for example, commentaries of the Vilna Gaon and Joshua Falk (*Binyan Yehoshua*) on the text, printed in the Vilna Edition.

demands, and for which the verse was cited. Ginzberg[63] suggests that the preposition על may have been taken in the sense
of a comparative, and translates accordingly, 'Thou art a priest
forever, higher than the order – or office – of Malchizedek.' It
is not at all clear, however, according to this rendering, how
the proof-text would have served the purpose for which it was
intended, namely to demonstrate the primacy of the messianic
king over his priestly counterpart.

The precise interpretation of Zechariah 4:14 is not the only
issue raised by this passage. The unknown *Tanna* has clearly
identified שני בני היצהר, with two eschatalogical figures, the
messianic king and his priestly counterpart, with the implication that both are to be anointed in the hereafter. This forms
a striking contrast with the view propounded by the *Tanna*,
R. Judah b. Ilai, that this verse refers to two historical personalities, as there will be no reanointing of the high priest in
the messianic age:[64]

'This is the anointing of Aaron, and the anointing of his sons (Leviticus 7:35)' ... R. Judah said: 'You might think that Aaron and his
sons will require the oil of anointing in the hereafter. Therefore, it
says, "*This* is the anointing of Aaron, and the anointing of his sons."
How, then, am I to explain "These are the two anointed ones etc.
..."? It refers to Aaron and to David.'[65]

None the less, the contrary view is stated explicitly, albeit in
a late source, that the high priest will be anointed in the
hereafter. Moreover, this act is to be performed by the Messiah
himself. This imagery conforms with the widely recurring
tendency in both rabbinic and non-rabbinic sources, to parallel the events of the final, messianic redemption, with those of
the first redemption from Egypt. Thus the messianic king is
destined to anoint his priestly colleague, just as Moses, who

[63] *An Unknown Jewish Sect*, p. 240, note 131.
[64] See *Sifra Tzav* 18, p. 40a, to Leviticus 7:35.
[65] See further *Sifrei Zutta* 84, p. 253 (and the parallels cited there) to Numbers 7:18,
where the following phrase is added: 'this refers to Aaron and David, the one is
seeking his priesthood, the other his kingship'.

functioned as Israel's first monarch,[66] had consecrated his brother Aaron:[67]

'Oil for illumination (Exodus 25:6)' – this alludes to the King Messiah, who will illuminate the eyes of Israel. 'Spices for the oil of anointing (*ibid.*)', [with which] he will in future anoint the high priest.

The notion implied here of the dependence of the priestly office on that of the king, is more clearly expressed in an exposition of Zechariah 4:14, cited in *Midrash Ha-Gadol* to Leviticus 7:35.[68] Its source is unknown, but its language and style echo that of the tannaitic statements cited above, and may, therefore, be early:

'These are the two anointed ones who stand by the Lord of the whole earth' – this refers to Aaron and David who are destined to return to their pre-eminence in the hereafter. For as long as kingship functions, so does the priestly office. When the former is suspended, so is the latter, as it is said, 'Removal of the priestly mitre accompanies the taking off of the royal crown (Ezekiel 21:31).'[69]

These sources, we suggest, are the fragmentary remains of a more highly developed tradition regarding the anointing of the messianic king and priest, and the relationship between the two, which may have been suppressed for polemical reasons in the second century of the current era.[70] At least one early

---

[66] See above, note 44.

[67] See *Midrash Leqaḥ Tov* to Exodus 25:6, ed. Buber, p. 177. See further the sources cited by Ginzberg, *Legends*, vol. 6, p. 63, note 323; also p. 340, note 112, for the reference in Christian sources to a Jewish belief that the Messiah himself is destined to be anointed in the hereafter by Elijah. Although it is mentioned by later Jewish writers, this tradition is unknown in older rabbinic sources.

[68] See p. 193.

[69] Lit.: 'The mitre shall be removed and the crown taken off.' However, for the midrashic rendering of this verse, see *Targum* and Rashi.

[70] See Ginzberg, *Legends*, vol. 6, p. 72, note 371, where he suggests that the emphatic denial of the anointing of either the High Priest or the Messiah in the sources we have quoted, may be of a polemical nature, negating the idea of the Christian משיח (*viz.* 'Anointed One'). It is further possible that the rabbis saw some support in this idea of the consecration of a messianic High Priest, for Paul's teaching discussed subsequently, regarding the ultimate displacement of the Aaronite or Levitical Priesthood, by a new order of priests based on the pattern of Malchizedek (see below, p. 115). Therefore, they insisted that the original anointing of Aaron by Moses was of eternal validity.

source, however, has preserved a statement which may predate these polemical considerations, that of our anonymous *Tanna* cited above from *Avot d'Rabbi Natan*. He has expounded Zechariah 4:14 precisely in the manner which R. Judah b. Ilai sought to avoid. Moreover, he found support for the primacy of the messianic king over his priestly counterpart, in a verse from a messianic psalm, אתה כהן לעולם על דברתי מלכי צדק, which he took as a declaration to the scion of Aaron that 'thou art a priest in perpetuity *on account of the Righteous King*'.[71]

Two further verses from Psalm 110 are interpreted in graphic terms with reference to the messianic era, in a quotation from the lost *Midrash Yelammedenu*.[72] According to this source, verse 6, ידין בגוים מלא גויות implies that God dips His purple robe[73] in the blood of every soul slain by 'Esau' (= Rome) until it is dyed blood-red. This is to be reserved for the Day of Judgement, to be worn by God when He will call the nations to account, displaying His robe to them as irrefutable evidence of their crimes against Israel. The phrase מנחל בדרך ישתה in verse 7 is taken as an allusion to the rivers which will be formed in the hereafter from the blood of the wicked, from which the birds will drink. These rivers will well up into waves, which will threaten to engulf the birds, who will be obliged to raise their heads above the waves, as is indicated by the words, על כן ירים ראש. Hence David concludes the psalm with the exclamation הללוי־ה, as an expression of thankful praise for this final act of retribution.[74]

---

[71] Rendering מלכי צדק as מלך צדק, as in the *Targum* to this verse and in Hebrews 7:2.

[72] Preserved in *Yalqut Psalms* 869. See also *Midrash Psalms* 9, p. 89 – where this exposition is recorded in the name of R. Eleazar – and 111, p. 467.

[73] פורפוריון = *Porphyrion*, the imperial purple robe. The reading in *Midrash Psalms* is הקב׳ה כותבו בפורפורא שלו, which Buber emends to פופוריא = *Papyros*, a scroll or book, hence, 'God records him on His scroll'. However in the context of the *Yelammedenu* passage, the reading פורפוריון is preferable, as it evokes the imagery of the emperor robed in his *porphyrion*, enthroned upon a *bema*, or *tribunal*, dispensing justice to his subjects.

[74] The version of this *aggadah* in *Midrash Psalms* 111, reads 'I am to render praise and thanks to You *in the future*', thus locating David's act of thanks-giving in the eschatalogical period.

The Abrahamic motif

The text of the psalm itself provides an obvious link with Abraham, as it refers to Malchizedek, who figures prominently in a notable event in the patriarch's life, recorded in Genesis 14. It is hardly surprising, therefore, that at an early period, Psalm 110 was treated as a commentary on the patriarch's life and experiences, as can be seen from tannaitic sources, where verses 1–4 are quoted in a noteworthy context. In the *Mekhilta d'Rabbi Ishmael*,[75] an anonymous aggadist cites the following example to illustrate the nature of God's response to those who dare to assault His children:

You have exalted Yourself exceedingly over such as have risen up against You! Who are they? Those who have risen up against Your children.[76] Who belongs in this category? '... Chedorlaomer [king of Elam] and Tidal king of Goiim etc. ... (Genesis 14:1)'. 'And he divided himself against them by night, he and his servants and he smote them... (*ibid.*, v. 15)'. 'Who hath raised up from the east, one at whose steps victory attendeth? [He giveth nations before him and maketh him to rule over kings; his sword maketh them as dust, his bow as the driven stubble] (Isaiah 41:2).' What does it state further? 'He pursueth them, and passeth on safely etc. (*ibid.* v. 3)'. And similarly it says, 'The Lord sayeth unto my lord: Sit at My right hand, [until I make thine enemies thy foot-stool]. The rod of thy strength I will send out of Zion: [rule thou in the midst of thine enemies]. Thy people offer themselves willingly in the day of thy warfare; [in adornments of holiness, from the womb of the dawn, thine is the dew of thy youth]. The Lord hath sworn and will not repent: Thou art a priest forever after the manner of Malchizedek (Psalm 110:1–4).'

This passage is little more than a collection of quotations taken, significantly, from the three main sections of the Hebrew Bible, the relevance of which the anonymous aggadist clearly expected his listeners to recognise without further explanatory comment. This may be due initially to the fairly obvious

[75] *Beshallaḥ, Shirta* 6, p. 135; also *Mekhilta d'Rabbi Shimon b. Yoḥai* to *Exodus* 15:7, p. 85.
[76] Or 'Your friends' = ידידיך; so MS Oxford, *Yalqut, Midrash Hachamim*, and *Mekhilta d'Rabbi Shimon b Yoḥai*. This reading is confirmed further by an extra-European source, *Midrash Ha-Gadol* to Exodus 15:7, p. 298.

thematic links between the three passages. Abraham is
explicitly mentioned in Isaiah 41:8, while verses 2 and 3
describe a glorious victory over kings. This theme of victory is
dominant in Psalm 110 which, as we observed earlier, mentions
a key figure in the pentateuchal narrative in Genesis 14,
Malchizedek. Moreover, a *haphtarah* list for the triennial cycle
discovered in the Cairo *Genizah*, enables us to identify Isaiah
41:1–13 as the corresponding prophetic reading for Genesis
14:1ff (= *Seder* 11).[77] Our tannaitic source, therefore, may be
early evidence for a lectionary link between the pentateuchal
and prophetic passages, which may have included a corresponding psalm.[78]

None the less, the preacher – or the redactor – has given no
indication of the actual exposition of his texts, relying, once
again, on his audience's familiarity with some well-known
traditional interpretation of Isaiah 41 and Psalm 110 with
reference to Abraham and his war with the kings recorded in
Genesis 14. It is possible that elements of this exegesis have
been preserved in extant sources, notably *Genesis Rabbah* 43:3,
which records tannaitic interpretations of Isaiah 41:2–3 relating to the miracles performed by Abraham in the course his
battle with the kings.[79] Similarly we find tannaitic expositions
of verses from Psalm 110. R. Joshua b. Qorha took verse 3 as an
allusion to God's support for Abraham in his preparations for
battle referred to in Genesis 14:14: David said: 'עמך נדבות

---

[77] See Mann, *The Bible as Read*, vol. 1, p. 562.
[78] Once again, see Mann, *The Bible as Read*, vol. 1, p. 105, where he argues that the
association between Genesis 14:1ff and Isaiah 41:1–13 was established before the
destruction of the Second Temple! As to the possibility that Psalm 110 was linked
with these two readings as part of a lectionary cycle from the Hagiographa, we can
only refer once again to a phenomenon discussed below in Appendix 3 (pp. 187f)
that in *Aggadat Bereshit*, this psalm is linked with five consecutive *sedarim* of the
triennial cycle, excluding *Seder* 11. Consequently, we should not place too much
value on the above source as evidence of a lectionary cycle involving components
from the *Torah*, the Prophets and the Hagiographa.
[79] See also the numerous parallels cited by Theodor, p 418. For the evidence in our
sources of the extensive interpretation of Isaiah 41 with reference to Abraham in
general, see the material cited by Mann, *The Bible as Read*, vol. 1, p. 105, note 101, to
which we may add the *Targum* to Isaiah 41:2–3, which gives us some indication of
the public exposition of this passage in the ancient synagogues.

ביום חילך וגוי [which means that] God said to him, 'I was *with you*[80] on the day that you armed your soldiers.'[81]

A particularly significant comment on the key verses 1 and 4, by the early *Tanna*, R. Ishmael, is recorded in a *Baraita* preserved in *Leviticus Rabbah* 25:5.[82] We referred earlier to the importance attached to these two verses in New Testament sources, notably in the writings of Paul.[83] In his exposition of verse 4, Paul depicts Malchizedek as the prototype for Jesus, an immortal, without genealogy, and a model for the perfect priesthood, functioning beyond 'the law of a carnal commandment' and superior to the priesthood of Levi, which it was destined to replace.[84] It is all the more poignant, therefore, that the rabbinic response to these claims was propounded by a member of the high-priestly family, R. Ishmael b. Elisha. Not only does R. Ishmael provide Malchizedek with a clearly defined genealogy within the frame-work of the patriarchal family, as Shem the son of Noah,[85] he also emphasises the imperfection of his performance as a priest, with the result that he forfeited the priesthood to Abraham and his descendants in perpetuity:[86]

R. Ishmael taught: 'God intended to make Shem the source of priesthood, as it is said, "And Malchizedek (= Shem) the king of Salem etc. ... and he was a priest of God the Most High (Genesis 14:18)". However, when he gave priority to the blessing of Abraham over that of God, Abraham said to him: "Does one give priority to the blessing of a servant over that of his master?!" The Omnipresent then deprived Shem [of the priesthood] and granted it to Abraham, as it is said, "The Lord hath sworn and will not repent: Thou art priest forever – על דברתי מלכי צדק", [which means] on account of Malchizedek's words. Hence it is written, "And *he* was a priest of God the Most High (but not his descendants)."'[87]

---

80   Reading *'im⁽cha* for *'am⁽cha* in the Masoretic Text.
81   See *Tanḥuma*, ed. Buber, 1, p. 60 and particularly comments in note 32.
82   See Margulies, p. 580, for parallels.   83   See the sources cited in note 52 above.
84   See Hebrews 7:1ff; see further, Justin Martyr, *Dialogue* 33 and 96.
85   This identification evidently gained wide currency in talmudic times, as is suggested by both Palestinian *Targumim* to Genesis 14:18 and the numerous sources, both Jewish and Christian, cited by Ginzberg, *Legends*, vol. 5, pp. 225f, note 102.
86   See *Leviticus Rabbah* 25:6, p. 580.
87   As is expressly stated in the parallel passage in *BT Nedarim* 32b: 'He was a priest, but his descendants were not!' The reading והוא כהן לא־ל עליון is found in all the MSS cited by Marguliues.

The actual context in which this *baraita* occurs is also note-worthy, as it relates to a crucial issue in Jewish-Christian polemics, the circumcision of Abraham. In a statement follow-ing that quoted above, R. Ishmael emphasises the inseparable link between Abraham's circumcision and his fitness to func-tion as a priest, thus negating the concept of an uncircumcised priesthood advocated by the early teachers of the Church:[88]

R. Ishmael said: 'Abraham was a high priest, as it is said, "The Lord hath sworn etc. (Psalm 110:4)" and it is written, "And you shall be circumcised in the flesh of your ערלה[89] (Genesis 17:11)." Where was he to be circumcised? If he were to be circumcised from his ear, then he would not be fit to offer sacrifices (since he would be physically blemished) etc. ... Consequently, where was he to be circumcised, and yet remain fit to offer sacrifices? You must conclude that [ערלה in this context relates to] the foreskin of the membrum.'

In later sources, we find Isaiah 41:2–3 and Psalm 110 midrashically interrelated in connection with the war with the kings in Genesis 14. *Midrash Psalms* to Psalm 110 consists mainly of a complex proem based on the two *Haphtarah* verses.[90] The first interpretation, recorded in the name of R. Reuben, comprises two distinct aggadic elements interpolated into the expression העיר in the first proemial verse. Referring to the widely current tradition of Abraham's missionary activity, R. Reuben depicts him as 'arousing' the slumbering gentiles to acknowledge the one true God. The second element

---

88 See particularly Jerome, *Epistola* 73, 2 (Migne, vol. 22, 677), where he records the views of a number of Church Fathers on the performance of the sacrificial rite by those who predated circumcision, the priesthood of Aaron and the Levitical code, namely, Abel, Noah, Enoch, Malchizedek and Job. It is interesting to compare this with the list of biblical personalities recorded in *Avot d'Rabbi Natan* Version A, chapter 2, p. 12, who were deemed to have been born circumcised: Job, Adam, Seth, Noah, Malchizedek (= Shem) Jacob etc. The biblical source cited for Shem-Malchizedek's circumcision is Genesis 14:18, ומלכי צדק מלך שלם, the term שלם – like its synonym תמים – being taken to connote the perfection of circumcision. See also the comment on this verse in *Genesis Rabbah* 43:6, p. 420; see further *Pirqei d'Rabbi Eliezer* 8, where Psalm 110:4 is connected with a tradition that Malchizedek instructed Abraham in the principles of intercalation.
89 R. Ishmael is exploiting here the use of this term in the Bible, where it occurs in connection with the four parts of the human body to which he refers, as is stated subsequently by his colleague, R. Aqiva (p. 581).
90 See p. 465; also *Yalqut Psalms* 869.

is more obscure. Treating צדק as the direct object of העיר,
R. Reuben asserts that the attribute of צדקה itself was also
slumbering until Abraham awakened it.[91] In older sources,
both these elements are introduced into the aggadic exposition
of Psalm 110 itself. Thus an anonymous aggadist rendered,
עמך נדבות ביום חילך (verse 3) as, 'I was with you[92] when
you offered yourself willingly for the sake of My name, to
descend into the fiery furnace. ביום חילך [alludes to] your
gathering to Me all those crowds (who witnessed your act of
martyrdom)'.[93] As to R. Reuben's second comment that
Abraham was responsible for arousing צדקה, this has its
counterpart in an equally obscure exposition of Psalm 110:1,
preserved in *Aggadat Bereshit*:[94]

God said: 'Righteousness (צדקה) normally sits at My right hand, as
it is said, "Thy right hand is full of righteousness (Psalm 48:11)."
Abraham, however, made it consequential [upon himself],[95] as it is
said, "For I have known him [... to do righteousness and justice]
(Genesis 18:19)". If so, sit in the place of righteousness! As it is said,
"Sit thou at My right hand ... The rod of thy strength the Lord will
send out of Zion (Psalm 110:1–2)."'

We can assume that underlying both these sources, is a
tradition discussed earlier regarding Abraham's role as the
advocate of the Sodomites, seeking divine clemency on their

---

[91] See *Genesis Rabbah* 43:3, p. 418, where the version of R. Reuben's statement is
substantially different:
Righteousness was crying out saying, 'If Abraham will not practise me, then
there is no-one else to do so!'
[92] Reading עמך once again as *'im'cha*, as did R. Joshua b. Qorha cited earlier, see
p. 115.
[93] See *Genesis Rabbah* 39:8, p. 370. It is noteworthy that this same motif is interpolated
into the aggadic exposition of Isaiah 41:7 (see *Genesis Rabbah* 44:7, p. 430).
Moreover, in the graphic account of the mass conversion inspired by Abraham's act
of martyrdom recorded in *Midrash Ha-Gadol* to Genesis 11:28 (p. 206) 14:14, וירק
את חניכיו is cited to suggest that the babes deposited with Abraham at that time
ultimately provided him with his warriors for his battle against the kings. See
further, *Sepher Ha-Yashar Noah*, which states that *some 300 men* accompanied
Abraham when he departed from Nimrod following his trial. See also Rav's
interpretation of Genesis 14:14 in *BT Nedarim* 32a.
[94] Chapter 24, p. 49.
[95] Which is one possible rendering of the Hebrew phrase, עשה אותה עקב, which
might also be rendered as, 'Abraham relegated it to a secondary position'.

The midrashic process

behalf.[96] This was associated with Psalm 45:8, **אהבת צדק**
ותשנא רשע, which was rendered midrashically as, 'You love
to justify [My creatures] and you hate to condemn [them]'.
Thus the references to **צדקה** in these sources is to the Divine
attribute of clemency, which Abraham sought to arouse. This
is borne out by the context from which the above quotation
from *Aggadat Bereshit* is taken. It is from the conclusion to the
Psalm-homily which corresponds to the *Torah*-homily on
Genesis 18:25ff, the *seder* which deals with Abraham's intercession on behalf of the Sodomites.

The second exposition in *Midrash Psalms* of the proemial
verses from Isaiah 41, is a parallel account to that found in
Genesis Rabbah,[97] of Abraham's miraculous performance in his
battle against the kings. In the former source, however, it
concludes with the following:

... And who waged all these battles? It was God, who said to
[Abraham], 'Sit at My right hand and I will wage war on your
behalf!' However, this is not explicitly stated here (viz in Isaiah).
Who, then, has explicitly stated it? David, [when he said,] 'The Lord
said unto my lord: Sit thou at My right hand [until I make thine
enemies thy footstool].' Similarly, it is said with reference to the
Messiah, 'And his throne is established through mercy, and he will sit
thereon in truth in the tent of David (Isaiah 16:5).' God Said: 'He
will remain seated, and I will wage war!' Hence, '... and he will sit
thereon in truth in the tent of David'...

The passage as a whole is significant, as it endeavours to
establish the interdependence of the triad of biblical texts.
While the *haphtarah* verses serve to amplify the miraculous
nature of Abraham's conflict with the kings – few details of
which are recorded in the Pentateuch – Psalm 110 emphasises
God's authorship of these events.[98] Moreover, it introduces a

[96] See above, pp. 95f.   [97] 43:3, p. 418.
[98] On the miraculous nature of Abraham's encounter with the kings, see, for example,
Genesis Rabbah 42:2 p. 416, for the view that Abraham's army consisted only of
Eliezer, as the figure 318 referred to in Genesis 14:14, is the numerical value of his
name. On God's role in assuring Abraham's victory, see particularly *Midrash
Ha-Gadol* to Genesis 14:20 (and the parallels cited by Margulies, pp. 237f) where,
in conjunction with Isaiah 41:2 and Psalm 110:1, Eliezer relates to Shem-
Malchizedek God's conduct of the war on behalf of his master. See further, *Tanḥuma*,
ed. Buber, 1, p. 74, and Buber's comments in note 170.

further, important notion that Abraham's battle with the kings is a prefiguration of the events in the messianic era. This reflects a highly developed motif in rabbinic *Aggadah*, which portrays the life of the patriarch as a prototype for his descendants' experiences throughout the course of their history, culminating in the messianic age.[99]

In the context of this broader motif, Abraham's struggle with the kings was perceived to be an indication of the events leading to the advent of the Messiah. Thus the exposition in *Genesis Rabbah*[100] of the opening verse of Genesis 14, concludes with the following:

'And it came to pass in the days of Amraphel king of Shinar' – this alludes to Babylon,[101] 'Arioch king of Ellasar' – this alludes to Greece,[102] 'Chedorlaomer king of Elam' – this alludes to Media,[103] 'Tidal king of Goiim' – this alludes to the wicked kingdom, which conscripts a levy of soldiers from all the nations of the world. R. Eleazar b. Abina said: 'If you see kingdoms in conflict, look out for the advent of the Messiah! You may know that this is so, since in the days of Abraham, greatness came to him because kingdoms were in conflict with each other.'

[99] This is an aspect of the aggadic treatment of Abraham which still requires further study and analysis in order to establish its scope and importance. Nonetheless, in this context, we may at least note the main sources for this motif, in which Abraham is portrayed as a prototype for the events relating to four major periods in the history of his descendants: a) the Egyptian Bondage; b) the Wilderness; c) the settlement in the Land of Israel; d) the Hereafter, or Messianic Age. There are relatively few examples in midrashic literature of aggadic expositions relating to four, or even three of these periods. This makes *Genesis Rabbah* 48:4 (p. 487f) all the more unusual, as it contains no less than six consecutive expositions of phrases from Genesis 18:4–8, relating Abraham's meritorious actions to the rewards which resulted for his descendants in the wilderness, in the land of Israel and in the Hereafter (במדבר וביישוב ולעתיד לבוא; so MS Munich, and similarly MS Oxford 2). In the exposition of verse 4 in the parallel passage in *Tanḥuma* Buber 1, p. 87, allusions are found for all the four periods. In a number of sources, Abraham is portrayed as the prototype for his children's experiences specifically in
  a) *Egypt*: see for example, *Genesis Rabbah* 40:6 (pp. 385f); 42:3 (p. 417); 43:9 (p. 423).
  b) *The Wilderness*: see *Genesis Rabbah* 43:9 (pp. 423–4); 55:8 (p. 594); *Tanḥuma*, ed. Buber, 1, p. 110.
  c) *The Hereafter*: see *Tanḥuma*, ed. Buber, 1, pp. 71 and 76; *Genesis Rabbah* 41:2 (p. 399) and 56:9 (p. 605).
[100] 41:4, p. 409.   [101] See *Genesis Rabbah* 36:4 and Theodor's note, p. 346.
[102] Theodor offers the plausible suggestion that this identification is based on the similarity between אלסר and *Hellas*.
[103] See Daniel 8:2.

Similarly, the homily to this *seder* in *Midrash Tanḥuma*[104] concludes with an extensive statement by the fourth century aggadist, R. Levi, who asserts that 'God gave Abraham a sign that all which happened to him, would happen to his children.' R. Levi continues to list the numerous parallels between Abraham's experiences and those of his descendants, from the time of their arrival in Egypt until their redemption and concludes:

Just as the four kings attacked Abraham, so it will be with Israel in the future age, that the nations will make an alliance[105] against them, as it is said, 'The kings of the earth stand up [and the rulers take counsel together against the Lord and His anointed] (Psalm 2:2).'[106] Just as with Abraham, God went forth and fought before him and slew his enemies, so will He fight for Israel. In the hereafter, God is to go forth and fight their battles, as it is said, 'Then shall the Lord go forth and fight against those nations, as when He fought in the day of battle (Zechariah 14:3).'[107]

This association in aggadic tradition between Abraham's battle and the messianic conflict may have additional significance for the midrashic treatment of Psalm 110 in our sources as a whole. As we indicated above, this is a further example of the development of several independent exegetical traditions relating to the same biblical passage, based on a common denominator. As in the case of Psalm 45, a royal psalm has been linked exegetically with three royal figures in biblical and rabbinic tradition. In this instance, however, they do not appear to be three disparate exegetical motifs, arbitrarily associated with the same psalm. It is possible that the early rabbinic exegetes – and, presumably, their audiences – recog-

---

[104] Ed. Buber, vol. 1, pp. 70f.   [105] המוניה = Greek: *Homonia*.
[106] The messianic interpretation of this psalm is well known and occurs in both rabbinic and New Testament sources. See for example Acts 4:25f (where verses 1 and 2 are taken as a reference to the attack on Jesus by Herod, Pontius Pilot and the 'peoples of Israel'); also 13:33; Hebrews 1:5, 5:5; *Leviticus Rabbah* 27:11, p. 646; *Exodus Rabbah* 1:1; *BT Berakhot* 7b. We may also note Rashi's opening comment to this psalm: 'Our Rabbis expounded the passage with reference to the King Messiah, but according to its plain meaning *and as a refutation to heretics*, it is correct to interpret it with reference to David himself... (see Maarsen, *Parshandatha* 3, p. 1).'
[107] The messianic character of the context from which this verse is taken is, once again, well known. See also *Tanḥuma*, Old Version, *Lekh Lekha* 9.

nised an inner organic link between these three strands of interpretation, connecting David and his messianic heir with Abraham, the original source of Israel's monarchy. There is no explicit statement to this effect in early sources. Rashi, however, who states at the outset of his commentary to Psalm 110, that he proposes to adhere to its traditional rabbinic interpretation as an 'Abrahamic' psalm, gives the following exposition of the key verse 4:[108]

From you shall issue priesthood and kingship, so that your descendants shall be heirs to the priesthood and kingship granted to Shem (= Malchizedek) your ancestor. ... 'Thou art a כהן' – The term כהן [also] contains the implication of greatness and rulership, as it is said, 'And the sons of David were כהנים – *viz.* princes (II Samuel 8:18)'.

It is possible that Rashi made use here of midrashic material which is no longer extant, as his statement contains aggadic elements found in much older sources. His interpretation of כהנים as שרים in particular, is very early and gained wide currency in talmudic times, notably in connection with Jethro.[109] Citing the same proof-text as Rashi, the early *Tanna*, R. Eleazar of Modi'in explained Jethro's title, כהן מדין as שר, which is clearly reflected in the *Targumim* to Exodus 18:1.[110] Similarly, the coupling of Abraham's priesthood and kingship occurs widely in our sources, in a statement by the *Tanna*, R. Joshua b. Qorḥa, who lays great emphasis on Abraham's unique role as the founder of Israel's priestly and royal lines in an unusual context. Moses, who, according to rabbinic tradition, exercised both royal and priestly offices,[111] sought to retain them for his descendants. However, he was rebuked by God with the words of Proverbs 25:6, אל תתהדר לפני מלך ובמקום גדולים אל תעמוד,[112] for daring to aspire to the

---

108 Ed. Maarsen, p. 103.
109 Who was regarded in a number of respects as a parallel figure to Abraham; see my article, 'Literary Motifs in the Testament of Job', pp. 4ff.
110 See *Mekhilta d'Rabbi Ishmael, Yitro, Amaleq* 1, p. 190.
111 In connection with Moses' kingship, see above, note 44. On his functioning as a priest, see Ginzberg, *Legends*, vol. 5, p. 422, note 139.
112 The selection of which, presupposes once again the tradition of Abraham's royal status, as R. Joshua has evidently identified the king referred to in the text with Abraham.

patriarch's privileged position as the progenitor of Israel's priests and kings:[113]

R. Joshua [b. Qorḥa][114] said: 'In two respects Moses compared himself to Abraham. God said to him, "Glorify not thyself[115] in the presence of the king (*viz.* Abraham) and stand not in the place of the great ones."[116] Abraham employed the expression הנני [implying,] "I am ready [to receive] priesthood, I am ready [to receive] kingship!"[117] He merited priesthood, [as it is said,] "The Lord has sworn and will not repent: Thou art a priest forever on account of the words of Malchizedek."[118] He merited kingship, [as it is said,] "Thou art a mighty prince among us (Genesis 23:6)."[119] Moses employed the expression הנני (Exodus 3:4) [implying] "I am ready [to receive] priesthood, I am ready [to receive] kingship!" God said to him, אל תקרב הלם ("Draw not nigh hither", *ibid.* 3:5). Now the expression קרב implies priesthood, as it is said, "And the common man that draweth nigh (הקרב) to sacrifice shall be put to death (Numbers 1:51)." Similarly, the expression הלם implies kingship as it is said (in

---

113 See *Genesis Rabbah* 55:6, and the numerous parallels cited by Theodor, p. 589.
114 This is the reading of the majority of MSS cited by Theodor and occurs also in early printed editions.
115 Or, perhaps, 'aspire not to regal splendour!', which would reflect the association of הדר specifically with the notion of kingship in biblical texts.
116 Presumably גדול here has been taken as an allusion to the high priest on the basis of Leviticus 21:10, והכהן הגדול מאחיו.
117 The writer is obliged to concede that he has not yet found a completely satisfactory explanation for this interpretation of the expression הנני. Pseudo-Rashi on the text, suggests the two offices were implied in the double נ of הנני, since the conjectured form הני (*sic*!) – comparable with הנך, – would have sufficed. A more plausible suggestion is made by Einhorn that this notion was derived from the reduplication of names which occurs in connection with both Abraham (Genesis 22:14) and Moses (Exodus 3:4). Since Moses received a similar call to that of the patriarch, he assumed that he was also being offered both kingship and priesthood.
     We may note in conclusion, that the two offices were evidently regarded as part of the patriarchal patrimony, as is indicated by a tradition which, once again, gained wide currency in the talmudic period. According to all the *Targumim* to Genesis 49:3, Jacob informed Reuben that, as the first-born, he should have inherited from his father both priesthood and kingship for his descendants. However, as a result of his unworthiness, the former was allotted to Levi and the latter to Judah (see *Genesis Rabbah* 98:4, p. 1,253; also *Midrash Ha-Gadol* to Genesis 49:3 and the numerous parallels cited by Margulies, p. 836).
118 Compare R. Ishmael's exposition of this verse above, p. 115.
119 In the parallel passage in *Deuteronomy Rabbah* 2:7, the proof-text cited is Genesis 14:17, אל עמק שוה הוא עמק המלך, which no doubt presupposes the midrashic exposition of this verse cited on p. 214.

connection with David) "... that Thou hast brought me הלם[120] (2 Samuel 7:18)".'

Finally, we may note that Abraham's investiture with both kingship and priesthood is connected in rabbinic tradition with the one significant event, closely associated in midrashic sources with Psalm 110, his battle with the kings recounted in Genesis 14. We have already cited R. Ishmael's view that it was as a result of his encounter with Malchizedek in the aftermath of this battle (Genesis 14:18ff) that Abraham was granted the priesthood in perpetuity. We may now add that the location of their meeting, recorded in verse 17, עמק שוה הוא עמק המלך, is widely interpreted in our sources as a direct allusion to Abraham's elevation to kingship:[121]

R. Berechiah and R. Helbo [said] in the name of R. Shemuel b. Nahman: '[The vale was so called,] because there all the nations concurred (השוו) [and cut down cedars, made a great platform and enthroned Abraham thereon; and they were hailing him saying, נשיא אלהים אתה בתוכנו (Genesis 23:6)]. They were saying to him, "Be thou a king over us, [be thou a god over us]!"[122] He said to them, "The world does not lack either its King or its God!"'

Moreover, there is at least one source which actually cites Psalm 110:1 in conjunction with this traditional exposition of Genesis 14:17, to support the identification of Abraham with the king referred to in the verse:[123]

---

[120] This exposition of II Samuel 7:18 is a particularly good example of that most extrinsic device in early rabbinic Bible interpretation, climatic exegesis (see above, p. 4). As the expressions קרב and הלם occur in a context, or climate of priesthood and kingship respectively, each has been invested with meaning of its climate, and taken in this new sense in a completely different context. In the parallel passage in *Exodus Rabbah* 2:6 (to Exodus 3:4) it is stressed that Moses did actually function as both a priest and a king, but his appointment was *ad personam*, without the hereditary rights which he sought by his exclamation הנני. See Einhorn's comment on the text, also *BT Zevahim* 101b–102a, for an extensive discussion on this point.

[121] See *Genesis Rabbah* 43:5 and the variants cited by Theodor, p. 419; also 41:3, p. 410 for parallels; see further, *Midrash Ha-Gadol* on this verse, p. 236; *Leqah Tov* to Genesis 14:3, p. 63; *Deuteronomy Rabbah* 2:7 and 33; and *Ecclesiastes Rabbah* to 4:13.

[122] Presumably taking the phrase as two separate proclamations. נשיא אתה, אלהים אתה!.

[123] See *Tanhuma*, Old Version, *Lekh Lekha* 13.

'And the king of Sodom went forth to meet him etc. . . . [to the Vale of Shaveh,] the same is the King's Vale.' From that time on it was called the King's Vale. Who is the king in question? Abraham, who was victorious over all the kings and their soldiers and concerning whom it is said, 'The Lord hath said to my lord: "Sit at My right hand, until I make thine enemies thy footstool."'[124]

We would conclude, therefore, that for the early rabbinic exegetes, the three distinctive motifs in the interpretation of Psalm 110 were entirely compatible. Its contents could refer equally to any one of three royal personages, who were inseparably linked, David, the founder of Israel's line of kings, his messianic heir, or Abraham the priest-king and prototype for the Messiah.

It is impossible to determine with any certainty which of these motifs is the oldest. It is likely, however, that the 'historicisation' of the psalm as Davidic or Abrahamic was due to polemical considerations. As can be seen from the material cited above, Psalm 110 figured in Jewish–Christian polemics already in tannaitic times. The adoption by the Church of the messianic interpretation of the psalm to support and propagate its teachings, may have led to a predictable reaction among the early rabbinic scholars. They transferred the psalm from an eschatalogical to a historical setting, relating it either to David, or to Abraham, the aboriginal monarch, to whom the pledge of a unique and exclusive priesthood had been given.

The tradition of Abraham's priesthood and kingship may also be presupposed by the second of our original series of proems relating to *Seder* 10 in *Genesis Rabbah* 39:2:

R. Berechiah opened [with the following proemial verse], לריח שמניך טובים שמן תורק שמך – "Thine ointments have a goodly fragrance; thy name is as oil poured forth (Canticles 1:3)." – To what was Abraham comparable? To a phial of balsam sealed with a tightly fitting lid and deposited in a corner, so that it did not exude its aroma. Once it was moved about, it exuded its aroma. Thus God said to Abraham: "Move about from one place to another, so that your

---

[124] This version of the statement occurs also in MS Vatican 2, cited by Buber in his edition of *Midrash Tanḥuma*, 1, p. 74, note 170.

name may become great in the world!" [Hence the opening words of the *seder*,] "Get thee out etc. ... ."'[125]

Following his own thesis, Mann[126] endeavours to link שמך in the proemial verse with Isaiah 63:15, 'So didst Thou lead Thy people to make Thyself a glorious *name* (שם תפארת)', which, he conjectures, formed part of a corresponding *haphtarah* for *Seder* 10. There is, of course, a more obvious verbal link directly with the *seder* itself, in Genesis 12:2, ואגדלה שמך, which is clearly presupposed by the theme of the proem. We would suggest, however, that R. Berechiah's selection of Canticles 1:3 was not based on verbal links alone. Firstly, there is evidence to show that the opening verses of Canticles were traditionally associated with the patriarchs, especially Abraham.

The opening word שיר – the numerical of which, is 510 – was taken as an allusion to the total number of years of the patriarchs' lives, plus the Decalogue.[127] Similarly the expression

---

[125] A fuller version of this proem is recorded in the name of R. Joḥanan b. Nappaḥa in *Canticles Rabbah* to 1:3. This includes an exposition of the final phrase of the verse על כן עלמות אהבוך, which introduces the well-known theme of Abraham's missionary activity, the scriptural source for which actually occurs in *Seder* 10, Genesis 12:5:

> God said to [Abraham]: 'You have many maidens!' – as it is written, 'And Abram took Sarai his wife and Lot his brother's son and all their substance that they had gathered,' ואת הנפש אשר עשו בחרן (lit.: 'and the souls that they had gotten in Haran'). Surely, if all the inhabitants of the world assembled to create a single gnat, they could not do it! However, this refers to the proselytes which Abraham and Sarah made, therefore [the verse] says, 'and all the souls which *they* made in Haran'. R. Hunia said: 'Abraham was converting the men and Sarah the women. What then does [the phrase] אשר עשו בחרן imply? It indicates that Abraham was gathering them to his house, giving them to eat and to drink, imbuing them with a love [for God], bringing them near, converting them and gathering them beneath the wings of the Divine Presence. Thus you may infer that anyone who gathers a single being to the protection of the Divine Presence, is regarded as having created him, fashioned him and formed him [like an embryo in the womb].'

It is noteworthy that this version of Abraham's proselytising activities, describes him as instilling love for God into his converts. This clearly echoes the oldest source for this tradition, *Sifrei Deuteronomy* 32 (see the numerous parallels cited by Finkelstein, p. 54) where ואהבת in 6:5 is interpreted as a positive commandment to convert one's fellow men, as did Abraham.

[126] *The Bible as Read*, vol. 1, p. 100

[127] 180 (= Abraham) + 175 (= Isaac) + 147 (= Jacob) + 10, excluding the two years of famine. See *Canticles Rabbah* to 1:1 (end) and Einhorn's commentary, on the inclusion of the Decalogue with the lives of the patriarchs.

דודיך in verse 2, in its more common meaning of 'thy friends', was treated as an allusion to the three patriarchs: 'Thy friends' – which refers to the patriarchs, 'are better than wine' – which alludes to the princes [of the tribes].[128] The evidence for an association of verse 4 with the patriarchs, particularly Abraham, is more extensive, occurring both in midrashic sources and early *piyyutim*. *Midrash Zutta*[129] – although a comparatively late source – preserves an interesting interpretation of this verse, which reflects very early traditions:

[נזכירה דודיך מיין][130] – This refers to Abraham, Isaac and Jacob. When we enter into [a period of] trouble, we make mention of the deeds of the patriarchs before You, and memory of them is more admissible to You than the libations of wine which were poured out on the altar. מישרים אהבוך [means] that they loved You with an integrity of heart.[131] They did not harbour any misgivings in their

---

128 See *Canticles Rabbah* to 1:2 (end). On the application of the expression דודיך, 'friends', to the patriarchs, see Katz's (*Matnot Kehunah*) commentary to the text and note 131 below, in connection with the interpretation of דודיך in verse 3. The basis for identification of מיין with the princes is more difficult to determine. Strashun (*R'Shash*) emends the text to מעשיהם on the basis of the comment in *Canticles Rabbah* to 1:3 (end), which does not yield a more plausible rendering. Einhorn suggests that it is an allusion to the offerings of the princes, which did include libations. Thus the מ of מיין was taken midrashically as a מ privative as well as a מ of comparison, hence, 'without wine'. However, this in no way clarifies the point the preacher is endeavouring to make.

129 Ed. Buber, p. 11. The section relating to *Canticles* was also published by Schechter in *JQR* (OS) vols. 6–7 and subsequently as a separate work (Cambridge 1896) under the title *Agadath Shir Ha-Shirim*, which is quoted hereafter. The parallel for our passage occurs in *Yalqut Canticles* 982, with several substantial differences which are discussed subsequently.

130 According to its context here, this is to be rendered midrashically as 'We shall mention Thy friends [which is more efficacious] than wine libations'. This is the reading of the *Yalqut*, which is clearly substantiated by the continuation of the passage. In *Midrash Zutta*, the comment is attached to clause B, מישרים אהבוך, which is inappropriate and, presumably, a copyist's error.

131 The application of this phrase – like the expression דודיך in both this and the preceding verse – to the patriarchs, presupposes the early tradition that all three patriarchs were designated as אוהבים, lovers of God, even though this epithet in biblical sources is reserved for Abraham alone. As we have noted subsequently (p. 148, note 11) this is expressly stated in the Zadokite Document and is reflected in the writings of Philo. In rabbinic sources, R. Meir portrays the three patriarchs as prototypes for the three aspects of love for God implied in Deuteronomy 6:5: בכל לבבך = Abraham, בכל נפשך = Isaac, בכל מאדך = Jacob. Although this topic and the relevant sources are discussed fully below, in this context we must note that the particular quality associated with Abraham is his ability accept God's will without protest, thus serving Him with both his good and his evil inclinations,

heart, nor did they complain[132] at Your demands. You promised Abraham to give him the land, as it is said, 'For all the land which thou seest, [to thee will I give it, and to thy seed for ever]... Arise, walk through the land in the length of it, and in the breadth of it, [for unto thee will I give it] (Genesis 13:15 and 17).' Then You said to him, 'Buy a burial place [for Sarah]!' and he did not murmur[133] against You.

The passage has apparently been recorded in *Midrash Zutta* in a truncated form.[134] The anonymous aggadist[135] began his exposition of מישרים אהבוך with a reference to all three patriarchs. It is highly probable, therefore, that the passage originally contained illustrations of unquestioning submission to God's will for Isaac and Jacob, as well for Abraham. This is actually found in talmudic-midrashic sources dating back to tannaitic times. In a *baraita* cited in *BT Sanhedrin* 111b,[136] R. Eleazar b. R. Jose depicts God as criticising Moses' lack of faith in challenging His treatment of Israel, citing the example of the three patriarchs, all of whom had been promised possession of the Land of Israel, yet each in turn had suffered humiliation without complaint. Abraham had to purchase a burial place for Sarah, Isaac became involved in a dispute over watering rights, and Jacob was obliged to pay for the privilege of pitching his tent, yet none of them harboured any misgivings regarding God's conduct.

However, the version of this *aggadah* in *Midrash Zutta* may be

as is implied in the uncontracted form לבב. Hence the reading of *Agadat Shir Ha-Shirim* (p. 14) ביש לבב, in our passage, which proceeds to elaborate on this very theme, is superior to that of *Midrash Zutta* and the *Yalqut*.

132 Reading רגנו (or, better the *pi'el*, ריגנו, see Jastrow, s.v. רגן p. 1,484) as in the *Yalqut*, which was accepted by Buber in preference to the reading of *Midrash Zutta*, דגנו (דיק√, 'they challenged'?).

133 *Viz.* רגן, so *Yalqut*; *Midrash Zutta*: דק.

134 *Yalqut* adds a reference to the *Aqedah*. This occurs also in *Canticles Rabbah* (*ibid.*), although this source contains no reference to the death and burial of Sarah. It is difficult to determine whether the compiler of the *Yalqut* actually had this statement in his *vorlage* of *Midrash Zutta*, or has simply introduced a more familiar example of Abraham's total submission to the will of God.

135 See, however, *Yalqut* and *Canticles Rabbah*, where this exposition is attributed to the *Amora*, R. Aibu, although in the latter source, it is drastically curtailed.

136 See also *Exodus Rabbah* 6:4; *Tanḥuma* Old Version, *Va-Era'* 1; *Midrash Ha-Gadol* to Exodus 6:3, pp. 93f, also *Midrash Aggadah* to this verse, ed. Buber, p. 134; *Yalqut Va-Era'* 176.

unique in one respect. As far as the present writer is aware, it is the only rabbinic source to associate Abraham's conduct at the burial of Sarah with his love for God. This is found only in one other source of great antiquity, the Book of Jubilees, where this event figures prominently as Abraham's climactic trial, and is depicted in terms which have their obvious affinities with *Midrash Zutta* and other rabbinic sources:

This is the tenth trial wherewith Abraham was tested, and he was found faithful, patient in spirit. And he said not a single word regarding the rumour in the land how that God had said that He would give it to him and to his seed after him and he begged a place there to bury his dead; for he was found faithful and recorded on the heavenly tables as the friend (= אוהב) of God.[137]

The text of *Midrash Zutta* continues with a further exposition of מישרים אהבוך, in the name of R. Joshua b. R. Joḥanan,[138] which presupposes a different exegetical motif:

R. Joshua b. Jonathan used to say concerning those whom the wicked Tineus Rufus slew: 'They loved You more than the first Righteous Ones, [as it is said,] "They have loved You more than the Upright Ones."'[139]

Buber, surprisingly, found this comment unintelligible. Yet it can be readily interpreted in the light of both exegetical traditions, and the historical period to which it clearly refers.

[137] See Jubilees 19:8–9. One further statement which bears a striking resemblance to the passage in Jubilees, is recorded in *BT Bava Batra* 15b. The context itself is interesting and warrants further analysis, as it is a midrashic commentary to the narrative section of Job in chapters 1 and 2. In the exposition of 1:6, Satan is cast in the unusual role of Abraham's advocate. In his efforts to prevent the transfer of God's especial affections from Abraham to Job, Satan declares:

I have wandered throughout the entire world and I have found none as *faithful* as Your servant Abraham, to whom you said, 'Arise, walk through the land in the length of it and the breadth of it, for unto thee will I give it (Genesis 13:17).' Yet, when he sought to bury Sarah, he could find no place to bury her (see MSS cited by Rabbinovicz, *Diqduqei Sopherim* p. 71; also *BT Bava Batra* 16a) but he did not harbour any misgivings regarding your conduct!

See also the comment on *Mishnah Avot* 5:3 by R. Jonah Gerondi, who lists the burial of Sarah as Abraham's tenth trial, as in Jubilees.

[138] Schechter (*Agadath Shir Ha-Shirim*, p. 56, note to lines 351–2) suggests that this may be Joshua Ha-Garsi, the devoted pupil of R. Aqiva, a view accepted by Bacher, *Die Agada der Tannaïten*, vol. 1, p. 265, note 4.

[139] Which is the reading in *Agadath Shir Ha-Shirim*, p. 15, taking מישרים midrashically as *miyy'sharim*.

As is well known, the biblical term יש is taken in rabbinic sources dating back to the period of the Second Temple, as an epithet for the patriarchs, particularly Abraham.[140] In keeping with this exegetical tradition, ספר הישר mentioned in Joshua 10:13 and II Samuel 1:18, was identified as the Book of Genesis, which deals primarily with the lives of the patriarchs.[141] Thus, R. Joshua b. Jonathan interpreted מישרים as an allusion to the patriarchs, who – as is stated in the preceding comment in *Midrash Zutta* – manifested their love for God ביושר לבם, enduring trials without complaint. However, he asserts that the generation which endured the worst excesses of the Hadrianic Persecution, manifested an even greater love in their readiness to surrender their lives rather than their allegiance to the Law of God.[142]

Although the application of the epithet יש to Abraham is found in very early sources, like the term חכם discussed earlier, it is never employed in the Bible itself to describe the patriarch. It is interesting to note, therefore, that Canticles 1:4 was apparently regarded as the *locus classicus* for this tradition, and is cited as the proof-text to substantiate the application of יש or מישרים in other biblical contexts to Abraham. Thus דבר מישרים in Isaiah 33:15 is equated with Abraham on the basis of אהבוך מישרים.[143] Similarly, Abraham is identified with the ישרים mentioned in Proverbs 3:32: This Abraham is an upright man (יש) as [it is said] מישרים אהבוך.[144]

Moreover, in *Midrash Ha-Gadol* to Genesis 12:1 (p. 217) the

[140] See *Genesis Rabbah* 6:9 (p. 49) where ישרים in Numbers 23:10, is taken as an allusion to Abraham, Isaac and Jacob. In connection with Abraham, this exegetical motif can be traced back to the last years of the Second Temple. R. Eliezer b. Hyrkanos expounded psalm 37:14–15 with reference to Abraham and his war with the kings, in the presence of the leaders of that generation, assembled in the school-house of Rabban Johanan b. Zaccai at Jerusalem. See *Genesis Rabbah* 42:1 (*viz. Seder* 11) and the parallels cited by Theodor, pp 397–8. See also the proem to this same *seder*, based on Proverbs 2:7, in *Tanhuma*, ed. Buber, 1, p. 71, also the parallels cited there in note 148, to which we may add Mann, *New Midrash on the Torah, The Bible as Read*, vol. 1 (Hebrew Section), p. 157.
[141] See *Genesis Rabbah* 6:9, (p. 49); *PT Sotah* 1:10, 17c; *BT Avodah Zarah* 25a; Rashi to II Samuel 1:18.
[142] For a fuller evaluation of R. Joshua's exposition of Canticles 1:4 in *Midrash Zutta*, see below Appendix 4, pp. 190ff.
[143] See *Genesis Rabbah* 48:6, p. 481.   [144] *Genesis Rabbah* 49:2, p. 498 for parallels.

opening verse of our original *seder*, Canticles 1:4 is treated as an
allusion by Solomon to Abraham's ready response to God's
charge לֶךְ לְךָ: 'Here I am before You, to the place which You
desire, I will go!' And it was concerning [Abraham] that
Solomon said, 'Draw me, we will run after Thee etc. . . .'[145]
In the light of this evidence, we would suggest that R.
Berechiah's selection of Canticles 1:3 as his proemial verse was
not based on verbal links alone. It also reflects an exegetical
tradition associating the opening verses of Canticles with
Abraham and patriarchs in general. We would suggest,
further, that there may have been another factor which influenced R. Berechiah's choice. The early rabbinic exegetes were
highly sensitive to any anomaly in the biblical text. They
would have noted, therefore, that although the singular שֶׁמֶן
occurs in clause B of Canticles 1:3, clause A contains the plural
שְׁמָנֶיךָ,[146] a form which occurs only in this verse. That this
anomaly did not escape the attention of the early exegetes can
be seen from *Canticles Rabbah* to this verse, where two expla-
nations are recorded. According the anonymous 'rabbis', the
plural form alludes to the two *Torot*, the Written and the Oral
Laws.[147]

R. Tanhum b. Ḥiyya, however, preserved the more literal
implications of שְׁמָנֶיךָ, referring it to Israel's two sacred offices
which require the oil of anointing: [שְׁמָנֶיךָ indicates that] there
are two 'oils', *the oil of priesthood, and the oil of kingship.* It is
unlikely to be mere coincidence, therefore, that R. Berechiah
chose to associate this anomalous phrase with Abraham, the
first priest-king of Israel, and the progenitor of its priestly and
royal lines.

---

[145] As Margulies observes (*Midrash Ha-Gadol*, p. 217), the source for this comment is
not known. Nonetheless, it could be early, as Yannai was evidently familiar with a
midrashic exposition of Canticles 1:4 relating to *Seder Lekh Lekha*, since he includes
it in the initial series of verses of his *Qedushta* for this *seder*, virtually all of which are
expounded with reference to Abraham in extant sources (see Zulay *Piyyutei Yannai*,
p. 17).
[146] *Viz.* the plural noun with the second person masculine singular suffix.
[147] On the imagery of שֶׁמֶן = *Torah*, see *Deuteronomy Rabbah* 7:3 on Canticles 1:3; also
Midrash Zutta to this verse, p. 8 (*Agadath Shir Hashirim* p. 12). See further *BT
Sanhedrin* 24a, where R. Isaac – in connection with *Zechariah* 4:14 – designates the

However, as we indicated earlier, the tradition of Abraham's priesthood and kingship was associated particularly with *Seder* 11 (Genesis 14:1ff) while R. Berechiah's proem relates to *Seder* 10. We may note, therefore, that our sources record the notion that these two offices were actually implied in God's promises to Abraham in the opening verses of Genesis 12. R. Berechiah himself took the phrase **ואגדלה שמך** as an allusion to Abraham's exercising the royal prerogative of minting his own coinage.[148] In a similar vein, an anonymous aggadist interpreted the expression **גדול** in the same verse, as a veiled promise to Abraham of his elevation to the high-priesthood:[149]

[**לך לך**] Another interpretation. To what may it be compared? To a king who entered a province, and saw a comely young man heating the furnace room[150] in the bath-house. The king said to him: Come with me and I will grant you a position in my palace! He went with him and [the king] made him a palace official.[151] The courtiers said: 'Yesterday he was heating a furnace room, now he is a palace official?'[152] Thus God said: 'Come after Me and I will make you a high priest like Adam.' As it is said, 'And I will make of thee a great (**גדול**) nation', and it is written, 'And the priest that is the greatest (**הגדול**) etc. ... (Leviticus 21:10)'. Moreover it is written, 'Thou art a priest forever on account of the words of Malchizedek (Psalm 110:4).'[153]

In conclusion, we may note that Canticles 1:3 is also quoted by Yannai in his *Qedushta* for *Seder Lekh-Lekha*, in conjunction with a further verse containing the expression **שמן**, Ecclesiastes 7:1, **טוב שם משמן טוב**.[154] The coupling of these two verses is

---

scholars of the Holy Land as 'sons of oil', who, like olive oil, 'mollify' each other in their halakhic disputes (see Bacher, *Agada der Palästinischen Amoräer*, p. 223).

[148] See *Genesis Rabbah* 39:11 (p. 374).
[149] *Midrash Abkir* quoted in *Yalqut Lekh Lekha* 63.
[150] **קמון** = Greek *Kaminos*.
[151] *Viz.* **בקסטר**. MS Oxford (Bod. 2637) on which the critical edition of Y. N. Lerrer and Y. Shiloni is based (Jerusalem 1973, p. 246) reads **פוקוסטר**, which the present writer cannot identify. Consequently, the rendering 'palace official' is purely tentative. Buber (see *Liqqutim Midrash Abkir*, Vienna 1883, p. 5) suggests that **בקסטר** is derived from the Latin *castrum*, a camp or fortress, hence 'he had him appointed to a post in a camp (or fortress)'. Alternatively, Buber suggests that we read **קסדור** or **קויסטור**, a quaestor.
[152] This is not found in MS Oxford; however, see Lerrer's observations on the text.
[153] See above, p. 115.   [154] Zulay, *Piyyutei Yannai*, pp. 17–18.

interesting, as the interpretations of Ecclesiastes 7:1 in our
sources are strikingly similar to that cited above for Canticles
1:3. The *Tanna*, R. Shimon b. Yoḥai, initially equates שמן
with the Ark of the Covenant, but adds a further interpretation: 'A good name is better than priesthood and kingship, for
the latter can cease, while the former never ceases.'[155] This
interpretation of שמן as an allusion to priesthood and kingship
may have gained wide currency, as it was incorporated into the
Targum to Ecclesiastes 7:1.[156] It is conceivable, therefore, that
Yannai was familiar with similar interpretations for both these
verses relating to Abraham's role as a priest-king, which are no
longer extant.[157]

[155] See *Ecclesiastes Rabbah* to 7:1. This second interpretation clearly accords with R.
Shimon's maxim in *Avot* 4:12: There are three crowns, the crown of *Torah*, the
crown of priesthood and the crown of kingship; but the crown of a good name
transcends them all! However, in the *Yalqut Ecclesiastes* 973, it is ascribed to R.
Shimon b. Menasia.
[156] In addition, we may note the following interpretation of this verse, which is also
recorded in *Ecclesiastes Rabbah*:
God said: 'The names of the tribes (engraved on the High Priest's breast-plate)
are more precious to Me than the oil with which priests and kings are anointed!'
[157] See *Midrash Zutta*, p. 133 and Rashi to Ecclesiastes 7:1.

CHAPTER 6

Popular legends and traditions III: the regenerating tree

As we have observed above,[1] the remaining proem to be discussed from the series of *petiḥot* in *Genesis Rabbah* 39, appears to lend the strongest support for Heinemann's theory regarding the element of surprise in the selection of proemial verses:

R. Berekhiah opened [with the following proemial text]: '"We have a little sister (Canticles 8:8)" – this alludes to Abraham, who united (lit.: sewed together) the whole world for Us (in an acknowledgement of divine authority). Bar Qappara [observed that Abraham was] like one who sews together a tear (in a garment). [The term] קטנה [indicates] that while he was still young, he was accumulating *mitzvot* and good deeds. "And she hath no breasts (*ibid.*)" – no breasts suckled him[2] either with *mitzvot* or good deeds. "What shall we do for our sister in the day she shall be spoken for?" – on the day when the wicked Nimrod decreed that he should be cast into the fiery furnace. "If she be a wall, we will build upon her...(*ibid.* verse 9)" – if he sets firm his deeds as a wall, We[3] will build thereon. ואם דלת היא נצור נליה לוח ארז (lit. 'And if she be a door, we will enclose her with boards of cedar' *ibid.*) – [which means,] If he be poor[4] in *mitzvot* and good deeds, we shall engrave [him] as an image on a board of cedar! Just as such an image is only temporary, so I will only abide with him temporarily. [Abraham] said to Him: "Lord of all worlds, 'I am a wall (*ibid.* verse 10)' – I make firm my deeds as a wall! 'and my off-spring[5] are like towers (*ibid.*)', [meaning] my descendants,

---

[1] See p. 81.
[2] *Viz.* he had no tutors to instruct him. On the imagery of breast as a teacher, see pp. 190f below.
[3] Reading נבנה for יבנה, as in *Canticles Rabbah* and *Yalqut* to this verse, also *Tanḥuma*, ed. Buber, 1, p. 59.
[4] Reading *deleth* (דלת) as *dallath*, feminine of דל.
[5] Treating שד as a transferred epithet, implying the child that suckles at the breast.

Ḥananiah, Mishael and Azariah."[6] "Then was I in His eyes as one
that is brought forth[7] in peace (*ibid.*)" – [meaning] that he entered in
peace, and came forth in peace...'

Mann, in keeping with his thesis regarding the selection of
proemial verses, endeavoured to link the concluding phrase of
verse 10, כמוצאת שלום, with comparable expressions in the
corresponding *Haphtarah* for *Seder* 10, Joshua 24:3ff, הוצאתי
and ואוציא (verses 5 and 6).[8] However, in the context of
Joshua, these two expressions refer to the Exodus from Egypt
and not to Abraham's departure from Ur of the Chaldees.[9] We
would suggest, therefore, that the application of Canticles
8:8–10 to Abraham should be viewed in a broader context of
aggadic imagery and exegesis.

The midrashic commentary to *Seder* 22 (= Genesis 25:1ff) in
Genesis Rabbah[10] opens with the following three proems, which
highlight the main theme of the lection, Abraham's marrying
Keturah and producing a new family in old age:

'And Abraham took another wife etc. ...' It is written, 'Happy is the
man that hath not walked in the counsel of the wicked ... (Psalm
1:1)'. 'Happy is the *man*' – this alludes to Abraham;[11] 'who hath not
walked in the counsel of the wicked' – this alludes to the Generation
of the Division [of the Tongues];[12] 'nor stood in the way of sinners
(*ibid.*)' – this alludes to the Sodomites, as it is said, 'Now the men of
Sodom were wicked and *sinners* (Genesis 13:13)'; 'nor dwelt in the
abode of the scornful (*ibid.*)' – this alludes to Abimelek, who said to
[Abraham], 'Behold my land is before thee; [dwell where it pleaseth
thee] (*ibid.* 20:15)', but he did not accept it;[13] 'But his delight is in the

[6] Who were prepared to share the same fate as their ancestor.
[7] Taking מוצאת, the feminine singular participle of the *qal* of מצא, as מוצאת, the
feminine singular participle of the *hoph'al* of יצא.
[8] *The Bible as Read*, vol. 1, p. 99.
[9] To which R. Berechiah clearly refers, taking מוצאת as an allusion to Genesis 15:7,
אני יי אשר הוצאתיך מאור הכשדים, which was widely accepted in talmudic times
as a direct reference to Abraham's experiences in the fiery furnace of Nimrod (see all
Targumim to this verse, also *Genesis Rabbah* 44:13, p. 435).
[10] 61:1–2, pp. 657–9.
[11] For the identification of איש with Abraham, see above p. 89, note 29.
[12] In the parallel passage in *Midrash Psalms* 1, p. 12, this is derived by means of climatic
exegesis, from Judges 20:7: Now the expression הבה connotes counsel, as it is said,
'Give here (הבו) your advice and counsel (עצה).'
[13] The precise implications of this phrase are not clear. Luria (*R'dal*) in connection
with its original context, *Genesis Rabbah* 54:2 on Genesis 21:23, observes that

law of the Lord (v. 2)' as it is said [of Abraham], 'For I have known him [to the end that he may command his children etc. . . . that they may keep the way of the Lord to do righteousness and justice]. (Genesis 18:19)'; 'and in His law doth he meditate day and night (*ibid.*)'. R. Shimon b. Yoḥai said: 'His father did not teach him, nor did he have a teacher, [consequently,] whence did he learn? However, God conditioned his two kidneys [to act] like two teachers, and they were flowing forth, teaching him Wisdom (*viz. Torah*) thus it is written, "I will bless the Lord who has counselled me, even by night my kidneys have instructed me (Psalm 16:7)."'[14] 'And he shall be like a tree planted by streams of water (v. 3)' – [this alludes to] God's planting him in the land of Israel;[15] 'that bringeth forth its fruit in its season (*ibid.*)' – this [alludes to] Ishmael; 'and whose leaf doth not wither (*ibid.*)' – this [alludes to] Isaac;[16] 'and in whatsoever he doeth he shall prosper (*ibid.*)' – this [alludes to] the children of Keturah. [Hence it is written,] 'And Abraham took another etc. . . .' 'They shall still bring forth fruit in old age (Psalm 92:15)' – this [alludes to] Abraham; 'they shall be full of sap and richness (*ibid.*)' – [hence it is written] 'And Abraham took another etc. . . .'

'For there is hope of a tree (Job 14:7)' – There was hope for our father Abraham; 'if it be cut down (יכרת) it will sprout again (*ibid.*)' – if [God] will say to him, 'Cut the covenant [of circumcision], and he will do it',[17] then he will produce [additional] *mitzvot* and good deeds; 'and its sucker shall not cease (*ibid.*)' – this [alludes to] his sap.[18] 'Though the root thereof wax old in the earth, (v. 8)' – [which alludes to] 'And Abraham was old (Genesis 24:1)'; 'and the stock thereof dieth in the ground (Job *ibid.*)' – [this alludes to] 'And Sarah died etc.

Abraham continued to reside in Beer Sheba rather than in the royal city of Gerar, thus rejecting Abimelek's invitation to live in the best location. However, see also the comments of S. Jaffe (*Ypheh To'ar*) and Theodor (p. 578).

[14] See above, p. 84f.

[15] Luria suggests that the reference to the land of Israel is contained in the phrase פלגי מים, which echoes the description of the Holy Land in Deuteronomy 8:7, ארץ נחלי מים.

[16] The order here, which gives Ishmael, as the first-born, precedence over Isaac, is supported by all the MSS and the majority of the parallels cited by Theodor. However, the *Yalqut* (*Hayyei Sarah* 109) reverses the order, giving precedence to Isaac.

[17] Reading אם יאמר עליו כרות ברית והוא כורת, so MS London (margin); MSS Oxford 1 and 2; MS Commentary to *Genesis Rabbah* (cited by Theodor, p. 658) and *Yalqut*.

[18] *Viz.* seminal fluid, which the preacher compares to the moisture absorbed by a plant through its suckers.

(Genesis 23:2)';[19] 'Yet through the scent of water it will bud, (Job 14:9)' – through the scent of *mitzvot* and good deeds[20] he will bud; 'and put forth boughs like a plant (*ibid.*)' – it is not written 'like a נוטע', but נטע, the addition exceeded the original.[21] [Hence it is written,] 'And Abraham took another etc. ....'

The significant feature of these three proems is their common imagery. In each case, the preacher has applied to Abraham – and to Sarah – a proemial text containing the imagery of a tree. This may not be immediately apparent in the second proem, as it appears in *Genesis Rabbah* in a defective form, expounding only one of the series of verses in Psalm 92 which depicts the righteous in terms of a palm and a cedar. A fuller version has been preserved in the *Yalqut* to this psalm,[22] containing an exposition of verse 14, which clearly echoes the theme developed in the first proem in *Genesis Rabbah*:

'Planted in the house of the Lord' – this [alludes to] Abraham, whom God planted in the Land of Israel; 'They shall flourish in the courts of our God' – this [alludes to] Ishmael; 'They shall still bring forth fruit in old age' – this [alludes to] Isaac; 'They shall be full of sap and richness' – this [alludes to] the children of Keturah. [Thus it is written,] 'And Abraham took another etc. ....'

In the material to be cited subsequently, we shall see that the key verse 13, צדיק כתמר יפרח כארז בלבנון ישגה, was also associated with Abraham in aggadic exegesis, as were other verses in Psalm 92, suggesting that it was, at least in part,

---

[19] S. Jaffe suggests that imagery of the wife as the stem which grows from the trunk of the tree is based upon the creation of the first woman from Adam's rib.

[20] This reflects the well-known and widely recurring exegetical tradition that the biblical expression מים is an allusion to *Torah* (אין מים אלא תורה).

[21] As Theodor notes, whatever reading we adopt here the text remains obscure and it is difficult to determine how the preacher interpreted the phrase. Consequently, we would offer the following conjectural reading, which appears to yield some sense: אין כתיב כאן אלא 'כמו נטע' התוספת מרובה על העיקר – ; 'It is written here כמו נטע, (implying that each of its branches functions like an independent plant, yielding its own branches, with the result that) the subsidiary [branches] outnumber those of the original stock.' See the MS Commentary cited by Theodor, also *Etz Yoseph* on the text.

[22] This fuller version is also partially preserved in MSS Paris and Munich and is presupposed by the commentary of Pseudo-Rashi to *Genesis Rabbah*.

regarded as an Abrahamic psalm.[23] We may note initially, however, that the application of the tree imagery to Abraham and Sarah is not limited only to the context of *Seder* 22. It occurs again in three of the series of proems which introduce the midrashic commentary to Genesis 21:1ff (= *Seder* 18) in *Genesis Rabbah* 53,[24] relating to the parallel event of the birth of Isaac. The opening proem is based on Ezekiel 17:24, the context of which is significant. It is part of the prophet's parable of the cedar, in which he employs imagery and terminology which closely resemble those found in the verses applied to Abraham from Psalms 1 and 92.[25] In the third proem of the series, the fig tree and the vine of the proemial verse (Habakuk 3:17) are identified with Abraham and Sarah respectively. This midrashic device occurs again in the sixth proem, where the vine in Psalm 80:15, is equated once more with Sarah:[26]

'And the Lord visited Sarah etc.': Thus Scripture states, 'And all the trees of the field shall know that I the Lord have brought down the high tree, have exalted the low tree and have made the dry tree to flourish; I the Lord have spoken and have done it.' (Ezekiel 17:24): R. Yudan said: [God is] not like those who say, but do not do! R. Berechiah said: [The verse states,] 'I the Lord have spoken and have done it.' Where [are we informed that] He spoke? [In the verse,] 'At the set time I will return unto thee... [and Sarah shall have a son.] (Genesis 18:14)'; 'and have done it', [hence,] 'and the Lord did unto Sarah as He had spoken'; 'And all the trees of the field shall know' – this [alludes to] mankind, just as you say, 'for the tree of the field is man (Deuteronomy 20:19)'; 'that I the Lord have brought down the high tree' – this [alludes to] Abimelech; 'have exalted the low tree' –

---

[23] This is supported further by the writings of Yannai, who was evidently familiar with an exposition of verses 8–10 with reference to Abraham's battle with the kings in Genesis 14 (*Seder* 8 in his lectionary cycle; see Zulay, *Piyyutei Yannai*, p. 22).

[24] See Theodor, pp. 554ff for parallels.

[25] Notably verse 23, 'in the mountain of the height of Israel will I plant it (אשתלנו) and it shall bring forth boughs, and bear fruit (פרי) and be a stately cedar (ארז); and under it shall dwell all fowl of every wing, in the shadow of the branches thereof shall they dwell'. It also possible that the early exegetes saw an allusion to Abraham in the expression רמה in verse 22, מצמרת הארז הרמה, which may have been equated midrashically with Abraham, like the expression רם in Job 32:2 (*PT Sotah* 5:8, 20d): 'ממשפחת רם', בן אברם – 'of the family of Ram', [which means] the son of Abram.

[26] On the imagery of גפן as a woman, see also *Mishnah Niddah* 9:11, 'Women, with regard to [the blood of] their virginity, are like *vines* ...'

this [alludes to] Abraham; 'have dried up the green tree' – this [alludes to] Abimelech's womenfolk, as it is said, 'For the Lord had fast closed up [all the wombs of the house of Abimelech] (Genesis 20:18)'; 'I have made the dry tree to flourish;' – this [alludes to] Sarah;[27] 'I the Lord have spoken and have done it.' etc. . . .
'For though the fig-tree shall not blossom' – this [alludes to] Abraham, just as you say, 'I saw your fathers as the first ripe in the fig tree in her first season; (Hosea 9:10)'; 'neither shall fruit be in the vines' – this [alludes to] Sarah, just as you say, 'Thy wife shall be as a fruitful vine, in the innermost parts of thy house; (Psalm 128:3)' etc. . . .
R. Menahamah and R. Naḥman of Yafo, in the name of R. Jacob of Caesarea opened [with the following proemial verse]: ' "O God of hosts, return, we beseech Thee (Psalm 80:15)", [which means,] return and do that which you said to Abraham. "Look (הבט) from heaven and behold (*ibid.*)" – [which refers to,] "Look now (הבט נא) toward heaven and count the stars etc. (Genesis 15:5)". "And visit this *vine*" – [hence it is written,] "And the Lord visited Sarah as He had promised . . ." '

This by no means exhausts the examples in talmudic-midrashic sources for the application of the tree imagery to Abraham and Sarah. In a homily based on Psalm 1:3, recorded in the name of the *Tanna*, R. Jose, in a late midrashic source,[28] Abraham is compared to a shady, fruitful tree situated by a stream in arid country, upon whom the grateful traveller invokes the blessing that all its saplings should be like the parent-tree. Similarly, the Yemenite *Midrash Ha-Gadol* to Genesis 18:11, records an exposition of Psalm 92:15, taken from an unknown source, associating this verse with Abraham and Sarah's rejuvenation, and the currency they issued to commemorate this miracle.[29]

There is, therefore, substantial evidence in our sources for this exegetical motif. However, there is no clear indication for

---

[27] The imagery of the 'high tree' as the king is self-explanatory. As to the equation of עץ יבש with the childless Sarah – and conversely עץ לח with Abimelech's women-folk who were originally fertile – this is based presumably on Isaiah 56:3, 'Neither let the eunuch say: "Behold I am a *dry tree.*" '

[28] See *Pirqei d'Rabbi Eliezer* 7, also *Seder Eliahu Zutta*, ed. Friedmann, p. 46 and *Midrash Ha-Gadol* to Genesis 15:1, p 243f, on Psalm 1:3.

[29] See *Midrash Ha-Gadol* to Genesis 18:11 and Margulies' comments, p. 300.

its basis. Although trees figure in the pentateuchal narrative of the patriarch,[30] the term is never used as an epithet for Abraham. The simple explanation may be that the tree imagery was regarded as appropriate to the theme of Abraham producing off-spring, particularly in an agricultural society, which made extensive use of horticultural imagery in describing sexual relationships.[31]

None the less, we cannot discount the phenomenon of popular tradition, particularly in the light of a recently discovered, early source, the Genesis Apocryphon,[32] which may be representative of the popular amplifications of biblical narratives even before the beginning of the current era. As in rabbinic *Midrash*, the author provides the necessary background information which highlights and resolves a problem in the biblical narrative.[33] The issue in question relates to Abraham's sojourn in the land of Egypt, recounted in Genesis 12:10ff. As he is about to enter Egypt, Abraham has a 'premonition' that his life will be in danger, when the Egyptians will observe the beauty of his wife Sarah. Therefore, he asks her to affirm that she is his sister, in order to save him. It is strange, however, that Abraham seemed oblivious of this potential danger at the outset of his journey. Moreover, the biblical account does not indicate how he became aware of it, when it was imminent. Consequently, the author of the Apocryphon provides the following explanation in form of a declaration by Abraham:[34]

13. ...now we passed through our land and entered the land of the sons of Ham, the land of Egypt.

14. And I, Abram, dreamed a dream on the night of our entering the land of Egypt, and lo! I saw in my dream one cedar and one palm

---

[30] See, for example, Genesis 13:18 and 21:33.
[31] See above p. 33, note 33. and see the parable employed by R. Isaac in blessing R. Naḥman (*BT Ta'anit* 5b–6a): 'May it be [God's] will that all the saplings which are planted from you, should be like you!' See also the description of R. Jose b. Ḥalaphta's relations with his late brother's wife in *PT Yevamot* 1:1, 2b, 'He ploughed five furrows and planted five saplings.'
[32] Published with facsimiles, transcription and translation, by Naḥman Avigad and Yigael Yadin, Jerusalem 1956.
[33] Compare, for example, the midrashic treatment of Exodus 2:16ff cited above, p. o.
[34] Column 19, English translation, p. 41.

15. ... And men came and sought to cut down and uproot the cedar and to leave the palm by itself.
16. And the palm cried out and said, 'Cut not down the cedar, for cursed is he who will fell ...' And for the sake of the palm the cedar was saved.
17. And no ... And I woke from my slumber that night and I said to Sarai, my wife, 'A dream
18. Have I dreamt ... and I am frightened by this dream.' And she said to me, 'Tell me thy dream that I may know.' And I began to tell her that dream.
19. '... the dream ... that they will seek to slay me and to save thee alive. This day all the good ...
20. ... that he is my brother and I shall live because of thee and my soul shall be saved for thy sake'

Although this legend may indicate the antiquity of the tree motif in the midrashic development of the Abraham narrative, it is not to be found in any extant rabbinic source. This, however, does not preclude the possibility that the story of the palm and the cedar was part of that corpus of popular traditions current in talmudic times, to which, as we suggested earlier, preachers might allude in the course of their homilies and expositions. Chapter 41 of *Genesis Rabbah*,[35] which forms part of the midrashic commentary to the account of Abraham's sojourn in Egypt in Genesis 12, opens with the following proem:

'And the Lord plagued Pharaoh and his house with great plagues Genesis 12:17)': 'The righteous shall flourish like a palm tree; he shall grow like a cedar in Lebanon (Psalm 92:13).' – Just as the palm and the cedar do not have curves[36] or excrescences,[37] nor do the righteous. Just as the palm and the cedar cast their shade afar, so the reward of the righteous is far off. Just as the 'heart' of the palm and the cedar is directed upwards, so the heart of the righteous is directed towards God, thus it is written, 'Mine eyes are ever toward the Lord; for He will bring forth my feet out of the net (Psalm 25:15).' Just as the palm and the cedar experience desire, so the righteous experience desire, and what is the object of their desire? God! R. Tanḥuma said: 'It once

[35] See Theodor, pp. 386ff for parallels.
[36] עוקמי. MS Stuttgart, *Yalqut* and *Arukh* read עומקי, 'depths', or possibly 'hollows'.
[37] סיקוסים = Greek *sykosis*. Some MSS and parallels read פיקוסים, 'coils', hence knots in the wood (see Pseudo-Rashi and *Matnot Kehunah* on the text).

happened with a palm that was standing in Ametho,[38] and was not producing fruit. A palm-gardener passed by and saw it. "This one – he said – is without grafting, it looks [to one] from Jericho."[39] Once they had grafted it, it produced fruit.' However, just as they do not make utensils from the palm, [are we to infer from the simile in the palm,] that the righteous [suffer from a similar deficiency]?! Therefore, the verse states [that the righteous] are like a cedar [from which, utensils are made]. Similarly, just as the cedar does not produce fruit, so it is with the righteous?! Therefore, the verse states, 'The righteous shall flourish like a palm-tree.' Just as the palm contains nothing which is useless, the dates are for eating, the branches [may be used] for *Hallel*, the twigs for hedging, the bast for ropes, the ribbed leaves for sieves, the large beams for the construction of houses, so Israel contains no individual who is useless! There are among them, masters of Scripture, masters of *Mishnah*, masters of *Talmud*, and masters of *Aggadah*. Moreover, just as when one climbs to the top of the palm or the cedar and does not take due care, he can fall and die, so any one who comes to attack Israel, he will receive from them his just desserts. You may know that this is so, because Pharaoh, having seized Sarah for only one night, was smitten together with his household with diseases. Hence it is written, 'And the Lord plagued Pharaoh etc. . . .'

This homily is unusual in its structural development. The preacher has not only presented his proemial verse without a word of explanation to justify its selection – as is the case with virtually every *petiḥah* we have quoted thus far – he does not even attempt to relate the imagery of his text to the main characters of the *seder*. He simply proceeds to explore in minute detail the significance of the biblical simile for the qualities of the righteous. Clearly, he expected his audience to recognise the appropriateness of his text, and the relevance of its imagery for the hero and heroine of the morning's lection. It is highly probable, therefore, that both he and his audience were familiar with the legend of the palm and the cedar, which was lost for centuries, until its rediscovery in the Genesis Apocryphon.

The rabbinic homily and the apocryphal passage pose a further question. Was the legend of the palm and the cedar inspired by the imagery of Psalm 92, which may, therefore,

---

[38] Situated in Trans-Jordan, see Theodor's comments, p. 387.
[39] Reading מיריחו צופה זו ארככבה אי; ארכבה being a noun like אגדה, or אזהרה.

have been regarded – at least in part – as an Abrahamic psalm
at a very early period? Or was the association of this psalm with
the patriarch in rabbinic sources influenced by the older
legend? While it not possible to resolve this question, we may
be able to account for the identification of **ארז** with Abraham,
in the light of the symbolism of the cedar in talmudic-
midrashic sources. 'Cedar' occurs in rabbinic sources as an
epithet for three distinctive types, **מלך**, **חכם**, and **צדיק**.

מלך = ארז

This device is biblical in origin as can be seen from King
Joash's parable of the trees,[40] in which he is represented by the
cedar of Lebanon. Similarly, in Ezekiel's parable (17:1ff) 'the
top of the cedar' (**צמרת הארז**) represents the king of Jerusalem.[41] In talmudic times, the symbolism of the cedar for
kingship was widely popularised through the medium of the
Targum, as can be seen from the following:

a) *Jeremiah 22:23*	*Targum*
'O inhabitant of Lebanon,	'You who dwelt in the
that art nestled in the	Temple,[42] among the
cedars',	*kings* ...'
b) *Ezekiel 17:22*	*Targum*
'I will take, even I, of	'And I will bring near,
the lofty top of the	even I, [a scion] of the
cedar',	kingship of David, who
	is likened to a lofty
	cedar',[43]
c) *Zechariah 11:2*	*Targum*
'... for the *cedar* is	'behold, the *rulers* are
fallen',	broken',[44]

---

[40] See 2 Kings 14:9ff (= 2 Chronicles 18:25ff).   [41] See verse 12.

[42] This identification of **לבנון** with the temple reflects an exegetical motif which
occurs widely in talmudic-midrashic – particularly tannaitic – sources. See particularly *Sifrei Deuteronomy* to 1:6 and 3:25 (*pisqa'ot* 6 and 28) and the sources cited by
Finkelstein, pp. 15 and 45. See also the extensive material cited by Vermes, *Scripture
and Tradition*, pp. 28ff.

[43] Compare also *Targum* to 1 Kings 5:13.

[44] See also *Avot d'Rabbi Natan* Version B, 4 p. 21, where **ארז** in this verse is taken as an
allusion to King Zedekiah.

חכם = ארז

a) The *Tanna*, R. Jose, described his singular achievement of producing five scholarly sons in the following terms:[45] 'Five times did I engage in the sexual act, and I planted five *cedars*.'
b) On the death of Ravina, Bar Kippuk proclaimed:[46] 'If fire has fallen among the *cedars*, then what shall the hyssop on the wall do?'
c) R. Judah b. Pazzi saw in Canticles 5:15, an allusion to the fate of those who are ardently devoted to the study of the Torah in this world:[47] 'Anyone who blackens his face for the study of the Torah in this world, God will cause his radiance to shine forth in the world to come, as it is said, "His aspect is like Lebanon, excellent as the cedars."'[48]

צדיק = ארז

The primary example for this motif is the lengthy homily based on Psalm 92:13, which we have quoted in full above. To this we may add the following, significant comment, recorded in the name of R. Levi in *Genesis Rabbah* 68:11 (p. 783): '"The beams of our houses are cedars (Canticles 1:17)" – this alludes to the righteous men and women, prophets and prophetesses.'

We see, therefore, that the cedar in rabbinic thought symbolised specific qualities, for which Abraham is portrayed in our sources as the archetype, kingship, *Torah*-scholarship and righteousness. We have already analysed fully the material relating Abraham's kingship and scholarship. As to his role as a צדיק, we may note that this once again, is rooted in biblical tradition, Genesis 15:6, 'And he believed in the Lord and it was accounted to him for righteousness (צדקה).' In talmudic times, Abraham, the embodiment of so many of the ideals of rabbinic Judaism, was also regarded as the supreme example of

---

[45] See *BT Shabbat* 118b.   [46] See *BT Moed Qatan* 25b, 47.
[47] *BT Sanhedrin* 100a, also *Leviticus Rabbah* 19:3, p. 423.
[48] The allusion to *Torah* is contained in the expression פו in clause B and particularly in the imagery of verse 14; see *Canticles Rabbah* to this verse, also *Leviticus Rabbah* 25:8, p. 583.

the צדיק, as is suggested by the following anonymous exposition of Canticles 4:6:[49]

'I will get me to the mountain of myrrh' – this alludes to Abraham,[50]
who is the head of all the righteous ones!

Abraham, therefore, is the Cedar, the majestic tree which casts
its giant shadow over all subsequent generations of his
descendants, symbolising his role as the source of kingship in
Israel, its archetypal sage and צדיק. This image of the patriarch, we would suggest, loomed large in popular tradition,
even before the beginning of the current era. Thus the early
preachers might select proemial and proof-texts containing the
cedar, or tree imagery in general, and rely upon their audiences' ability to recognise the relevance of their quotations for
the patriarch and his family. This was also the case, we would
suggest, with R. Berechiah's selection of Canticles 8:8–10 as the
basis for his *petiḥah* in *Genesis Rabbah* 39. Although the curiosity
of his audience may have been aroused, and they waited to
hear with interest the precise interpretation he would place on
his proemial text, the key term ארז was sufficient to indicate its
relevance for the patriarch.

---

[49] See *Canticles Rabbah* to 4:6 end.
[50] On this identification of מור with Abraham, see *Canticles Rabbah* to 1:13:
　　'My beloved is unto me as a bag of myrrh' ... R. Azariah in the name of R. Judah
　　expounded the verse with reference to our father, Abraham. Just as myrrh is
　　preeminent among all the various types of incense, so Abraham is preeminent
　　among all the righteous ones. Just as myrrh does not exude its aroma save in the
　　open air, so Abraham's deeds were unknown until he was cast into the fiery
　　furnace!
　　In all probability, this is based on the identification of הר המור as הר המוריה, the
　　scene of Abraham's greatest trial; see *Genesis Rabbah* 55:7 (p. 592) on Genesis 22:2:
　　'To the land of Moriah (מוריה)' ... The Rabbis said: 'To the place where the
　　incense is offered, as it is said, "I will get me to the Mountain of Myrrh (הר המור
　　– Canticles 4:6).'"

CHAPTER 7

The midrashic background for James 2:21–23

In his article 'Midrashim in the New Testament',[1] Dr M. Gertner has endeavoured to prove that the Epistle of James is essentially midrashic in origin and character. In support of this thesis, it is possible to show that certain difficulties arising from the comments on Abraham in 2:21–23 can be resolved in the light of early Jewish exegesis.

Abraham is cited in these verses as a biblical prototype for the ideal of the justification of faith by works: 'Was not Abraham our father justified by works, in that he offered up Isaac his son upon the altar? Thou seest that faith wrought with his works, and by works was faith made perfect: And the scripture was fulfilled which saith, "And Abraham believed God, and it was reckoned unto him for righteousness"; and he was called the friend of God (= אוהב א־להים).'[2]

The theme reflected here is well known. The association of Abraham's love for God with his faith in trial – the *Aqedah* in particular – and its significance for the development of Jewish thought in general, has been subjected to detailed study and analysis.[3] However, the exegetical processes presupposed by

---

[1] *JJS*, vol. 7 (1962), pp. 267–92; see particularly pp. 285f.

[2] For the references to Abraham as an אוהב in early sources, see Strack-Billerbeck, *Kommentar zum neuen Testament aus Talmud und Midrasch*, vol. 3, p. 755; see further Ginzberg, *Legends*, vol. 5, pp. 207–8, note 4.

[3] See G. Vajda, *L'amour de Dieu dans la theologie juive du Moyen Age*, Paris 1957. The Book of Jubilees, where the theme of Abraham as the friend or lover of God, faithful and long-suffering in trial, occurs in a highly developed form (see 17:15–19:9), is frequently cited as an early parallel for James. It is to be noted, however, that there is no reference in Jubilees to the notion that Abraham was designated a friend of God specifically on account of the *Aqedah*. Even before this event Abraham was regarded as a faithful lover of God in heavenly circles, according to the author of Jubilees

145

this passage have received little attention. The author of the Epistle has apparently disregarded the literal meaning of Genesis 15:6, and its original context, treating this verse as a prognostication of Abraham's faith in trial, referring specifically to the sacrifice of Isaac in chapter 22. Secondly, in disagreement with the biblical account of the *Aqedah*, where Abraham is expressly designated as a ירא א־להים (22:12), the author of the Epistle asserts that for this act of faith, Abraham was called an אוהב א־להים! Both these peculiarities of the text presumably reflect some early traditions of interpretation as New Testament commentators suspected.[4] Moreover, the absence of any explanatory comment in the text suggests that the author expected his readers to be fully conversant with his background material. It is necessary, therefore, to examine our extant sources for some trace of these early traditions.

A significant comment on the epithet ירא א־להים in Genesis 22:12 was noted by Billerbeck.[5] According to R. Meir, this epithet, as applied to both Abraham and Job, is not to be taken in its restricted meaning of 'God-fearing'. Since Abraham is characterised as an אוהב, a lover of God, the epithet ירא א־להים must similarly be construed as an expression of his love for God: 'It is said of Job that he was God-fearing, and it is said of Abraham that he was God-fearing. Just as "God-fearing", when predicated of Abraham [connotes a

---

(17:15), who stresses that God already acknowledged Abraham to be 'faithful and a lover of the Lord' on account of his preceding trials (17:17–18), the purpose of the *Aqedah* being primarily to refute the allegations of Mastema (see *BT Sanhedrin* 89b, cited by Rashi on Genesis 22:1). In the Book of Jubilees, it is the burial of Sarah, not the *Aqedah*, which constitutes Abraham's tenth trial for which he was formally acknowledged (*viz.* 'recorded on the heavenly tables') as the friend of God (19:3–9). Consequently the relationship between Jubilees and James on this subject requires closer examination to determine, if possible, whether the author of James has employed a modified version of an earlier theme, or whether he has preserved in its more original form an ancient tradition which the author has developed in his more elaborate treatment of the subject. In either case, the Epistle of James remains our earliest extant source for the notion that Abraham was called the friend of God as a direct result of the *Aqedah*.

4 See B. S. Easton, *The Epistle of St. James*, in *The Interpreter's Bible*, New York 1957, vol. 12, p. 44; E. M. Sidebottom, *The Century Bible* (New Edition): *The Epistle of James*, London 1967, p. 45.

5 *Kommentar zum neuen Testament*, vol. 3, p. 755.

virtue born] of love for God, so "God-fearing" when predicated of Job [connotes a virtue born] of love for God.'[6]
Although in its original context R. Meir's comment refers
initially to Job,[7] through his interpretation of ירא א-להים, he
has introduced the notion of Abraham's love into the context of
God's own words of acknowledgement following the *Aqedah*.
This is formulated in more explicit terms by an unknown
aggadist, who actually renders כי עתה ידעתי כי ירא
א-להים אתה, as 'Now I have made known to all that you love
me.'[8]

It is possible that this interpretation of ירא א-להים is
already presupposed in the writings of Philo. In his treatment
of the *Aqedah*, Philo elaborates upon Abraham's emotional
reactions to the command to sacrifice Isaac in the following
terms: 'He, though devoted to his son with a fondness which no
words can express, showed no change of colour, nor weakening
of the soul, but remained steadfast as ever with a judgement
that never bent nor wavered. *Mastered by his love for God, he
mightily overcame all fascination expressed in the fond terms of family
affections.*'[9]

6　*BT Sotah* 31a, where the *Gemara* adds the following: 'Whence do we know that
Abraham himself [loved God]? From that which is written, "... the offspring of
Abraham my friend (= אוהבי, *viz.* 'who loved me' – Isaiah 41:8)".' See further
Büchler's observations on the above *baraita*, *Studies in Sin and Atonement*, Oxford 1928,
p. 126; and more recently, E. E. Urbach, *The Sages – Their Concepts and Beliefs*
(Hebrew), Jerusalem 1969, p. 354.
7　R. Meir's statement indicates that he subscribed to the view formulated by R.
Joshua b. Hyrkanos in *Mishnah Sotah* 5:5, that Job served God out of love. By means
of his definition of ירא as a more comprehensive epithet, he sought to eliminate the
difficulty posed by the scriptural testimony to Job's character as a 'blameless and
upright man, *who fears God* and turns away from evil (Job 1:8)', upon which Rabban
Johanan b. Zaccai based his view that Job served God only from fear (*Mishnah Sotah*
5:5).
8　See *Genesis Rabbah* 56:7, and the variant readings cited by Theodor, p. 603. Although
the date of this passage cannot be determined, it may be very early, as it clearly
echoes Jubilees 18:16, 'And I have shown to all that thou art faithful unto Me ...'
On the rendering of ידעתי with a causative meaning, as is presupposed already
by Jubilees (see also 18:11), see further *Peshitta* on Genesis 22:12; also Pseudo-Philo's
paraphrase of this verse (*Liber Antiquitatum Biblicarum*, ed. G. Kisch, Indiana 1949,
p. 204): 'Non interficias filium tuum, neque disperdas fructum ventris tuum. *Nunc
enim manifestavi* ut appareres ignorantibus te ...', which is comparable with the Latin
version of Jubilees (see H. Rönsch, *Das Buch der Jubiläen*, Leipzig 1874, p. 20): 'quod
quo *nunc manifestavi* quia times Deum tuum'.
9　See *De Abrahamo* xxxii, 170 (trans. F. H. Colson, The Loeb Classical Library, vol. 6,
pp. 85–6).

As in James and in rabbinic *Midrash*, Philo has introduced the notion of Abraham's love for God into the context of the *Aqedah* story. However, may we assume that he was familiar with the exegetical basis for this motif preserved in rabbinic sources? This possibility cannot be entirely discounted in view of certain notions expressed by Philo on the subject of love and fear of God in connection with Abraham. In a lengthy homily which, significantly, forms part of his deliberations on the opening verses of Genesis 15, Philo implies that Abraham's attitude in the service of God was, like that of Moses, a synthesis of both love and fear,[10] a notion which is echoed in R. Meir's statement cited earlier. It is conceivable, therefore, that Philo, like R. Meir a century later, regarded the epithet ירא א־להים in Genesis 22:12 as a more comprehensive term connoting also the notion of Abraham's love for God.

This would be in keeping with other parallels between Philo and rabbinic sources relating to this subject. In the passage cited above, Philo portrays Abraham as having mastered his natural affections through his love for God. He develops this imagery further in connection with all three patriarchs, whom he compares to athletes, 'fostering the robustness of their soul' in order to achieve victory over their passions and who are, therefore, designated lovers of God, and God-beloved.[11] This imagery clearly corresponds with that employed in the early *baraita* enumerating the seven types of Pharisee. Abraham is cited in this source as the biblical prototype for the פרוש אהבה, the Pharisee motivated by love for God, as he was able

---

[10] See *Quis Haeres Sit*, vi, 19ff. For a full evaluation of this homily and its possible links with Palestinian *Aggadah*, see J. Amir, 'Philo's Homilies on Love and Fear, and their Relationship to Palestinian Midrashim', *Zion*, vol. 30 (1965), pp. 47–60.

[11] See *De Abrahamo* x, 48; see further 4 Maccabees 14:20. The tradition that all three patriarchs were designated lovers of God occurs also in the Zadokite Fragments (p. 3, lines 2 and 3–4, ed. Ch. Rabin, Oxford 1954, p.11), and is presupposed by R. Meir in *Sifrei Deuteronomy* 32 (pp. 58–9), where he presents each of the three patriarchs as an example for one of the three aspects of love for God suggested by Deuteronomy 6:5, 'with all your heart, and with all your soul, and with all your might'. See further Vajda, *L'amour de Dieu*, p. 44, note 1.

to suppress his evil nature, so that his heart was found faithful by God:[12]

Of all of them none is beloved save the Pharisee from love [of God] like Abraham! Abraham made the evil inclination good. What is the scriptural basis for this? 'And you found his heart faithful before you (Nehemiah 9:8)'.[13]

This statement forms a significant link in the chain of ideas connecting Philo and James. Like Philo, the anonymous author of the *baraita* emphasises Abraham's ability as a lover of

---

[12] See *PT Berakhot* 9, 14b; *PT Sotah* 5, 20c. Although the *Aqedah* is not explicitly mentioned in this source, it may be presupposed, as the terminology employed in the *baraita* is found in both midrashic and liturgical sources in connection with the sacrificing of Isaac. See *Pesiqta de Rav Kahana*, ed. Mandelbaum, vol. 2, p. 342:

Abraham our father said before God: 'Lord of [both] worlds, it was revealed and known before You that when You said to me, "Take your son, your only son, etc ... (Genesis 22:2)", I had in my heart the appropriate answer to give to You! I had it in my heart to say to You, "Yesterday You said to me, 'For through Isaac shall your descendants be named (Genesis 22:12)', and now You say to me, 'Take your son'!" But, just as I had in my heart the appropriate answer to give to you, yet *I suppressed my inclination* (כבשתי את יצרי) and I did not answer you, so when the descendants of Isaac etc. ....'

See further the parallels cited by Mandelbaum; see also the Fragmentary *Targum* to Genesis 22:14, and particularly the concluding doxology of the *Zikhronot* (i.e. the second of the three special benedictions introduced into the additional *Amidah* for the New Year; *Authorised Daily Prayer Book* (new edn, London 1962), p.342): 'And may the binding with which Abraham our father bound his son Isaac on the altar, appear before You, *how he suppressed his compassion in order to perform your will with a perfect heart* (וכבש רחמיו לעשות רצונך בלבב שלם).'

[13] For the interpretation of לבב – as opposed to the contracted form לב – as an allusion to the two natures or inclinations in man, see *Sifrei Deuteronomy* 32, p.55, on Deuteronomy 6:5: '"with all your heart (לבבך)" – [this implies] with your two inclinations, with the good inclination, and with the evil inclination'. See further R. Meir's statement in this same source (p. 58) that Abraham is the biblical prototype for the whole-hearted love for God as enjoined in this verse: 'And you shall love the Lord your God with all your heart – Love him with all your heart like Abraham your father!' In conjunction with these sources, see Jubilees 21:2–3, where Abraham declares to Isaac, 'throughout all the days of my life I have remembered the Lord, and sought *with all my heart to do His will* ... and I have given *my heart and my spirit* that I might observe to do the will of Him who created me'. The phrase 'my heart and my spirit' which is preserved in the Latin version of Jubilees (See Charles, *The Apocrypha and Pseudepigrapha of the Old Testament*, vol. 2, p. 43, note 3), may be purely stylistic. However, in the light of the material, rabbinic, liturgical and sectarian, cited in this chapter, as well as the significant terminology לב and רוח = יצר, some serious consideration should be given to the possibility that the Book of Jubilees is the earliest source for the motif reflected in all the passages cited above, portraying Abraham as the faithful lover of the Lord, subjecting both his evil and his good inclinations to the whole-hearted service of God.

God to control his passions. However, by means of his proof-text, Nehemiah 9:8, he also introduces the element of Abraham's faith which forms the core of James's argument in the Epistle. In this same context we may note a further passage from a sectarian source, the Zadokite Fragments. Although it is couched in the peculiar terminology of the Judaean Scrolls, the passage's affinities with the sources cited earlier are quite clear. Abraham was designated a friend of God because of his obedience to Divine commands, rather than to the dictates of his own 'spirit', *viz.* רוח, a term comparable with the rabbinic יצר.[14] 'Abraham did not walk in it, *and he was recorded as a friend* (= אוהב) through keeping the commandments of God and not choosing the desire of his own spirit.'[15]

We see, therefore, that the reference to Abraham in the Epistle reflects a complex of ideas widely current in early times, relating to Abraham's love for God as characterised by his faith-obedience, his total submission to the Divine will. Moreover, the author's use of the epithet 'friend of God' in connection with the sacrificing of Isaac, presupposes an early exegetical device, investing the biblical phrase ירא א־להים, used in the context of the *Aqedah*, with the broader connotations of love as well as fear.

As to the meaning of Genesis 15:6 presupposed in the Epistle, Abraham's faith in trial, modern scholars have noted the parallels for this notion in early sources,[16] which indicate that this interpretation of the verse had been established centuries before the author of James, and was, in all probability, widely accepted in his day.[17] Thus the author of 1 Maccabees, writing

[14] See Driver, *The Judaean Scrolls*, Oxford 1965, p. 551.
[15] P. 3, lines 2–3, ed. Rabin, pp. 10–11.
[16] See A. Meyer, *Das Ratsel des Jacobusbriefes*, Giessen 1930, pp. 135ff; see also Urbach, *The Sages*, p. 353. The biblical source for this interpretation of Genesis 15:6, as Meyer notes, is Nehemiah 9:8, cited above in the *baraita* of the seven types of Pharisee. In view of the possible common authorship of Ezra-Nehemiah and Chronicles, it is interesting to note that the Chronicler had already summarised the life and character of Abraham as related in Genesis, in the two terms נאמן and אוהב (2 Chronicles 20:7), neither of which occurs in the pentateuchal narrative, indicating that this motif, which is already found in a highly developed form in Jubilees, has its origins early in the period of the Second Temple.
[17] See *Targum Pseudo-Jonathan* to Genesis 15:6: 'And he had faith in the Word of the Lord, and it was accounted unto him for merit, because he did not reproach Him

a century before the current era, paraphrased Genesis 15:6, 'Was not Abraham found faithful in trial, and it was accounted unto him for righteousness?' (2:52). Virtually the same phrase, 'and in trial he was found faithful', was employed by Ben Sira in a context worthy of note. In the following passage, Ben Sira links Abraham's faith in trial with a poetic paraphrase of Genesis 22:16–17, God's oath to Abraham following the *Aqedah*, which suggests that he already associated Genesis 15:6 with the sacrificing of Isaac over two centuries before the author of James:

> In his flesh He engraved him an ordinance,
> And in trial he was found faithful.
> Therefore, with an oath He promised him
> 'To bless the nations in his seed',
> To multiply him 'as the dust of the earth'
> And to exalt his seed 'as the stars'.[18]

We see, therefore, that the application of Genesis 15:6 in the Epistle, as well as its interpretation, may be very early. However, the application of a biblical verse to a specific theme – which is a common feature of rabbinic *Midrash* – is usually based upon an allusion to that theme either in the verse itself, or in its context. Did the author of James – and possibly Ben Sira before him – conform with midrashic method in their application of Genesis 15:6? This possibility deserves some consideration, as there are a number of parallels between Genesis 15 and 22, both in content and language, which may have provided an ancient exegete with the necessary textual links for interrelating these two chapters,[19] as can be seen from

with words.' The concluding phrase which the Targumist has added to his rendering has an interesting parallel in Jubilees 19:3, relating to the climactic trial of Abraham, the burial of Sarah (see above, note 3): 'And Abraham went to mourn over her and bury her, and we tried him to see if his spirit were patient *and he were not indignant in the words of his mouth.*' See further Bowker's remarks on the above rendering of the Targum, *The Targums and Rabbinic Literature*, Cambridge 1969, pp. 202f; also Philo's rendering of Genesis 15:6, *Quis Haeres Sit* xix, 94.

[18] 44:20–1 (*Apocrypha and Pseudepigrapha*, ed. Charles, vol. 1, p. 483). See also Segal's comments on the Hebrew text (44:25–7), *Sepher Ben Sira Ha-Shalem*, Jerusalem 1953, pp. 308f.

[19] Both chapters open with almost identical phrases in the Hebrew text. The promise of progeny as numerous as the stars (15:5) is reiterated in 22:17, also the promise of

at least one early source, Pseudo-Philo's *Liber Antiquitatum Biblicarum*.[20] The following passage forms part of a dialogue in which God demands of Balaam:

Was it not concerning this people that I spake unto Abraham in a vision saying: '*Thy seed shall be as the stars of heaven*', when I raised him up above the firmament and showed him all the orderings of the stars, and required of him his son for a burnt offering and he brought him to be laid upon the altar, but I restored him to his father. And because he resisted not, his offering was acceptable in my sight, and for the blood of him[21] did I choose this people. And then I said unto the angels that work subtly: 'Said I not of him: "*To Abraham will I reveal all that I do* (= Genesis 18:17)"?'

M. R. James, whose translation is quoted here, identified the quotation, 'Thy seed shall be as the stars of heaven', as Genesis 22:17, 'and I will multiply your descendants as the stars of heaven', presumably on the basis of subsequent references to the *Aqedah*. This identification was accepted by Kisch in his critical edition of the Biblical Antiquities. However, from the text it is quite clear that this quotation is a paraphrase of Genesis 15:5, 'And He brought him outside and said: "Look toward heaven, and number the stars, if you are able to number them." Then He said to him: "So shall your descendants be."' This is indicated initially by the reference to God speaking to Abraham in a vision, which clearly presupposes Genesis 15:1, 'After these things the word of the Lord came to Abram *in a vision*.' Moreover, Pseudo-Philo has actually introduced an aggadic comment on Genesis 15:5, which has its parallel in a rabbinic source. Thus R. Johanan b. Nappaḥa interpreted 'And He brought him outside', to mean,

ultimate triumph over the enemy in this verse is an allusion to the covenant in 15:18f regarding the possession of Canaan and its inhabitants. Moreover, the expression כה, which occurs in an unusual context in 22:5 actually forms the basis of an aggadic association with 15:5, 'So (כה) shall your descendants be' (see *Tanḥuma*, ed. Buber, 1, p. 113; also *Targum Pseudo-Jonathan* and Rashi on Genesis 22:5).

20 18:5, ed. Kisch, p. 159; trans. M. R. James, London 1917, pp. 123–4.
21 On the notion presupposed here, that Isaac was actually slain by Abraham, see S. Spiegel, *Me-Aggadoth Ha-Aqedah, Alexander Marx Jubilee Volume*, Hebrew Section, New York 1950, pp. 471–547, particularly pp. 493–7 (= *The Last Trial*, trans. J. Goldin, New York 1967, repr. 1979, pp. 51ff; also G. Vermes, *Scripture and Tradition in Judaism* Leiden, 1961, pp. 204ff.

'He raised him above the vault of the heavens'.[22] Pseudo-Philo, therefore, has interrelated the accounts of God's promise of progeny to Abraham, and the sacrificing of Isaac.

It is interesting to note further that Pseudo-Philo has introduced a second passage which has obvious verbal parallels with Genesis 22. In keeping with the rabbinic maxim 'There is no "earlier" or "later" (i.e. strict chronological order) in the Torah', he has disregarded the historical sequence of the biblical narrative, and has presented God's communication with Abraham, recounted in Genesis 18:17ff, as a direct result of the *Aqedah*. The textual basis for this is not difficult to perceive. God's prognostications regarding Abraham in Genesis 18:18, 'seeing that Abraham shall become a great and mighty nation, and all the nations of the earth shall bless themselves by him', are clearly echoed in His subsequent utterances to Abraham in 22:17–18.[23] It is possible, however, that Pseudo-Philo's reference to 18:17 may be of further significance, in view of the aggadic amplification of this verse which apparently gained wide currency in early times, as it is found in a *Targum*, in the writings of Philo, and in later rabbinic *midrashim*. All these sources introduce into their renderings of 18:17 the operative expression אוהבי, 'Shall I conceal from Abraham *my friend* ...'[24] In the context of Pseudo-Philo's homily, this rendering would be most apt. Because Abraham was prepared to sacrifice Isaac despite the former promise of progeny, he was deemed a friend of God, in whom He confided His intentions. If this interpretation of the passage is correct, then it forms a striking parallel with James 2:21–3, both with regard to content and exegetical background.

---

[22] *Genesis Rabbah* 44:12, p. 432.

[23] Similarly the phrase, 'For I have known him' (verse 19) may have been taken as a pointer to 22:12, 'for now I know that you fear God'.

[24] Fragmentary *Targum* to 18:17: 'And the Lord through His Word said: Shall I hide from *Abraham My friend* (אוהבי = רחמי)'; Philo, *De Sobrietate* 55–6 (trans. Colson and Whitaker, vol. 3, p. 473):

For wisdom is rather God's friend than his servant. And therefore he says plainly of Abraham: 'Shall I hide anything from *Abraham my friend?*'

On this passage, see S. Sandmel, 'Philo's Place in Judaism', *HUCA*, vol. 26 (1955), pp. 165–6, note 130; *Midrash Ha-Gadol* on Genesis 18:17, p. 303: 'God said: "I am about to perform a great deed in My world, and I do not tell Abraham *My friend*?"'
See further *Pirkei d'R. Eliezer* 25, and *Midrash Sekhel Tov*, ed. Buber, p. 28.

CHAPTER 8

Elements of Near-Eastern mythology in rabbinic '*Aggadah*'

No systematic attempt has yet been made to analyse fully the mythological material preserved in rabbinic literature in the light of ancient Near-Eastern sources. It is generally recognised that the early rabbinic exegetes have introduced into their exposition of biblical texts notions and motifs of high antiquity. Some of these can be traced back to Assyrian-Babylonian sources, and may have been introduced into Jewish tradition at the time of the Babylonian Exile.[1] Other motifs in rabbinic literature clearly echo the indigenous traditions of Palestine, dating back centuries before the beginning of the current era, possibly to the very sources presupposed by the Bible itself.[2]

---

[1] Ginzberg, who has collected all the relevant material in rabbinic sources, called attention to a number of parallels for rabbinic traditions in ancient Near-Eastern sources. However, his invaluable work predates the developments in scholarship resulting from the publication of the Ugaritic texts. Consequently, a fresh analysis of rabbinic mythology in the light of more recent scholarship is still required. See Ginzberg, *Legends*, vol. 5, p. 26, note 73 and pp. 43–6, note 127. See also H. Gunkel, *Schopfung und Chaos in Urzeit und Endzeit*, Gottingen 1895, pp. 141–69; and T. H. Gaster, *Thespis*, revised edn, Harper Torchbook, New York 1966, p. 142. Gaster has allotted a place to rabbinic tradition in his analysis of the development of the combat myth (pp. 137 and 150–1), but his remarks are of a general nature.

[2] As has been suggested by Cassuto in connection with his thesis regarding the existence of epic poetry in ancient Israel, comparable with that of Ugaritic and Mesopotamia, of which only fragments are preserved in biblical literature. Although this ancient poetry disappeared – possibly in the obscure period following Ezra and Nehemiah, Cassuto conjectures – the essential theme of the poem lived on in the memory of the people, re-emerging in the popular legends of the talmudic period. See, 'Epic Poetry in Ancient Israel' (Hebrew), in *Keneseth – Dedicated to the Memory of H.N. Bialik*, vol. 8, pp. 121–42. This article has been reprinted in Cassuto's *Studies on the Bible and Ancient Orient – Vol. 1: Biblical and Canaanite Literatures*, Jerusalem 1972, pp. 62–90, which is quoted hereafter. For an English summary of Cassuto's thesis, see U. Cassuto, *The Goddess Anath* (trans. I. Abrahams), Jerusalem 1971, pp. 71–5. See further Cassuto's *Commentary on the Book of Genesis – Part I: From Adam to Noah* (trans.

Moreover, the rabbis exhibit a remarkable degree of accuracy in associating their store of mythological traditions with the fleeting, and often obscure references in biblical literature, which the modern scholar has only recently evaluated in the light of archaeological discoveries. This may be illustrated best by the well-known statement of Rav, based on Job 26:12, בכחו רגע הים ובתבונתו מחץ רהב. In the light of Ugaritic texts the full implications of this verse may now be ascertained. The author of Job is alluding to the primordial struggle between the Creator and the genius of the sea, Yam – or Rahab in Israelite tradition.[3] Rav was not only familiar with the cosmogonic event to which the biblical author alludes, he actually employs an epithet for the genius of the sea, for which there is no counterpart in biblical sources, but which is comparable with the Ugaritic *ZBL YM*, שר של ים, 'Prince of the sea':

When God desired to create the world, He said to the Prince of the sea: 'Open your mouth and swallow up all the waters of the world.' The latter answered, 'Lord of the universe, I have enough with my own!' Whereupon God trampled on him and slew him, as it is said, 'By His power He beat down the sea,[4] and by His understanding He smote Rahab.'[5]

Ginzberg, who noted the parallel between Rav's *Aggadah* and the Babylonian creation epic, regarded the Babylonian *Talmud* as the source for this motif in Palestinian *Midrashim*.[6]

1. Abrahams), Jerusalem 1961, pp. 36ff. Although Cassuto has discussed a number of passages in rabbinic literature which refer to the primordial conflict with the sea, he did not attempt to evaluate the more extensive material containing descriptions of the battle with the Leviathan.

[3] See M. H. Pope, *Job*, The Anchor Bible, New York 1965, p. 166.

[4] Modern translators usually render רגע as 'to still', or 'to stir up' (see Pope, *Job*, p. 166). However, the rendering presupposed by the *Midrash*, 'to beat', or 'to beat down', has some merit. It is linguistically plausible (רקע ‖ רגע, 'to beat') and forms a suitable parallel with מחץ in clause B. *Targum* to Job 26:12, renders clause A as בחיליה גזר ימא, 'By His strength He split the sea'. Although this rendering, which was adopted by several medieval commentators and the AV, is linguistically doubtful, the imagery of God splitting the sea in two at the time of the creation has its parallel in a very early source. In the Babylonian Creation Epic, Marduk divides the carcass of Tiamat, slitting her in two like a fish (*Enuma Elish* IV, lines 136–7, J. B. Pritchard (ed.), *Ancient Near Eastern Texts*, Princeton 1954, p. 67). See Ibn Ezra, Naḥmanides and Kimhi on Job 26:12; also Kimhi's *Sepher Ha-Shorashim*, s.v. רגע (ed. J. H. R. Biesenthal and F. Lebrecht, Berlin 1847, pp. 343–4).

[5] See *BT Bava Batra* 74b.   [6] *Legends*, vol. 5, p. 26, note 73.

However, he was unaware of the Ugaritic version of the primordial conflict, which, together with its parallels in biblical sources, clearly indicates that the combat with the sea formed part of the mythological heritage of Palestine centuries before Rav.[7] Moreover, on closer examination, it can be shown that the Palestinian sources have preserved a fuller version of the ancient myth than that recorded in the Babylonian *Talmud*.

The Babylonian creation epic relates how Marduk, having vanquished Tiamat, tramples on her carcass, from which he creates the primeval seas, which are barred and guarded to keep them in check.[8] Scattered allusions to these events are preserved in biblical writings, notably Job 9:8, which describes God as the sole creator of the heavens, who tramples upon the body of Yam,[9] and 38:8ff, which records the conception, birth and ultimate incarceration of the primordial sea. From Palestinian *Midrashim* it is clear that the early myth presupposed by the biblical text was known among the early rabbinic exegetes. Moreover, the *Midrash* employs a term for God's trampling upon the seas, כבש, which does not occur in biblical allusions to this event, but which has an exact parallel in the Enuma Elis epic, where the cognate root, KABASU[10] is used:[11]

Blessed be the name of the supreme King of kings, the Holy One, blessed be He, whose wonders are innumerable, and whose greatness

---

[7] Rav may have been responsible for introducing the legend of God's confrontation with the prince of the sea into Babylon, as he was the principal disseminator of Palestinian traditions in his native land. It is interesting to note that the legends of God's subjugation of both Yam, the sea, and the Leviathan apparently gained wide currency in Babylon during the Talmudic period, as can be seen from contemporary magical texts which refer to the mightiest of spells which hold the sea (*YM*) and Leviathan in check. See J. A. Montgomery, *Aramaic Incantation Texts from Nippur*, Philadelphia 1913, p. 121, lines 3–4; also C. H. Gordon, 'Aramaic Incantation Bowls', *Orientalia*, vol. 10, (1941), p. 273, lines 6–7 (the writer is grateful to Professor M. J. Geller of University College London, for calling his attention to this material).

[8] See *Enuma Elish* IV, lines 139–40, Pritchard, *ANET*, p. 67.

[9] For this rendering, see N. H. Tur-Sinai, *The Book of Job: A New Commentary*, Jerusalem 1957, pp. 157–8: also Pope, *Job*, p. 69.

[10] IV, line 129:

Ik-bu-us-ma be-lum sa Ti-a-ma-tum i-sid-sa.

[11] See *Tanḥuma*, ed. Buber, 4, pp. 97–8: also Old Version, *Ḥuqqath* 1; *Numbers Rabbah* 18:22; *Midrash Wa-Yoshha* in A. Jellinek, *Bet ha-Midrasch*, vol. 1, p. 46; see also *Pirqei d'R Eliezer* 5.

is unsearchable,[12] 'He gathered the waters of the sea as in a bottle; He put the deeps in storehouses (Psalm 33:7).' What does [the phrase] 'He gathered the waters of the sea as in a bottle' mean? When God created the world, He said to the Prince of the sea, 'Open your mouth and swallow all the waters of creation!' The latter answered, 'Lord of the universe, I have enough with my own!', and he began to weep.[13] Whereupon God trampled on him and slew him, as it is said, 'By His power He beat down the sea, and by His understanding He smote Rahab (Job 26:12)' – [from this verse] you may ascertain that the name of the Prince of the sea is Rahab. What did God do then? He trampled on [the waters], and trod on them, and thus the sea[14] received them, as it is said, 'He trod on the back of the sea (*ibid.* 9:8)'[15], and He set the sand as a bar and doors against them, as it is said, 'Or who shut in the sea with doors … [and prescribed bounds for it, and set bars and doors]?[16] (*ibid.* 38:8 and 10)' …

The rabbinic version of the combat myth is by no means limited to the primordial conflict between the Creator and the genius of the sea. The battle with Leviathan figures more extensively in rabbinic literature, and may be of some special significance for the study of the mythological traditions of Palestine in general. For in striking contrast with the cursory allusions to this incident in biblical sources, and the terse references in Ugaritic texts to the smiting of Lotan, the slaying of Leviathan is portrayed in rabbinic literature in detailed and graphic terms. Although these descriptions are highly coloured by the popular religious beliefs of the talmudic period, none the less, they preserve an imagery and terminology which has

---

[12] *Tanḥuma* (both versions) and *Numbers Rabbah* read:

ולנפלאותיו אין חקר ולגדולתו אין מספר

However, the reading adopted above is preferable as it is clearly an allusion to Job 9:10, which refers to God's activities at the time of the creation.

[13] On the allusion to the weeping of the waters in this context, see Ginzberg, *Legends* vol. 5, p. 26, note 73.

[14] *Viz.* the Primordial Ocean, ים אוקייעוס as in *Genesis Rabbah* 5:2, cited in the next note.

[15] So *Midrash Wa-Yosha*. All other sources cited above (note 11) read ודורך על במתי ארץ (Amos 4:13). However, the sense of the passage clearly requires Job 9:8, and Luria corrects the text of *Numbers Rabbah* accordingly. This emendation is supported further by the version of this *Aggadah* recorded in *Genesis Rabbah* 5:2 (p. 33), where God's trampling upon the waters is likened to the deflating of blown-up skin bottles, which are compressed and relegated to a convenient place.

[16] So *Tanḥuma*, Old Version.

evidently been drawn from much older sources. It is possible, therefore, that rabbinic *Aggadah* has preserved in a fuller, albeit adapted form, a significant aspect of the ancient combat myth, presupposed by the oldest literary sources of Palestine.[17]

THE BATTLE WITH LEVIATHAN

As is well known, the brief references to Lotan in Ugaritic texts have added considerable support to the contentions of those scholars who have argued that the biblical Leviathan is a mythical rather than a natural creature.[18] Among the early rabbinic exegetes the supernatural character of Leviathan was never questioned, as can be seen from their expositions of numerous verses particularly from Job 40:25–41:26.[19] This passage is essentially a description of Leviathan's awesomeness. However, the author of Job has employed a number of terms and expressions which leave little doubt regarding the context from which he has taken his imagery. In 40:32, Job is enjoined to remember the battle, 'don't try again!' This theme is resumed in 41:18–21, where a veritable armoury of weapons is enumerated, all of which are ineffective against Leviathan. Moreover, this sequence of verses is preceded by an allusion to

---

[17] As to the nature of the sources used by the Rabbis for their store of mythological traditions, this is largely a matter for conjecture. Undoubtedly some traditions were received in oral form. However, one rabbinic source (*Canticles Rabbah* to 1:4) refers to חדרי בהמות ולויתן, 'the secrets of Behemoth and Leviathan', in the same context as חדרי מרכבה, 'the secrets of the *Merkavah*' (for this rendering of the expression חדרי, see Margulies, *Leviticus Rabbah* 16:4, p. 354). It is conceivable that just as there was a *baraita* devoted to the subject of *Ma'aseh Merkavah*, so some kind of compilation may have existed containing material relating to Behemoth and Leviathan. We do find collections of *aggadot* relating to these monsters in existing sources: see *Pesiqta de Rav Kahana* 6, pp. 57b–58a, and 187b–188b (ed. Mandelbaum, pp. 112–13, and 455–7); also *BT Bava Batra* 74b–75a). In view of the expositional character of these collections, it is conceivable that they are the remains of a more extensive aggadic commentary, possibly on Job 40–41, which incorporated many early mythological traditions.

[18] See Pope, *Job*, pp. 268f and 276f.

[19] In addition to the material cited in this study, see further R. Joḥanan b. Nappaḥa's description of the devastating methods by which Leviathan obtains its food, based on 41: 23–24 (*BT Bava Batra* 75a; see also *Pesiqta d'Rav Kahana* 29, p. 188a; (ed. Mandelbaum, p. 456) for a further description based on 41: 17. See also the detailed accounts of Leviathan's fate in the messianic era based on 40: 30–31, in the *Pesiqta* and *BT Bava Batra* 75a.

the terror of the gods at the presence of Leviathan, a motif which has its parallels in both the Akkadian and the Ugaritic versions of the combat myth.[20]

The early rabbinic exegetes clearly recognised the full significance of these allusions and, by means of aggadic exegesis, transformed the passage from a mere description into a highly dramatised account of the battle between the celestial beings and the primordial monster of the deep. In keeping with the general tendency in rabbinic literature, the setting for the combat is an eschatalogical rather than a cosmogonic one,[21] the slaying of Leviathan being projected from its original setting in the drama of the creation and establishment of God's kingship, to the messianic age, the period of the new cosmos and re-establishment of divine sovereignty. Similarly, the terrified gods are transformed into angels[22] who, like Ea and Annu in the Babylonian epic,[23] are first dispatched in an unsuccessful attempt to subdue the dragon of the sea, before a more capable combatant is summoned:[24]

---

[20] See Pope, *Job*, p. 286; also Gaster, *Thespis* (above, note 1).

[21] As in Isaiah 27:1, which forms the scriptural basis of one of the accounts of the slaying Leviathan cited on p. 307.

Rabbinic sources do preserve one or two allusions to a primordial conflict with Leviathan. *BT Bava Batra* 74b records the tradition – once again in the name of Rav – that God created both a male and a female Leviathan, but He slew the latter and castrated the former in order to avert the danger to the world that might have resulted from their mating. Gaster equated the castration of Leviathan in Jewish tradition with the incarceration of the serpent or dragon, which figures in other ancient versions of the combat myth. We would suggest, however, that the castration of Leviathan resembles more closely the imagery employed in Egyptian sources to describe the destruction of the serpent Apophis, 'He is not and his heirs are not. His egg shall not last nor shall his seed knit together'. (*The Book of Knowing the Creations of Re and of Overthrowing Apophis*, 27:11, Pritchard, ANET, p. 7). Moreover, Gaster has not noted a much more obvious parallel in rabbinic sources for the incarceration-motif, recorded, once again, in the *Pesiqta* (p. 188a; ed. Mandelbaum, p. 456), where the *Amora*, R. Berekhiah interprets the obscure phrase, צר סגור חותם (Job 41:7), as God's declaration that He has safely and securely immured Leviathan (see also *Tanḥuma* (Old Version) *Niẓẓavim* 4).

[22] Compare, for example, *Targum* to Psalm 29:1; also *Targum* and *LXX* to Job 1:6, 2:1 and 38:7.

[23] See *Enuma Elish* II, lines 50ff, (Pritchard, *ANET*, pp. 63f).

[24] See *Pesiqta d'Rav Kahana* 29, p. 188a (ed. Mandelbaum, p. 456) also *Tanḥuma* (Old Version), *Niẓẓavim* 4.

'On account of its glory, He brings forth His armed ones (Job 41:7)'.[25]
Because Leviathan possesses a celestial glory, God says to the ministering angels, 'Go down and wage war with it!' Whereupon they
descend and wage war with it. But Leviathan rears its head, and when
the angels see it, they are terrified by its awesomeness and they flee, as
it is said, 'When he raises himself up, the angels[26] are afraid (41:17)' –
elim connotes 'angels', as it is said, 'For who in the skies can be compared unto the Lord? Who among the *angels*[27] is like the Lord? (Psalm
89:7)' . . . Then God says to the angels, 'Take up swords and go down
against it!' Thereupon they take up swords and set upon it, but it does
not affect Leviathan,[28] as it is said, 'Though they overtake him with
the sword, it will not hold (Job 41:18)'. 'He diverts the spear as chain-
mail[29] (*ibid.*)', just as the spear is diverted from chain-mail, so it is
diverted from the hide of Leviathan. Moreover, iron weapons are
accounted by it as straw, as it is said, 'He regards iron as straw, and
brass as rotten wood (*ibid.* 19).' They take up bows and shoot arrows
at it, but it does not affect Leviathan,[30] as it is said, 'The arrow cannot
make him flee (*ibid.* 20).' Then they take up sling-stones and cast them
at it, but Leviathan regards them as stubble, as it is said, 'Slingstones
are turned with him into stubble (*ibid.*)' . . . What does God do then?
He brings together Behemoth and Leviathan and they do battle with
one another, as it is said, 'They draw near to one another, and there is
no space between them (*ibid.* 8)' . . . Immediately Behemoth and
Leviathan cleave to one another, as it is said, 'They are joined one to
the other (*ibid.* 9)', and once they are joined together, they do not
separate from one another, as it is said, 'They stick together that they
cannot be sundered (*ibid.*).' What does God do? He signals to Leviathan who smites Behemoth with its fins and slaughters it, and He
signals to Behemoth who smites Leviathan with its tail and kills it!

The imagery and language employed in the opening lines of
this passage require further evaluation, particularly the phrase
גאוה של מעלה, 'celestial glory'.[31] This unusual formulation

[25] AJ: 'His scales are his pride'. Presumably אפיק was taken midrashically as אפיק,
the *aph'el* of נפק.

[26] So *Vulgate*, 'angeli'.   [27] So *Targum*.

[28] ולא איכפת ליה which is the reading of *Yalkut Job* 927. *Pesiqta* reads: ואיכפת
לך בהן.

[29] AJ: 'Nor the spear, the dart, nor the pointed shaft'. However, the *Midrash* has taken
מסע as מסיע, and שריה as שריון, 'body armour'.

[30] So *Yalkut*; *Pesiqta* reads: ואיכפת לו.

[31] Taking גאוה in the positive sense in which it is found in both biblical and rabbinic
Hebrew, compare the phrase גאותה של מלכות שמים, 'the glory of the Kingdom
of Heaven' (*BT Ḥagigah* 5b).

occurs, apparently, only in the above context, from which it is difficult to determine its precise significance. We may assume, however, that our unknown aggadist is alluding to an ancient tradition – possibly biblical in origin[32] – that Leviathan is endowed with a supernatural splendour. According to an early tannaitic source, Leviathan's eyes are great orbs of light illuminating the depths of the sea.[33] *Pesiqta d'Rav Kahana*, from which the quotation is taken, also records the tradition that Leviathan's fins alone could dim the light of the sun with their brilliance.[34] In this respect, the splendour of Leviathan is

---

[32] See E. Kimron, תחתיו חדודי חרש (Job 41:22), *Leshonenu* 37 (1973), pp. 96–8.
Kimron has endeavoured to prove that the correct rendering of the phrase חדודי הרש, is 'the brightness of the sun', as suggested in midrashic sources (see note 34, below), an early piyyut of Qaliri (see note 47, below), and Rashi on Job. If this is correct, then rabbinic legend has preserved in a fuller form, an early mythological tradition to which the biblical author merely alludes.

[33] See *BT Bava Batra* 74b.

[34] See ed. Buber, 29, p. 187b–188a, and ed. Mandelbaum, p. 455, for parallels:
Behold the skin of Leviathan which I am to use for the righteous in the hereafter, if I were to omit a single patch from it, I would be obliged to make it good, as it is said, 'Can you make good its skin with patches? (Job 40:31)'. Should you say that the skin of Leviathan is nothing remarkable, R. Pinḥas ha-Kohen b. Hama and R. Jeremiah in the name of R. Shemuel b. Isaac said: 'Even its fins could dim the light of the sun! As it is said, "Beneath him are sun-like fins (*ibid.* 41:22)", for חרש means the "sun" as it is said, "Who commands the sun – חרס – and it rises not (*ibid.* 9:7)".'
Presumably the rendering of שכות in Job 40:31, as 'patches', presupposed by the *Midrash*, is based on the parallel between the Aramaic מטללא (= סוכה; see *Targum* on Job) and מטלית, two nouns from the cognate roots טלל and טלי. Moreover, we actually find מטליותא (= מטלית) as the Aramaic rendering for the Hebrew סוכה, see A. Berliner, *Targum Onkelos* 2, p. 37, on Leviticus 23:43. For the reading חדודות שלו, see Buber's comments; also Lieberman's additional note, ed. Mandelbaum, p. 476, on the additional expression פופסים or פופסיס (= Greek: *apopsis*, 'appearance'), found in MS Oxford.
The theme of Leviathan's splendour is developed further in the *Pesiqta* in conjunction with Job 41:22b. While the resting-place of other fish on the sea-bed is most foul the resting-place of Leviathan is finer than gold, see also Rashi and *Ma'yan Gannim* on Job, ed. Buber, Berlin 1889, p. 133. It is possible that the tradition of Leviathan's splendour is presupposed in an early apocryphal work, the Testament of Job, where Elihu, who emerges as a demonic figure in the Testament, is depicted as a devotee of the dragon, loving the 'beauty of the serpent, and the scales of the dragon' (see 10:14ff, particularly verse 17, translated by K. Kohler, *Semitic Studies in Memory of Alexander Kohut*, Berlin 1897, p. 333; also ed. S. P. Brock, Leiden 1967, 43:5ff, particularly verse 8, p. 52). Compare also the rabbinic tradition that Elihu is the keeper of secret knowledge relating to Leviathan, *Canticles Rabbah* to 1:4, cited above, note 17.

comparable with that of the primordial light[35] which, according to rabbinic tradition, emanated from the mantle donned by
God at the time of creation.[36] Thus Leviathan radiates a
heavenly splendour. Our interpretation of this obscure phrase
is supported by a much older source, which may preserve the
prototype for the awesome, luminous monster of Jewish tradition. The Babylonian creation epic contains a description of
the dreadful dragons provided for Tiamat's army by Mother
Hubur. These monsters are garbed with a *pulhu*, the awesome,
fiery garment of the gods, and are crowned with a *melammu*, a
dazzling, divine aureole,[37] so that when they rear up – like
Leviathan – none can withstand them.[38]

> Roaring dragons she has clothed with terror,
> Has crowned them with haloes, making them like gods,
> So that he who beholds them shall perish abjectly,
> (And) that, with their bodies reared up, none might
>   turn them back.

As to the final conflict between Leviathan and the monster
bull, Behemoth, this is a much later development in the Jewish
version of the combat myth, inspired by the conditions prevail-

---

[35] See *Genesis Rabbah* 3:6 and the parallels cited by Theodor, p. 21. See also the sources
cited by Ginzberg, *Legends*, vol. 5, p. 80, note 24, relating to the tradition that the
splendour of Adam could likewise eclipse the sun; also *Genesis Rabbah* 19:4 (p. 173,
for parallels) for a similar tradition relating to the monster-bird Ziz. It is interesting
to note further that the parallel between the primordial light and the luminous hide
of Leviathan, is reflected in their respective eschatalogical roles. According to the
above passage, the primordial light was hidden away for the enjoyment of the
righteous in the hereafter. In *BT Bava Batra* 75a, a detailed description is given of
God's distribution of Leviathan's hide among the righteous in proportion to their
merits, the remainder being spread over Jerusalem so that its splendour can
illuminate the whole world.

[36] See *Genesis Rabbah* 3:4, and the parallels cited by Theodor, p. 19, and note the
striking parallel between the terminology employed here, in connection with the
primordial light, and that found in the description of Leviathan's hide in *BT Bava
Batra* 75a.

[37] For this interpretation of these terms, see A. L. Oppenheim, 'Akkadian *pul(u)h(t)u*
and *melammu*', *JOAS* vol. 63 (1943), p. 31. Oppenheim stresses (pp. 32 and 34, note
8) that demons as well as gods could be invested with the splendour of the *pulhu* and
melammu. This may provide the background for the phenomenon of Jewish tradition, that Leviathan, a satanic beast, is endowed with a splendour comparable with
that of God.

[38] See *Enuma Elis* I, lines 136–9; II, lines 23–6; III, lines 27–30, also lines 85–8
(Pritchard, *ANET*, p. 62).

ing in Palestine under Roman rule.[39] However, rabbinic sources preserve two further accounts of the final fate of Leviathan, which presupposes a much older tradition resembling more closely ancient Near-Eastern versions of the combat myth:

A[40]

וי'ה ד'ג[42] – This refers to Leviathan which is destined from the six days of creation to provide a banquet for the righteous in the world to come, as it is said, 'In that day the Lord with His hard and great and strong sword will punish Leviathan the fleeing serpent, Leviathan the twisting serpent, and He will slay the dragon that is in the sea (Isaiah 27:1).' When God brings Leviathan from the midst of the Great Sea, He has his messengers

B[41]

In the future, Gabriel will arrange a chase[43] of Leviathan as it is said, 'Can you draw out Leviathan with a fish-hook, or press down his tongue with a cord?' But, were God not to assist him, he could not prevail against it, as it is said, 'He who made it will bring his (= Gabriel's) sword near (Job 40:19).'

bind it until [He can draw it out] with a fish-hook, and press down its tongue with a cord, as it is said, 'Can you draw out Leviathan with a fish-hook, or press down its tongue with a cord? (Job 40:25)' By what means does He bring Leviathan? God sends Gabriel to bring it from the midst of the Great Sea, putting hooks in its cheeks, and pressing down its tongue with a thick cord two thousands parasangs in breadth – equal to the measurement of the Great Sea, as it is said,

---

[39] It is explicitly stated in the parallel passage (*Leviticus Rabbah* 13:3) that this spectacle of the great beasts in conflict will be reserved for those who resist the temptations of the arena in this world. In all probability, it was the beast-fights of the arena which actually inspired this imagery.

[40] See *Midrash Alpha Betot*, in A. J. Wertheimer, *Battei Midrashot*, Jerusalem 1950, vol. 2, pp. 437–8. Although this passage is preserved in a work of uncertain date, its language and style suggest that it may be based on early sources.

[41] See *BT Bava Batra* 74b–75a, where this statement is reported by R. Dimi in the name of the Palestinian *Amora*, R. Jonathan b. Eleazar.

[42] ד'ג = Leviathan, which is classified in Tannaitic sources as a דג טהור (i.e. a ritually 'clean' fish; see *Sifra* on Leviticus 11:10, p. 49b; also *Tosephta Ḥullin* 3:27, ed. Zuckermandel, p. 506) and, therefore, fit for consumption by the righteous in the hereafter.

[43] קעיגיא = Greek, *kynegia*, 'chase' or 'hunt'.

'And his body was as vast as the Sea of Tarshish (Daniel 10:6)'[44] and of infinite length. As he draws it and brings it forth, Leviathan's strength prevails over Gabriel, and it swallows him up, at which point God comes to his aid and brings it forth from the midst of the Great Sea of the mighty deep, and brings it before the righteous and slaughters it in their presence with His own hand, as it is said, 'He that made it will bring His sword near (Job 40:19)' . . .[45]

Although these two versions exhibit several significant differences, they share a common imagery which suggests that they are merely adaptations of an older, possibly fuller account. The significant feature of both versions is the introduction of a specific hero, Gabriel, a guardian angel of Israel in rabbinic tradition,[46] and a prince of the celestial regions, שר של מעלה,[47] an epithet comparable with that employed for the

---

[44] AJ: 'His body also was like the beryl.' However, the *Midrash* presupposes the traditional interpretation of Tarshish in this verse; see *BT Ḥullin* 91b, also Rashi and Saadiah Gaon on Daniel 10:6; compare also *Targum* to Ezekiel 38:13.

[45] The application of this verse to Leviathan in both versions is unusual, as it is quite clear from the context that Job 40:19 refers to Behemoth. We may note, however, that Ibn Ezra was familiar with a further midrashic interpretation of this verse, relating it to Leviathan which, presumably, was taken from older sources (see his introduction to his commentary on the Pentateuch: The world was created upon Leviathan, as it is said, 'It is the first of God's ways'). Moreover, there is a parallel for this peculiarity in a Tannaitic source, which describes the course of the Jordan from the Cave of Paneas down to the mouth of the Leviathan, in connection with Job 40:23 (see the *baraita* in *BT Bava Batra* 74b). This application of the verse already disturbed the *Amora*, Rava b. Ulla, who was obliged to place a rather forced interpretation upon the verse in order to justify the *baraita*. See further Tur-Sinai's efforts to prove that Job 40: 16ff forms part of the description of Leviathan (*The Book of Job*, pp. 557ff).

[46] A role which he shares with Michael (See Ginzberg, *Legends*, vol. 5, p. 4, note 8) who figures as the chief opponent of the dragon in Revelations 12:7. However, the obscure reference in I Enoch 20:7, to Gabriel's authority over the serpents, may presuppose an early tradition linking Gabriel with Leviathan.

[47] See *Genesis Rabbah* 78:1 (p. 916); see also the sources cited by Ginzberg, *Legends*, vol. 5, p. 70, note 13: 'Michael and Gabriel *are* the princes of the celestial regions (שרים של מעלה).' Although this epithet is not found in the two extant accounts of Gabriel's conflict with Leviathan, it may have been employed in the sources used by the early Palestinian poet, Qaliri, who gives the following description of the initial encounter between the angels and Leviathan in a *silluq* (ויכון עולם) composed for the 9th Ab, preserved in the Byzantine and Roman Rites:
   And when the great day cometh,
      The Great King shall command
   That it be given as food to the great nation.
      Then shall He send against it the *Great Prince*,
   And with him shall be troops, a great multitude,

genius of the sea, שר של ים, and therefore, particularly apt in the context of the combat myth. Both versions stress that the heavenly hero cannot subdue his monstrous opponent without divine aid, a theme common to many ancient versions of the combat myth.[48]

Gabriel's efforts, in Version A, to secure Leviathan with a rope and hooks, and the monster's tactic of swallowing the angel, clearly echo Marduk's battle with Tiamat, in which the divine hero spreads his net to ensnare the monster, which counters by opening its mouth wide to devour him.[49] Version A, however, conforms with biblical tradition in ascribing to God the final act of killing Leviathan. In this respect, Version B represents a significant departure from biblical sources. God is no longer the slayer of Leviathan, he merely supports Gabriel in his task by rendering the angel's weapon effective. While this is inconsistent with biblical tradition, it does conform more closely with other versions of the combat myth, where the dragon is subdued by a divine hero who is furnished with invincible weaponry by a supporting deity, or deities.[50]

In biblical writings, the combat has obviously been adapted under the dominant influence of Israelite monotheism. The divine supporters are understandably eliminated, so that the Hebrew God emerges as the sole hero of the exploit. Rabbinic

To spread over it the great net,
To drag it with a fish-hook by his great strength.

(See J. Schirmann, 'The Battle between Behemoth and Leviathan according to an Ancient Hebrew Piyyut', in *Proceedings of the Israel Accademy of Sciences and Humanities*, vol. 4, p. 330, note 9, and p. 350 for the sources for this *silluq*; also p. 355 for the excerpt quoted above). Qaliri has introduced here a new element, the 'great net', חרם גדול, which is to be spread out to ensnare Leviathan. While this is not found in extant biblical and rabbinic sources, it does resemble Marduk's tactic, referred to above, to ensnare Taimat: 'The Lord spread out his net to enfold her' (*Enuma Elish* IV, line 95; Pritchard, *ANET*, p. 67).

[48] See Gaster, *Thespis*, p. 150f.

[49] *Enuma Elish* IV, line 97; Pritchard, *ANET*, p. 67. See further the swallowing of Baal, either by Mot, or the netherworld, which opens wide its mouth, extending its tongue to the stars: *[spt la]rs.spt. lsmm [l]sn lkbkbm* (C. H. Gordon, *Ugaritic Textbook*, Rome 1965, 67, II, lines 2–3, p. 178; see also Gaster, *Thespis*, p. 206). Compare this imagery with the description in *Midrash Alpha Betot* (Wertheimer, *Batei Midrashot*, vol. 2, p. 434), of the swallowing of Satan and his band by Gehinnom, which extends its fiery tongue to the heavens, swallowing the dissident angels like a dragon.

[50] See Gaster, *Thespis*, pp. 150f.

legend, however, has preserved the more original form of the combat myth. The combination of the divine hero and his supporting deity is retained, although translated into acceptable terms. The national god and hero of the pantheon of the polytheistic versions, becomes a prince of the celestial beings, who exercises a special guardianship over Israel. The supporting deity is God himself, who enables Gabriel's sword to vanquish Leviathan.

THE MONSTER-BULL, BEHEMOTH

We observed earlier, in connection with the conflict between Leviathan and Behemoth, that this is a later development in the Jewish version of the combat myth. However, the implication that the Behemoth is a creature of combat is one of several traditions relating to the monster-bull in rabbinic literature which have their parallels in ancient Near-Eastern mythology.

As in the case of Leviathan, modern scholarly opinion is divided on the question of the natural, or supernatural character of Behemoth.[51] In support of the latter view, parallels have been noted between the biblical Behemoth and the bull-monsters of Mesopotamian and Ugaritic traditions. However, a significant feature of these monsters is their combative role, the Sumero-Akkadian 'Bull of Heaven' being slain by Gilgamesh and Enkidu, and the Ugaritic 'ferocious bullock of El' falling prey to Anat. Unless we accept the traditional Jewish interpretation of Job 40:19,[52] there is no evidence in biblical

---

[51] See Pope, *Job*, pp. 268–70, where he explores fully the possible parallels for the biblical Behemoth in Sumero-Akkadian and Ugaritic sources, citing all the relevant material relating to the character of these bull-monsters and their combative role, to which we refer above.

[52] See for example, the commentaries of Rashi, Samuel b. Nissim Masnuth (*Mayan Gannim*, ed. Buber, p. 130), and Isaiah of Trani, on this verse, on the basis of which, we may render it as, 'He who made it will bring His sword near' (*viz.* to slay it; see also Pope, *Job*, p. 272). As such, the verse may be taken as an allusion to a future confrontation between God and Behemoth, comparable with the slaying of Leviathan predicted in Isaiah 27:1, involving the same terrible weapon described by the prophet, God's invincible sword. (This identification of the sword in Job 40:19 with that mentioned in Isaiah 27:1, is suggested in Version A of the combat with Leviathan quoted above, where both the verses are cited.)

sources for a similar tradition relating to Behemoth. Even the bovine character of the monster is implicit rather than explicit. On the other hand, rabbinic traditions relating to Behemoth resemble ancient Near-Eastern mythology more closely. Behemoth is undoubtedly a bull-monster, possessing a voracious appetite like its Mesopotamian and Ugaritic counterparts,[53] and is clearly depicted as a creature of combat. This is indicated further by the following passage, which is the continuation of Version A of the battle with the Leviathan cited earlier:[54]

After this, God sends Gabriel and Michael to bring the two Behemoths from the midst of a thousand mountains, as it is said, 'For every beast of the forest is mine, even Behemoth upon a thousand mountains (Psalm 50:10)'. At that time Gabriel and Michael go and search after the Behemoths. As soon as they see them, they run after them and endeavour to seize them, but they cannot overpower them, and they flee from them ...

Although the text is incomplete, it is sufficient to indicate the existence of a further – possibly older – tradition regarding the final fate of Behemoth, independent of Leviathan. The interesting feature of this account is the combination of the two celestial princes,[55] Gabriel and Michael, in the pursuit of Behemoth. This may not be of any special significance, since the hunt is for a pair of monsters. However, in the light of other similarities between the rabbinic Behemoth and the Mesopotamian Bull of Heaven, we cannot discount the possibility that this imagery may be an echo of the Mesopotamian myth of the slaying of a bull-monster by the heroes Enkidu and Gilgamesh.

[53] See Pope, *Job*, p. 273, who notes the parallel for the ancient Near-Eastern myth in midrashic sources (see *Pesiqta d'Rav Kahana*, 6, p. 58a; ed. Mandelbaum, p. 112).
[54] See *Midrash Alpha Betot*, Wertheimer, *Batei Midrashot*, vol. 2, p. 438.
[55] See above, note 47.

CHAPTER 9

Conclusions

In the preceding pages, we have analysed only a limited selection of sources from the vast array of material preserved in talmudic and midrashic literature, in connection with relatively few themes. It may seem somewhat less than judicious, therefore, if on the basis of this, we would proceed to draw wide-ranging conclusions regarding the midrashic process as a whole. None the less, we would argue that the sources and the subjects we have chosen for analysis, are genuinely representative of that process, which we would describe in simple terms, as the authentication or 'biblicisation' of old traditions and the development of new ones, through the medium of a sophisticated apparatus for textual exposition.

As we observed at the outset of our discussions, some element of the plethora of aggadic traditions preserved in our extant literature, both rabbinic and non-rabbinic, must be of high antiquity, emanating from the same sources from which the biblical narratives themselves were derived. We could only demonstrate this with any degree of certainty in connection with rabbinic accounts of the Creation Drama and the mythical monsters, where we could actually observe the early rabbinic exegetes 'biblicising' ancient mythological material, connecting it with relevant or appropriate texts. In so doing, the rabbis of the talmudic period demonstrated a better awareness of the plain meaning of those texts than their counterparts in the middle ages.

As to the expansion and development of biblical narratives and personalities, the evidence is of course much more substantial, already in earliest apocryphal sources. We observed

168

above, that the essential elements in the aggadic presentation of the personality of Abraham and the Generation of the Flood in rabbinic literature, are already to be found in a highly developed form in early, pre-Christian works like Jubilees.[1] Moreover, the material we cited in chapter 7, suggests that the actual methodology employed by the rabbis to develop these *aggadot* in the talmudic period, already formed part of an exegetical legacy shared by non-rabbinic writers before the beginning of the Christian Era.

The early rabbinic exegetes were clearly not the first to recognise the dramatic expansion of biblical personalities and events as a highly effective means of influencing their listeners' religious, social and moral conduct. None the less, they developed this aspect of the midrashic process to a remarkable degree of creativeness and sophistication. By means of their exegetical skills, they linked the earlier traditions found in apocryphal sources, many of which have no explicit basis in the pentateuchal narratives, with selected passages in the later books of the Bible, creating scriptural supplements to the *Torah*. Our primary example for this is undoubtedly the Book of Job, which was established already in tannaitic times, as an extra-pentateuchal source for details relating to the Generation of the Flood and Israel's early history as a nation. In addition to lending scriptural authority to early traditions, this also served to emphasise the centrality of the Bible, the revealed word of God, as the ultimate and most comprehensive source for all Jewish teachings and traditions.[2]

However, the creative genius of the early rabbinic exegetes was not limited to 'biblicising' earlier traditions. Indeed, this may have been only part of a much wider agenda for their public teaching and exposition of the biblical text. As we stressed above, aggadic *Midrash* is in origin a product of the ancient synagogue. It has its roots in the teaching and preaching of living preachers to live audiences. An essential com-

---

[1] See, for example, the extensive material cited by S. Sandmel, 'Philo's Place in Judaism', *HUCA*, vol. 26 (1955), pp. 151–332; also J. P. Lewis, *A Study of the Interpretation of Noah and the Flood in Jewish and Christian Literature*, Leiden 1968.
[2] See *Avot* 5:22, 'Turn it (= the *Torah*) over again and again, for everything is in it!'

ponent of this educative process, was the development of role models. The rabbis were highly sensitive not only to the social and economic conditions of their audiences, but also to their intellectual capacity. They realised that abstract ideological concepts could be most effectively and dramatically conveyed in the form of three-dimensional, familiar images. Therefore, they consciously built biblical heroes and anti-heroes into prototypes for the life-style, attitudes and conduct which they wished their followers to emulate, or to avoid. Similarly, the preachers in the ancient synagogues made extensive use of the powerful element of drama in amplifying a biblical narrative, in order to demonstrate to their listeners the consequences of righteous or wicked conduct.

We have only scratched the surface of this vast area of study, which still requires a comprehensive, wide-ranging review. We would emphasise, however, that it should be a review of the process as well as the end-product. Much scholarly effort has already been devoted to an analysis of the literary or ideological motifs in the aggadic treatment of biblical events and personal-ities, against the background of the religio-political conditions of the Holy Land. Although this remains a valid approach, due consideration must also be given to the issues which we have raised in the course of this study.

Midrash is Bible exegesis, therefore an analysis of the midrashic process must include an evaluation of the exegetical methodology and techniques developed by the rabbis in order to exploit the Bible as their central medium for the public communication of their ideals and beliefs. Moreover, it would not be sufficient to examine the interpretation of individual verses in isolation. It is equally essential to look for patterns of exegesis, to ascertain if other verses from the same context have been applied to a particular personality or theme. Having established the existence of such a pattern, it is then necessary to determine, where possible, the basis for it. For no matter how extrinsic the rabbis' treatment of the biblical text may appear to the modern reader, it was neither vicarious nor haphazard, as we have shown, for example, in case of Psalms 29, 45 and 110. It is the ultimate challenge to the student of

Midrash to find the פתח הדרש, the 'exegetical opening' within the plain meaning of the text as the rabbis perceived it, through which they could extract or introduce their desired message, or create thematic links.

What we have outlined is undoubtedly a painstaking and laborious task, but one which cannot be avoided if we are to gain a fuller insight into the early rabbinic perception of the Bible. Moreover, as the process was, in origin, largely a public one, the contribution and collaboration of the audience cannot be ignored. The shared knowledge of preachers and audiences, their mutual awareness of exegetical traditions and popular legends are, in the final analysis, indispensable to our understanding of the midrashic text.

In our view, this task was too great to be undertaken within the confines of a single book, or by a single author. Consequently, we have endeavoured to illustrate the major aspects of this midrashic process, principally through two key examples, for which there is a rich store of traditions, dating back to high antiquity and extensive aggadic exegesis in our extant sources. Abraham, who understandably loomed large in early Jewish tradition as the founding father of the Jewish people and their supreme role model, whose every action profoundly influenced the fate of his descendents. The Generation of the Flood, the archetypal sinners, whose graphically reconstructed life-style in talmudic-midrashic sources, was no doubt based on the worst excesses of the Graeco-Roman world.

There are, of course, numerous other illustrations of this process still awaiting exhaustive analysis, as might be seen from only a cursory study of the relevant material collected by Ginzberg in his *Legends of the Jews*, relating to biblical figures like Phineas or Mordechai on the one hand, and Esau or Balaam on the other. Similarly, a close reading, even in translation, of the midrashic treatment of the *Aqedah* in *Genesis Rabbah* 55–56, should prove sufficient to demonstrate the ancient preachers' use of drama to achieve their goal. Whole scenes are introduced into an already dramatic tale, to transform Isaac from object to subject in Abraham's ultimate trial of faith and to establish him as a co-hero. We have chosen

Abraham and the Generation of the Flood specifically, because they are, in our view, two of the best illustrations of this process. Moreover, we hope that our approach to the analysis of these two major topics has provided some useful guidelines for a similar study of other biblical personalities and events.

Job and the Generation of the Flood

ROBBERY AND VIOLENCE

In addition to the sources cited above on this subject, there is the following passage recorded in *Genesis Rabbah* 27:3 (see also the parallels cited by Theodor, p. 257). This source is note-worthy as it involves further verses from Job 24. In a sermon to the community of Sepphoris, R. Ḥanina cited verses 14 and 16 to illustrate the deceitful methods employed by the Generation of the Flood in perpetrating their crimes, with unfortunate consequences:

'[. . . and that every imagination of the thoughts of his heart] was only evil all the day. (Genesis 6:5)' – from the moment that the sun shone until it set, there was nothing to hope for in them! Thus it is written, 'The murderer riseth with the light to kill the poor and the needy; and in the night, he is like a thief.' (Job 24:14) But surely it is written 'In the dark they dig through houses'?! (*ibid.* 16 – which implies that they actually committed robbery). Why [then does it state '*like* a thief']? Because [they robbed houses] 'which they had marked out for themselves by day (*ibid.*)'. What did the Generation of the Flood used to do? They would bring balsam and rub it on the stones of the houses they intended to rob, then return by night, smell out the house and break in! Thus R. Ḥanina expounded in Sepphoris and that same night three hundred house-breakings were effected! (= כך דרש ר' חנינה בצפורין איתעביד ההוא ליליא תלת מאה חיתרין).

For this reading of the concluding statement, see Luria's comments on the text and the evidence cited by Theodor from MSS, early printed editions and parallels, particularly the version of this anecdote preserved in *BT Sanhedrin* 109a.

THE BIBLICAL TERM חמס

The identification of the biblical term **חמס** with robbery reflects the general usage of this expression in both its verbal and nominal forms in rabbinic literature, as can be seen from several of the passages we have cited. However, the following homily, based on Job 4:20–1, recorded in *Genesis Rabbah* 31:5 (p. 279) is particularly noteworthy, as the preacher offers a legal definition of **חמס** in order to illustrate the deviousness of the Generation of the Flood:

What does **חמס** connote as opposed to **גזל**? R. Ḥanina said: **חמס** [connotes the stealing of an article] worth less than a *perutah*, while **גזל** [connotes the stealing of an article] worth at least a *perutah*. Now this is what the Generation of the Flood used to do. One of them would take out a basket full of lupines, others would then come, each of them taking an amount less than the value of a *perutah*, with the result that [their victim] could not claim from them at law! Whereupon God said to them, 'You have not acted in accordance with the line of strict justice, therefore, I will not deal with you according to the line of strict justice!' Thus it is written, **הלא נסע יתרם בם ימותו ולא בחכמה** (lit.: 'Is not their tent-cord plucked up within them? They die, and that without wisdom.') 'Has not their excellency departed from them? They die without **חכמה**' – [which means] lacking the wisdom of the *Torah*! **מבקר לערב יוכתו מבלי משים לנצח יאבדו** (lit.: 'Betwixt morning and evening they are shattered; they perish forever without any regarding it.') 'They will be cut off from the evening (i.e. this world) and the morning (i.e. the world to come) they perish forever without justice being applied to them!' – **משים** connotes justice on the basis of the verse **ואלה המשפטים אשר תשים לפניהם** (Exodus 21:1. Since the term **שים** occurs here in the context or 'climate' of justice, it is invested with this meaning and taken as such in the context of 4:20)

This exposition of Job 4:20–1 is tannaitic in origin, as it can be traced back to R. Aqiva's pupil, R. Meir; see *Genesis Rabbah* 26:6 (p. 252).

REJECTION OF DIVINE AUTHORITY

In connection with this motif, we may note in particular the following homily of R. Meir – based on Job 34:29 – in which he

ascribes to the Generation of the Flood, Eliphaz's words in
22:14 (see *Genesis Rabbah* 36:1, p. 334; also *Leviticus Rabbah* 5:1,
pp. 98f, and *Yalqut Job* 909):

R. Meir expounded [the verse thus]: '"He has given Himself rest –
from His world, and has hidden His face – from His world", like a
judge before whom they spread a curtain (= בילון – so MSS Vatican
and Stuttgart – which is merely a variant for וילון, found in all MSS
of *Leviticus Rabbah*) so that he is ignorant of what is taking place
without. Thus the Generation of the Flood declared, "Thick clouds
are a covering to Him that He seeth not (Job 22:14)."' [His col-
leagues] said to him: 'Enough Meir!' He retorted to them: 'Why then
is it written, והוא ישקיט ומי ירשיע?' They answered: '[This verse
implies] that God bestowed tranquillity on the Generation of the
Flood, who then condemned them? What was the nature of the
tranquillity which He bestowed upon them? "Their seed is established in their sight with them, and their offspring before their eyes
(*ibid.* 21:8)... They send forth their little ones like a flock... (v. 11)".
Consequently, when He hid His face from them, who could say to
Him: "You have not acted correctly!"'

It is highly probable that R. Meir has not only based his
imagery of the judge on contemporary Roman practices (see S.
Lieberman, 'Roman Legal Institutions in Early Rabbinics and
in the Acta Martyrium', *JQR* 35 (1944–5) pp. 17ff) but was
also alluding to the heretical notions which were current in his
day. The destruction of the Second Temple, and particularly
the collapse of the Bar Cochba Uprising with its subsequent
persecution, brought in their wake a severe disillusionment,
resulting in apostasy and doubt regarding God's control over
the affairs of His world (see G. Allon, *Toldoth Ha-Yehudim
be-Eretz Yisrael bi-Tequfath Ha-Mishnah veHa-Talmud*, vol. 2, p.
58). This attitude of questioning and doubt is reflected particularly in the expositions of Exodus 17:7, 'Is the Lord among
us or not', by scholars who were active either in the troubled
years following the fall of Jerusalem, or in the oppressive period
of the Hadrianic persecutions. For our purposes, we may note
specifically the interpretation of R. Eliezer b. Hyrkanos,
repeated two generations later by R. Meir's colleague, R.
Nehemiah, which clearly echoes the sentiments in 21:15,
ascribed to the Generation of the Flood: 'If He provides us with

Appendix 1

our needs, we will serve Him, if not, *we will not serve Him!*' (See *Mekhilta Beshallaḥ, Massekhta d'Va-Yassa* 6, p. 175; also *Pesiqta d'Rav Kahana*, ed. Mandelbaum, p. 50, and the parallels cited there.)

The audacious declaration ascribed here to the rebellious Israelites was no doubt intended to portray the attitude of the Jewish heretic of the period who, despite his awareness of God, rejected His authority. Thus Elisha b. Abuya, a teacher of R. Meir and the classical example of the apostate at that time, is characterised as one who 'knew My power, yet rebelled against Me' (see *PT Ḥagigah* 2:1, 77b). Similarly, an anonymous *Tanna* interpreted Leviticus 26:14, 'But if you will not hearken unto Me', as referring to the man 'who knows his master, but is intent on rebelling against Him' (see *Sifra* to Leviticus 26:14, ed. Weiss, p. 111a). Finally, R. Tarphon, a contemporary of R. Eliezer b. Hyrkanos, relegated the Jewish heretic to a position lower than that of the pagan, because the latter does not know of God, and therefore denies Him, while the former denies God even though he knows of Him (see *BT Shabbat* 116a).

In all probability, such views were being voiced in certain sections of the oppressed and disillusioned population of the Holy Land, who found a plausible explanation for Israel's continued misfortune in the notion that God had actually abandoned His world, and had withdrawn from its affairs. R. Meir endeavoured to portray the Generation of the Flood as biblical prototypes for this heterodox outlook. His colleagues, on the other hand, apparently took exception to his finding a scriptural basis for the very notion they were obliged to combat. None the less, R. Meir was persistent in introducing the theme of God's abandoning His world into his exegesis relating to the Generation of the Flood, as can be seen from his interpretation of Genesis 6:3, לא ידון רוחי באדם לעולם. According to R. Meir, these are not God's words, as is suggested by the plain meaning of the text, but a declaration by the Antediluvians to the effect that 'there is no judge in the world! God has forsaken His world!' (see *Avot d'Rabbi Natan* Version A, 32, p. 93; also the view of Judah the Patriarch in *Genesis Rabbah* 26:6, p. 252). We may observe in conclusion, that in ascribing this sentiment to the Generation of the Flood, R. Meir was influenced by his master, R. Aqiva, who portrays them as declaring, 'There is neither justice nor a judge!' (see *Genesis Rabbah* 26:6, also the fuller version of this statement recorded anonymously in *Midrash Tehillim* to Psalm 10, ed. Buber, p. 95).

THE ANTEDILUVIANS' DESTRUCTION BY FIRE

Ginzberg endeavoured to find a very early background for this tradition in the much older concept of a world conflagration (מבול של אש) which is destined to engulf the world (see '*Mabul Shel Esh*', *Ha-Goren*, pp. 45ff). It seems more likely, however, that this tradition was modelled on the fate of the Sodomites, who are the classical example for punishment by fire. There is a close relationship in rabbinic thought between the Antediluvians and the Sodomites, which is reflected in the parallel traditions found already in early sources, regarding the nature and causes of their corruption, as well as the manner in which they were ultimately punished. For example, the three cardinal sins ascribed to the Antediluvians by R. Levi, idolatry, immorality and bloodshed (see p. 35, note 45) are likewise attributed to the Sodomites (see *PT Sanhedrin* 10:3, 29c; also *Avot d'Rabbi Natan* Version A, 12, and the sources cited by Schechter, p. 52). Similarly, in the tannaitic sources cited above (p. 28, note 22) the Sodomites are enumerated along with the Generation of the Flood, the Tower-builders etc., as examples for overbearing arrogance. It is interesting to note that in these sources, just as Job 21 is associated with the conduct and conditions of the Antediluvians, so 28:5ff is treated as a description of the Sodomites' social injustice and illicit dealings (see also *BT Sanhedrin* 109a-b, which contains a description of the Sodomites' corrupt conduct markedly similar to that of the Antediluvians' lawlessness, based on the same verses from Job, 24:2f and 16; see above, pp. 30f, also Ginzberg, *Legends*, vol. 5, p. 238, note 155).

We may note further that this association between these two prototypes for wickedness is reflected also in the writings of

Philo, who classifies the crimes of both Antediluvians and the Sodomites as 'knavery, injustice and other vices', which resulted in their destruction through unparalleled punishments by means of 'the most forceful elements of the universe ... fire and water' (see *Life of Moses* II, x, 53). Moreover, Philo refers to 'repeated destructions by fire and water (*ibid.* xlvii, 263)', which may presuppose the tradition found in rabbinic sources that the Antediluvians and the Sodomites were subjected to both a deluge and a conflagration (see the statement of R. Joḥanan b. Nappaḥa in *Genesis Rabbah* 27:3 and the parallels cited by Theodor, p. 257). See further *Mishnah Sanhedrin* 10:3, where the Sodomites, like the Antediluvians, are consigned to eternal oblivion; also *Mekhilta d'Rabbi Shimon b. Yoḥai* to Exodus 14:21 (p. 61) where the punishment of both the Antediluvians and the Sodomites is deduced from the same proof-text, Job 4:19.

Finally, we would emphasise that immorality does emerge in rabbinic sources as the main common feature in the degenerate conduct of both the Antediluvians and the Sodomites, a crime for which punishment by fire is specifically prescribed in early sources (see the statement of R. Shimon b. Yoḥai in *Mishnah Sanhedrin* 9:3, 'Had fire not been the more severe [punishment], it could have been prescribed for the daughter of a priest [who had committed adultery].' See also *Tanḥuma*, ed. Buber, 1, p. 93, where to illustrate the statement that the severity of the crime of immorality is indicated by its punishment through fire, R. Judah b. Nehemiah observes, 'Similarly the Sodomites, because they broke all bounds in their immoral conduct, were condemned to burning.' On the immorality of the Sodomites, see the sources cited by Ginzberg, *Legends*, vol. 5, p. 238, note 155).

APPENDIX 2

Job and Israel's early history as a nation

JOB 28:27–8

The text in *Genesis Rabbah* 24:5 (p. 234f) continues with a further interpretation of אדם in the name of R. Judah b. R. Simon, who once again associates Job 28:27–8 with the subject of the *Torah*. However, he has taken לאדם as לא אדם, 'not to Adam.' Despite His original intentions to bestow the Law upon Adam, when God saw his inability to observe six commandments, He decided to give the Torah with its 613 injunctions to Adam's descendants (see Theodor's observations, particularly the exposition of verses 27–8, which he cites from a manuscript commentary to *Genesis Rabbah*). It is interesting to note that R. Judah b. R. Simon has treated these two verses as a comment on the creation and not the Exodus. This is reflected further in a statement of R. Tanḥuma, who has associated verses 27–8 with the notion that the creation of the world was dependent on the *Torah* and its acceptance by Israel (see *Exodus Rabbah* 40:1, also *BT Shabbat* 98a). Presumably both these *Amora'im* based their expositions on the phrase אז ראה, which may have been taken as a verbal link with Genesis chapter 1, where the verb ראה occurs frequently.

One further passage which we may note in this context, presupposes the fuller expositions of Job 28:27 which we find in other sources, yet contains an interesting feature of its own (*Tanḥuma* Old Version, *Yitro* 15):

Thus we find with God, that He grants an answer to all creatures, and that the *Torah* is revealed before Him like a כוכב (or כתם) and when He came to give it to Israel, it is written of Him, 'Then did He see it and declare it etc. ...'

The operative expression here, which requires elucidation, is
כוכב. To translate it literally, 'the *Torah* is revealed before
Him like a *star*', yields no satisfactory meaning. Nor would this
translation be improved if we adopt the alternative reading,
כתם. We would suggest, therefore, that in this context, כוכב
is to be equated with *Hermes* = *Hermenous tou Nomou* (= דורש
התורה) = 'Law-Interpreter', hence 'the *Torah* is revealed
before Him, as before a master-expositor of the Law' (See N.
Wieder, 'The "Law-Interpreter" of the Sect of the Dead Sea
Scrolls: The Second Moses', *JJS* 4 (1953), pp. 165ff).

JOB 9

One further speech of Job which may have been associated
with Exodus and Wilderness themes is contained in chapter 9.
For example, the fragmentary *Midrash* cited earlier, published
by Mann (*ibid.*, p 237) preserves a proem based on verse 10,
'Who doeth great things (עושה גדולות) past finding out; yea,
marvellous things without number', relating to *Seder* 58 (=
Exodus 18:1ff) which presents a graphic picture of the gentile
reaction to the Exodus. According to an anonymous aggadist,
the nations of the world, on witnessing the miracle of the
Exodus, assembled in their legions to adjoin themselves to the
faith of the one true God. Following his own thesis, Mann
(*ibid.*) links the proemial verse with Isaiah 33:13, 'Hear ye that
are far off what I have done (עשיתי)' – from the corresponding
haphtarah for this *seder* – which, in turn, echoes Exodus 18:1, 'all
that God had done (עשה)'.

We would suggest, however, that the association of 9:10 with
the miracles surrounding the birth of Israelite nation, may
reflect the broader tradition that the drama of Job and his
companions was enacted against the backcloth of these events
(see pp. 24f). For the immediate context in which this verse
occurs, is a description of Job's experience of the Divine, 'Lo,
He goeth by me, and I see Him not; He passeth on also, but I
perceive Him not (v. 11).' As can be seen from the material
quoted in chapter 3, similar descriptions in the speeches of
Eliphaz and Elihu were taken as allusions to the revelation at

Sinai (see pp. 56f on 4:15–16, and pp. 59ff on 37:1ff). It is probable, therefore, that Job's comments on this theme were also treated as an allusion to the same historical events. Moreover, this has influenced the formulation of the *Ge'ulah* Benediction for the Evening Service, where the liturgical account of the miracles of the Exodus opens with 9:10. See also p. 73 , for the midrashic treatment of 9:22.

JOB 5:22FF

It is interesting to note that Masnut knew of further aggadic expositions of verses 22ff of this chapter for which no parallels can be found (see *Mayan Gannim* on Job, ed. Buber, p. 21). Quoting from an unidentified source, Masnut presents the opposing views of R. Joshua b. Levi and R. Shemuel b. Naḥman, the former applying these verses to Jacob, the latter to David's troubles with Saul, Doeg and Ahitophel. It is highly likely that an exposition of this type relating to Exodus and Wilderness themes also existed and was known to the Aramaic translator of Job. It is possible that a fragment of such an exposition has been preserved in older sources, which record a number of interpretations of verse 5, one of which does accord with the chronological order followed by the *Targum*. As we observed, the earlier verses of chapter 5 have been related specifically to the Exodus, this is reflected in the following passage, where verse 5 has been associated with Moses and Aaron and their triumph over Pharaoh (see *Pesiqta d'Rav Kahana*, ed. Friedmann, p. 70b, ed. Mandelbaum, pp. 139f, and the parallels cited there):

אשר קצירו ('Whose harvest') – referring to Pharaoh – רעב יאכל ('the hungry consumes') – referring to Moses and Aaron; ואל מצנים יקחהו (lit.: 'and taketh it even out of the thorns') [which means that they will seize it] without weapons or shields, but through prayers and supplications, as it is said, 'And the Lord said to Moses: "Why doest thou cry out (= pray) to Me? Speak to the Children of Israel and let them journey forward. (Exodus 14:15)"' ושאף צמים חילם (lit.: 'and the snare gapeth for their substance'.) – Who trampled upon the wealth of Pharaoh? Moses, Aaron and all their followers.

In all probability, the preacher has taken clauses B and C as, 'the unarmed ones will take it, and their associates will trample on their (= the Egyptians) wealth'. This presumes that **וְאַל מצנים** has been taken as **וְאַל מצנים**, associating **מצנים** with **צנה**, a shield, as is explicitly stated in *Esther Rabbah* 9:9, where Psalm 91:4, **צנה וסוחרה**, is cited as the proof-text. Similarly **שאף** has been taken in the sense of 'to tread' (see Amos 2:7 and 8:4). Finally, **צמים** has been associated with **צמת**, 'to heap', hence 'to gather together', 'to summon', the *pu'al* **מצמת**, therefore, connotes one who is summoned to follow (see Jastrow, s.v. **צמת**). On the allusion to Moses praying in Exodus 14:15, see *Targum Onqelos*, both Palestinian *Targumim* and Rashi to this verse. See also the further interpretation of Job 5:5 recorded in the sources cited above, alluding to Moses' defeat of Og and Sihon.

אור = RAIN

Although it is presupposed in several talmudic passages, the interpretation of the expression **אור** as an allusion to rain occurs explicitly in only one source, *BT Ta'anit* 7b. The *Amora*, R. Ammi, in expounding on the theme of robbery as a cause for drought, indicates that the *locus classicus* for this exegetical motif is Job 37:11, **יפיץ ענן אורו**, on the basis of which he explains a further utterance by Elihu in 36:32:

The rains are withheld only on account of the sin of robbery, as it is said, **על כפים כסה אור** (lit.: 'He covereth His hands with lightning'). Now **כפים** connotes robbery, as it is said, 'and from the robbery which is in their hands (**כפיהם**; Jonah 3:8)'; similarly **אור** connotes rain, as it said, '[Yea, He ladeth the thick cloud with moisture,] He spreadeth abroad the cloud of His rain (**אורו**).'

R. Ammi evidently rendered his proof-text as, 'On account of the sin of robbery He concealeth the rain', a rendering which is clearly reflected in the *Targum* to 36:32. This equation of **אור** in verse 32 with rain, is clearly pressuposed by R. Ammi's statement in *BT Ta'anit* 8a, where he cites the following verse **יגיד עליו רעו** as the scriptural remedy for a generation suffering from drought through the lack of those skilled in reciting incantations. See also the exposition of 37:13 preserved in both *Talmudim* (*BT Ta'anit* 8a, and *PT Ta'anit* 3:3, 66c) on the beneficial and punitive effects of rain-fall, which once again presupposes the interpretation of אור in verse 11, as rain.

In contrast with talmudic-midrashic sources, and the sparseness of its own aggadic content, the *Targum* to Job preserves no less than five examples of this exegetical motif in its rendering of 36:30 and 32, 37:11, 15 and 21. The survival of this material in a *Targum* which may have been divested of much of its former aggadic content, may not be too difficult to explain. Life-giving rain occupies a special place in the relationship between God and His worshippers in rabbinic thought, as in other early societies. Far from being a natural phenomenon, rainfall is a miracle comparable with the entire work of creation (see R. Hoshaiah's comment based on Job 5:9–10, in *Genesis Rabbah* 13:4, p 115). It is the instrument both of Divine anger and Divine pleasure. It is the manifestation of God's interest in His world and its inhabitants, whose need for rain ensures their attachment to Him (see initially *PT* and *BT Ta'anit* cited earlier; also *Genesis Rabbah* 13:3f, pp. 115ff, particularly the statement of R. Shemuel b. Naḥmani in connection with Job 5:11, in paragraph 9, p. 119). As a *Targum* was intended essentially for public usage, it is understandable that it should have been employed as a medium for the dissemination of such teachings. Thus the *Targum's* rendering of 37:11–13 is virtually a homily on the themes we have outlined.

MOSES' ABILITY TO COMMAND GOD

This notion which is developed in our sources in conjunction with Job 22:28, ותגזר אמר ויקם לך, which in its original context, contains a sentiment expressed by Eliphaz to Job. However, in the following proem, this verse is expounded by the *Amora*, R. Levi as a declaration by God to Moses (see *Exodus Rabbah* 21:2):

'[And the Lord said unto Moses:] "Wherefore criest thou unto me? (Exodus 14:15)"': Thus it is written, 'Thou shalt decree a thing, and He shall establish it for thee (Job 22:28)' – R. Levi said: 'Just as God was commanding Moses and speaking with him, so Moses was, as it were, commanding God. Thus the children of Joseph said to him, "The Lord hath commanded my lord, ... and my lord hath commanded (reading צוה, *pi'el*) the Lord (Numbers 36:2)". And just as God was calling to Moses and speaking with him, so Moses was calling to God and speaking with Him, as it is said, "And the Lord spoke to Moses, saying", and it is written, "And Moses spoke to the Lord, saying: 'Let the Lord, the God of the spirits of all flesh, set [a man over the congregation]. (*ibid.* 27:15–16)'" See how much power Moses could wield! When he saw Pharaoh pursuing after the Children of Israel, he came to cry out [to God], as it is said, "And the Lord said unto Moses: 'Wherefore criest thou unto Me?'" He said to him: "Why are you troubled?"' R. Joshua said: 'It may be compared to the friend of a king who had a cause [to plead]. He went to cry out before the king, who said to him: "Why do you cry out? Give an order, and I will do it!" Thus God said to Moses: "wherefore criest thou unto Me – speak, and I will do [whatever you say]!"'

The notion that Job 22:28 was addressed by God to Moses, giving him licence to formulate decrees which He would fulfil, can be traced back to a tannaitic source, notably the *Sifrei* to Numbers cited earlier. In conjunction with Deuteronomy 3:26, an anonymous teacher treats Job 22:28 as God's reassurance to Moses that he may still command Him in all matters save the question of his own fate (see *pisqa* 135, p. 182):

'Speak no more unto Me of this matter!' [God] said to him: 'Moses, do not make any request of me regarding this matter, but regarding any other matter, give Me your order and I will do it!' To what may it be compared? To a king who imposed a harsh decree upon his son, and he was seeking [pardon] from his father. He said to him: 'Do not make any request of me regarding this matter, but regarding any other matter, give me your order and I will do it!' Thus God said to Moses: 'Moses, do not make any request of Me regarding this matter, but regarding any other matter, give Me your order and I will do it!' [Hence it is said,] 'Thou shalt decree a thing, and He shall establish it for thee.'

It is interesting to note in conclusion, that in both *Talmudim*, Job 22:28 is applied to a further personality who was noted for his audacious behaviour towards God, Ḥoni the Circle-Drawer (see *BT Ta'anit* 23a and *PT Ta'anit* 3:12, 67a). It can hardly be mere coincidence that in rabbinic tradition, Ḥoni is regarded as a direct descendant of Moses (see *Tanḥuma*, ed. Buber, 2, p. 37).

AUDACIOUS COMMUNICATIONS WITH GOD

The present writer has attempted a partial analysis of this comprehensive and fascinating topic in an article entitled, 'The Historical and Religious Implications of *Mishnah Sotah* 5:5' (*Journal for the Study of Judaism* vol. 23, pp. 227ff). In this context we would only give some indication of the scope of this motif:

a) *Joshua*
   BT Sanhedrin 44a, the statements of R. Naḥman and Rav, who applies the Biblical term עזות to Joshua (see also Rabbenu Hananel on the text). The tradition of Joshua's bold speech can be traced back to the first century CE, when Josephus refers to his using 'freedom with God' (*Antiquities*, v, i, 13).

b) *Phineas*
   In *BT Sanhedrin* 82b, R. Eleazar b. Pedath depicts the ministering angels as seeking to attack Phineas for his audacity. However, God defends him claiming that he is 'zealot the son of a zealot' (compare R. Aqiva's *aggadah* relating to Moses cited below).

c) *Elijah*
   In *BT Berakhot* 31b–32a, Elijah, who is identified with Pinchas in rabbinic sources (see Ginzberg, *An Unknown Jewish Sect*, pp. 242ff) is depicted by R. Eleazar as blaming God for Israel's backsliding (see also *PT Sanhedrin* 10:1, 28a and, *Tanḥuma* ed. Buber, 4, p. 96, which refer also to Moses and Micah).

d) *Hannah*
   See the statement of R. Eleazar b. Pedath in BT *Berakhot* 31b.

e) *Moses*
   See initially the statements of R. Eleazar b. Pedath in *BT Berakhot* 32a (although the comment on *Exodus* 32:10 is ascribed in printed editions to R. Abahu, the reading 'R.

Eleazar' is found in MSS Munich and Paris, and is confirmed by *Midrash Ha-Gadol* to Exodus 32:10, p. 682). See
also *Numbers Rabbah* 18:12, where Moses threatens to deny
the authenticity of his mission if God were to permit
Korach and his associates to die a natural death; *Midrash
Tanna'im*, p. 14, and particularly *Exodus Rabbah* 5:22, where
in opposition to R. Ishmael who interpreted Exodus 5:23
literally, R. Aqiva amplifies Moses' offensive utterances,
and depicts the attribute of Divine Justice as seeking to slay
him.

f) *Abraham*

Of particular interest are the bold discourses ascribed to
Abraham on Mount Moriah were, according to the Biblical
narrative, he had remained silent; see *Tanḥuma*, ed. Buber,
1, pp. 114–15 (it is interesting to note the similarity
between Abraham's adamant refusal to depart from
Moriah and Ḥoni's confrontation with God in *Mishnah
Ta'anit* 3:8); see also *Genesis Rabbah* 56:8, p. 604; and 49:8–9,
pp. 506–11 (on Abraham's intercession on behalf of the
Sodomites) and particularly *Tanḥuma*, ed. Buber, 1, p. 90.

The archetypal sage

A LECTIONARY CYCLE FROM THE HAGIOGRAPHA

It would be difficult to find any support in the varied selection
of proemial verses cited above from *Genesis Rabbah* 39 for the
attractive theory that there was a cycle of readings from the
Hagiographa to complement the weekly pentateuchal and
prophetic lections, which may have provided the early
preachers with an immediate source for the verses upon which
they based their homilies (see I. Elbogen, *Ha-Tephillah b'Yisrael
b'Hitpathutah Ha-Historit*, trans. J. Amir and J. Heinemann, Tel
Aviv 1972, p. 139, and notes 8–10, p. 433). In the light of this
theory, what plausible explanation could be offered for the
phenomenon of five proems based on four different selections
from the Hagiographa, unless we assume that there were
diverse cycles of hagiographic readings in vogue at different
times, or in different locations. This, in the opinion of the
present writer, would be beyond the acceptable limits of conjecture.

Even the most obvious 'candidate' for a possible lectionary
role among the texts represented in these proems, Psalm 45,
was not linked exclusively with this *seder*. Verses 3–4 form the
basis of proem relating to *Seder* 14, and verse 3 occurs again as a
proemial text in connection with *Seder* 20. Consequently, if
Psalm 45 formed part of a lectionary cycle, with which *seder*
was it associated? We may also note a similar phenomenon in
Aggadat Bereshit in connection with Psalm 110. This comparatively late midrashic work apparently follows the Palestinian triennial cycle (see ed. Buber, Cracow 5663 (reprinted

Jerusalem 5733) Introduction, p. ix) and contains homilies not
only for each *Torah*-reading and its corresponding lection from
the Prophets, but also a homily based on a psalm. Psalm 110
has provided the texts for the psalm-homilies of no less than five
consecutive *sedarim*, all of which relate to Abraham (see chapters 18, 21, 24, 27 and 30). From the ample material we have
analysed in chapter 5, it is quite clear that both Psalm 45 and
110 were traditionally regarded as 'Abrahamic' psalms. We
would argue, therefore, that this was the determining factor
which influenced the choice of verses from these psalms when
dealing with the subject of Abraham, rather than a conjectural
lectionary cycle.

THE MIDRASHIC TREATMENT OF PROVERBS 11:30

The full text of *Midrash Ha-Gadol* to Genesis 18:1 is as follows:

Why [did God reveal Himself to Abraham] at an oak? To inform you
that just as a tree when it is pruned, produces fruit, so Abraham when
he was circumcised, had the merit of producing fruit, as it is said,
פרי צדיק עץ חיים ולקח נפשות חכם.

The proof-text has been left untranslated, because the anonymous exegete has simply not indicated how he related it to his
theme of the patriarch's circumcision. The expression צדיק in
clause A would have been sufficient to establish a link with
Abraham, who was regarded as preeminent among the righteous (see above, pp. 143f). We would suggest, however, that the
main verbal links were provided by clause B, which we have
incorporated into the text. Both the term חכם, and the phrase
לקח נפשות, could be regarded as epithets for Abraham,
particularly the latter which clearly recalls Genesis 12:5, ויקח
אברם וגו' ... ואת הנפש אשר עשו בחרן. As is well known,
this verse is traditionally interpreted as a reference to Abraham's proselytising activities (see *Genesis Rabbah* 39:14, and the
parallels cited by Theodor, p. 378). It is interesting to note,
therefore, the same interpretation was placed upon Proverbs
11:30 already in a tannaitic source.

Tosephta Pe'ah 4:18 (p. 24; see also *PT Pe'ah* 1:1, 15b) records
a remarkable act of charity by King Monobaz, who, together

with other members of the royal family of Adiabene, had
converted to Judaism (see Genesis 46:10, p. 467; also *JE* 1, pp.
191f). Contrasting his own conduct with that of his forebears,
he declares, 'My ancestors accumulated treasures of money,
but I have accumulated treasures of souls, as it is said, "The
fruit of the righteous is a tree of life, and the wise man acquires
souls."' The allusion here is probably to Monobaz's efforts to
win converts for his adopted faith from among his own subjects.
This conforms with the pattern of the convert-missionary type,
like Abraham, Jethro and Job, developed in early sources.
These are depicted as royal figures who, following their own
conversion, proceed to play a missionary role among their own
people, or former associates (see my article, 'Literary Motifs in
the Testament of Job', *JJS* vol. 20 (1970) pp. 4ff).

How the anonymous teacher interpreted clause A, which
apparently formed the basis of his comment, poses a more
serious problem. We would suggest initially that he identified
עץ חיים with *Torah*, an obvious aggadic device based on
Proverbs 3:18, 'It (referring to חכמה = *Torah* in verse 13) is a
tree of life to them that lay hold upon it.' However, he may
have taken the identification one stage further, equating *Torah*
in this context specifically with circumcision. This specific
interpretation of *Torah* is to be found in *Midrash Ha-Gadol* in
conjunction with Genesis 26:5, the pentateuchal source for the
wide-spread rabbinic tradition relating to Abraham's study
and observance of the Torah (see p. 447): תורתי – this refers
[specifically] to circumcision, which is of equal importance to
the whole of the *Torah*.'

Although this interpretation of Genesis 26:5 is not found in
any early source, the equation of *Torah* with circumcision does
occur in an addendum to *Mishnah Nedarim* 3:11, which was
known to *Tosaphot* and Rabbenu Nissim (*Ran*; see *BT Nedarim*
31b; also the *Mishnah* as cited in *PT Nedarim* 37d). Thus clause
A may be rendered midrashically as 'The fruit (i.e. progeny) of
the righteous [resulted from] circumcision.'

The archetypal priest-king

THE EXPOSITION OF CANTICLES 1:4 IN *MIDRASH ZUTTA*

We may note initially that R. Joshua's exposition of Canticles 1:4 is a further example of a well-known motif in early rabbinic exegesis to equate love for God primarily with the endurance of suffering and death, which received fresh impetus during the period of the Hadrianic Persecution. Its *locus classicus* is the *Sifrei* to Deuteronomy 6:5, the injunction to love God with all one's soul (*pisqa* 32, see Finkelstein, p. 55 for parallels). See further the graphic exposition of Exodus 20:6, לאהבי ולשמרי מצותי, by R. Aqiva's pupil, R. Meir, with reference to the heroism of his contemporaries in the Holy Land (*Mekhilta d'Rabbi Ishmael, Yitro, Massekhta d'Ba-Ḥodesh* 6, p. 227). See also R. Aqiva's own equally dramatic portrayal of the pagan nations' reactions to Israel's heroic and determined allegiance to God in the face of suffering and death (see *Mekhilta d'Rabbi Ishmael* to Exodus 15:2, *Beshallaḥ Massekhta d'Shirta* 3, p. 127). According to R. Aqiva, Canticles 1:3, על כן עלמות אהבוך, is descriptive of his own generation, who 'loved You unto death!' (אהבוך עד מות).

It is probably in this same context, that we should view the concluding interpretation of Canticles 1:4 in *Midrash Zutta*, which singles out the two scholars whose names are specifically associated with the interpretation of Deuteronomy 6:5 in terms of martyrdom, R. Aqiva and Ben Azzai (see *Sifrei* to Deuteronomy 6:5, p. 55 and *BT Berakhot* 61b):

נזכירה דדיך מיין, 'We proclaim your *scholars* to be better than wine!' Yet is it possible for a breast to produce wine?! However, just as a breast flows with milk, so R. Aqiva arose and revealed (פלש) the secrets of the Torah. מישרים אהבוך – this refers to Ben Azzai and his associates.

Although the passage is terse and its imagery elusive, it does not defy explanation. Firstly, we have phenomenon of an implied *al tiqrei*, *dodekha* being read as *daddekha*, 'thy breasts', a reading which was actually adopted by the LXX: *Agapesomen mastous sou hyper oinon*, 'we will love *thy breasts* more than wine'. This is also the rendering of verse 2, כי טובים דדיך מיין: *hoti agathoi mastoi sou hyper oinon*, '*Thy breasts* are better than wine', which is presupposed once more by *Midrash Zutta*, p. 8. As to the symbolism of the scholar as a breast, this reflects R. Aqiva's own imagery for the teacher-pupil relationship, which he employed in response to R. Shimon b. Yoḥai's request that he should teach even though he was incarcerated by the Romans: יותר ממה שהעגל רוצה לינק, הפרה רוצה להיניק, 'More than the calf wishes to suckle, the cow wishes to give its milk!' See *BT Pesaḥim* 112a; also the interpretation of שדים in the third proem in *Genesis Rabbah* 39, based on Canticles 8:8, which is discussed above, p. 133; see further the strophe in Yannai's *piyyut* for the first day of *Pesah* (Zulay *Piyyutei Yannai*, p. 265):

אלה דדי דברת דת \ דורות דיצת דורשי דבר יי

'These are the "masters" of the word of the Law; the joyous generations of expositors of the word of the Lord.'

A further problem is presented by the term פלש, the precise meaning of which is difficult to determine in this context (see, however, *Arukh Completum*, v, pp. 358f; Ben Yehudah, s.v. פלש II, p. 4967; Bacher, *Die Agada der Tannaïten*, p. 266). Our rendering is based primarily upon the use of this expression in early *piyyutim*, particularly with reference to the revelation at Sinai. Thus, in a *Qedushta* for *Shevuot* attributed to Yannai (Zulay, p. 366) we find:

אמנה פילשתה / בחדש אשר שילשתה
גובה הר תלשתה / דיברות כן דרשתה

'You expounded (or revealed) the Covenant (= *Torah*) in Your designated third month (Sivan). You plucked up the lofty mountain and thus You elaborated upon the Decalogue.' (See *Mekhilta d'Rabbi Ishmael*, *Yitro Massekhta d'Ba-Ḥodesh*, 3, p. 214)

A similar phrase is used by Qaliri to describe Ezra, the 'Second Moses', in a composition preserved in the Ashkenazi Rite for *Hosha'na Rabbah*: סופר מהיר מפלש אמנה, 'The ready scribe, expositor of the covenant' (see Nehemiah 10:1). Moreover, Qaliri actually employs פלש as a synonym for גלה in a *Yozer* preserved in the Ashkenazi Rite for the first day of *Rosh Ha-Shanah*:

מלך פלש סוד המעמיקים / לסתיר עצה במעמקים / יחשף ויגלה עמוקים

'The King who disclosed the secret of those who plot deeply to conceal counsel in the depths, He searches out and reveals deep matters.'

The use of this term in connection with Aqiva probably reflects his reputation as the outstanding interpreter of the Law in his generation, 'who brought to light matters which were [hitherto] concealed from mortals'. This is how he was described by his contemporary R. Tarphon, who applied to him a verse from a chapter significantly associated with Moses in early aggadic exegesis (see above, pp. 44ff) Job 28:11 (see *Avot d'Rabbi Natan* Version A, chapter 6, p. 29; in Version B, chapter 12, this is ascribed to R. Eliezer). As such, this may be a reference to Aqiva's innovative method of halakhic exegesis and not purely to his esoteric learning, as is suggested in the parallel passage in *Midrash Hallel* (see Jellineck, *Bet Hamidrasch*, 5, p. 97; this source reads פירש for פלש, which, as Schechter (*Agadath Shir HaShirim*, p. 57, note to lines 361–64) observes, is found also in Moses b. Samuel Ibn Tibbon's commentary to Canticles 1:4. However, this appears to be a case of replacing an obscure term with a more familiar one.) Finally the reference at the conclusion of the above passage to Ben Azzai and his associates, is possibly an allusion to those scholars who shared his heroic fate (see *Lamentations Rabbah* 2:2, ed. Buber, p. 100).

Select bibliography

PRINCIPAL RABBINIC TEXTS
(to which page numbers cited in the notes refer)

Avot d'Rabbi Natan, ed. S. Schechter, London 1886.

Babylonian Talmud (BT), ed. Romm, Vilna 1880–6 (of which most recent reprints are photocopies).

Diqduqei Sof'rim, Variae Lectiones in Mischnam et in Talmud Babylonicum, ed. R. Rabbinovicz, vols. 1–15, Munich 1868–86; vol. 16, Przemysl 1897; repr. 12 vols., New York 1960.

Genesis Rabbah, ed. J. Theodor and Ch. Albeck, Berlin 1913–32.

Leviticus Rabbah, ed. M. Margulies, Jerusalem 1953 *et seq.*

Mekhilta d'Rabbi Ishmael, ed. H. Horovitz and I. A. Rabin, Frankfurt 1931, 2nd edition, Jerusalem 1960.

Mekhilta d'Rabbi Shimon b. Yohai, ed. J. N. Epstein, Jerusalem 1955.

Midrash Ha-Gadol: Genesis, ed. M. Margulies, 2nd edition, Jerusalem 1967; *Exodus*, ed. M. Margulies, 2nd edition, Jerusalem 1967; *Leviticus*, ed. A. Steinsalz, Jerusalem 1975; *Numbers*, ed. Z. M. Rabinowitz, 2nd edition, Jerusalem 1973; *Deuteronomy*, ed. S. Fisch, Jerusalem 1972.

Midrash Psalms, ed. S. Buber, Vilna 1891.

Midrash Rabbah to the Pentateuch and the Five Megillot, ed. Romm, Vilna 1878 (of which most recent reprints are photocopies).

Midrash Tanhuma, Old Version or Ordinary Edition.

Midrash Tanhuma, ed. S. Buber, Vilna 1885 (repr. Jerusalem 1964).

Midrash Tannaim, ed. D. Hoffmann, Berlin 1908–9.

Palestinian Talmud (PT), ed. Krotoschin (repr. Jerusalem 1960).

Pesiqta d'Rav Kahana, ed. S. Buber, Lyck 1868; also ed. B. Mandelbaum, New York 1962.

Sifra, ed. J. H. Weiss, Vienna 1861.

Sifrei Numbers, ed. H. S. Horovitz, repr. Jerusalem 1966.

Sifrei Deuteronomy, eds. H. S. Horovitz and L. Finkelstein, Berlin 1939, repr. New York 1969.

194   *Select bibliography*

Tosephta, ed. M. S. Zuckermandel, Jerusalem 1937.
Yalqut Shimoni, ed. Romm, Vilna 1898. Ed. D. Hyman, D. N. Lerrer
  and I. Shiloni (to the Pentateuch), Jerusalem 1973.

ADDITIONAL RABBINIC TEXTS

Agadath Shir HaShirim, ed. S. Schechter, Cambridge 1896.
Aggadat Bereshit, ed. S. Buber, Cracow 1903 (repr. Jerusalem 5733).
Alphabet of Ben Sira (1 and 2), ed. M. Steinschneider, Berlin 1858.
Battei Midrashot, second edition enlarged and revised by A. J.
  Wertheimer (2 vols.), Jerusalem 1950.
Bereshit Rabbati, ed. Ch. Albeck, Jerusalem 1940.
Bet Ha-midrasch, ed. A. Jellineck (vols. 1–6), Leipzig 1853–77.
Liqqutim Mi-Midrash Abkir, ed. S. Buber, Vienna 1883.
Mayan Gannim, ed. S. Buber, Berlin 1889.
Midrash Leqah Tov, Genesis and Exodus, ed. S. Buber, Vilna 1884;
  Leviticus, Numbers and Deuteronomy, ed. M. Katzenellenbogen (of
  Padua), Vilna 1884.
Midrash Sekhel Tov (to *Genesis* and *Exodus*), ed. S. Buber, Berlin
  1900/1901.
Midrash Zutta, ed. S. Buber, Berlin 1896 (repr. Tel Aviv).
Parshandatha (The Commentary of Rashi on the Prophets and the Hagiographa) Part III: Psalms, ed. I. Maarsen, Jerusalem 1936.
Pesiqta Rabbati, ed. M. Friedmann, Vilna 1880.
Pirqei d'Rabbi Eliezer, Warsaw 1952 (repr. Jerusalem 1963); also the
  translation of G. Friedlander, London 1916 (repr. New York 1981).
Seder Eliahu Rabbah (including *Seder Eliahu Zuta*), ed. M. Friedmann,
  Vienna 1902 and 1904 (repr. Jerusalem 1960).
Seder Olam Rabbah, ed. B. Ratner, Vilna 1897 (repr. Jerusalem 1988).

EARLY NON-RABBINIC SOURCES

The Apocrypha and Pseudepigrapha of the Old Testament, ed. R. H.
  Charles, Oxford 1913.
Philo, trans. F. H. Colson and G. H. Whitaker, Loeb Classical
  Library, London/Cambridge (Mass) 1956–7.
Pseudo-Philo: Liber Antiquitatum Biblicarum, ed. G. Kisch, Indiana
  1949; for trans. see M. R. James, London 1917.
Sepher Ben Sira Ha-Shalem, ed. M. H. Segal, Jerusalem 1958.
The Testament of Abraham, trans. G. H. Box, London 1927.
The Testament of Job, ed. M. R. James, *Apocrypha Anecdota*, Cambridge
  1897, pp. 104–137.
  ed. K. Kohler (English translation)

Semitic Studies in Memory of Alexander Kohut, Berlin 1897, pp. 264–353.
ed. S. P. Brock, *Pseudepigrapha Veteris Testamenti Graece*, vol. 2, Leiden 1967.

MODERN LITERATURE

Albeck, Ch., *Mavo l'Mishnah*, Tel Aviv 1959.
Mavo l'Talmudim, Tel Aviv 1969.
Allon, G., *The History of the Jews in the Land of Israel in the Period of the Mishnah and the Talmud* (Hebrew), 2 vols., 3rd edition, Tel Aviv 1958.
Amir, J., 'Philo's Homilies on Love and Fear and their Relationship to Palestinian *Midrashim*', *Zion* vol. 30 (1965), pp. 47–60.
Avigad, N. and Yadin, Y., *A Genesis Apocryphon, A Scroll from the Wilderness of Judea*, Jerusalem 1956.
Bacher, W., *Die Agada der Tannaïten*, Strasburg 1884.
Die Agada der Palästinenischen Amoräer, Strasburg 1892.
Die Prömien der alten jüdischen Homilie, Leipzig 1913.
'Das Targum zu Hiob', *MGWJ*, vol. 20 (1871), pp. 208–23.
Bloch, P., 'Studien zur Aggadah', *MGWJ*, vol. 34 (1885), pp. 166–84.
Bowker, J., *The Targums and Rabbinic Literature*, Cambridge 1969.
Büchler, A., *The Political and Social Leaders of the Jewish Community of Sepphoris in the Second and Third Centuries*, London 1909.
Studies in Sin and Atonement, Oxford 1928.
Cassuto, U., *Commentary to the Book of Exodus* (Hebrew), 3rd edition, Jerusalem 1959.
Commentary to the Book of Genesis – Part I: From Adam to Noah, trans. I. Abrahams, Jerusalem 1961.
'Epic Poetry in Ancient Israel' (Hebrew), *K'neset l'Zekher H. N. Bialik* vol. 8 (5703), pp. 121–42 (subsequently republished in his *Studies on the Bible and the Ancient Orient – Volume 1: Biblical and Canaanite Literatures*, Jerusalem 1972, pp. 62–90).
The Goddess Anath, trans. I. Abrahams, Jerusalem 1971.
Churgin, P., *Targum Ketuvim*, New York 1945.
Driver, G. R., *The Judaean Scrolls*, Oxford 1965.
Easton, B. S., *The Epistle of St. James, Interpreter's Bible*, vol. 12, New York 1957.
Elbogen, I., *Jewish Prayer in its Historical Development* (Hebrew), trans. from the German and enlarged by J. Amir and J. Heinemann, Tel Aviv 1972.
Epstein, L. M., *Marriage Laws in the Bible and in the Talmud*, Cambridge (Mass.) 1942.

Finkelstein, L., *Mavo li-M'sekhtot Avot v'Avot d'Rabbi Natan*, New York 1950.
Fischel, H. A., 'Martyr and Prophet', *JQR* (NS) vol. 37, pp. 265–80 and 363–86.
Fishbane, M., *Biblical Interpretation in Ancient Israel*, Oxford 1985.
Frankl, Z., 'Die Zusätze in der LXX zu Hiob', *MGWJ*, vol. 21 (1872), pp. 306–15.
Fruedenthal, J., *Hellenistiche Studien* (parts 1 and 2), Breslau 1874–5.
Gaster, T. H., *Thespis*, revised edition, New York 1966.
Gelles, B. J., *Peshat and Derash in the Exegesis of Rashi*, Leiden 1981.
Ginzberg, L., *The Legends of the Jews* (7 vols.), Philadelphia 1909–55.
Ginzei Schechter (*Geniah Studies in Memory of Dr Solomon Schechter*) vol. 1: *Midrash and Haggadah*, New York 1928.
'*Mabul shel-Esh*', *Ha-Goren* vol. 8, pp. 35–51.
An Unknown Jewish Sect, trans R. Marcus, H. L. Ginsberg, Z. Gotthold and A. Hertzberg, New York 1976.
Gordon, C. H., 'Leviathan: Symbol of Evil', *Biblical Motifs: Origins and Transformations*, ed. A. Altmann, Cambridge (Mass.) 1966, pp. 1–9.
'Hebrew Origins in the Light of Recent Discovery', *Biblical and other Studies*, ed. A. Altmann, Cambridge (Mass.) 1963, pp. 3–14.
Ugaritic Textbook, Rome 1965.
Gunkel, H., *Schöpfung und Chaos in Urzeit und Endzeit*, Göttingen 1895.
Hartman, G. H. and Budick, S. (eds.), *Midrash and Literature*, Yale 1986.
Heinemann, I., *Darkhei Ha-Aggadah*, Jerusalem 1949 (3rd edition 1973).
Heinemann, J., 'The Proem in the Aggadic Midrashim – A Form-Critical Study', *Scripta Hierosolymitana* 22 (1971), pp. 100–22.
Jacobs, I., 'Literary Motifs in the Testament of Job', *JJS* vol. 21 (1970), pp. 1ff.
'Elements of Near-Eastern Mythology in Rabbinic Aggadah', *JJS* vol. 28 (1977), pp. 1ff.
'The Historical and Ideological Implications of *Mishnah Sotah* 5:5', *Journal for the Study of Judaism* vol. 23 (1992), pp. 227ff.
'Understanding Rabbinic Midrash', *L'Eylah* no. 21 (Spring 1986) pp. 53–7.
Jastrow, M., *A Dictionary of the Targumim, the Talmud Babli and Yerushalmi, and the Midrashic Literature*, London/New York 1903.
Kohler, K. 'Reading from the Law', *JE*, vol. 7, New York/London 1925, pp. 647–8.
Komlosh, Y., *The Bible in the Light of the Aramaic Translations* (Hebrew), Tel Aviv 1973.

Lachs, S. T., *A Rabbinic Commentary on the New Testament: The Gospels of Matthew, Mark and Luke*, Hoboken 1987.

Lauterbach, J. Z., 'The Ancient Jewish Allegorists in the Talmud and Midrash' *JQR* (NS) vol. 1 (1910–11), pp. 291–333 and 503–31.

Peshat, JE vol. 9, pp. 652f.

Levy, J., *Neuhebräisches und Chaldäisches Wörterbuch über die Talmudim und Midraschim*, Leipzig 1876–89.

Lewis, J. P., *A Study of the Interpretation of Noah and the Flood in Jewish and Christian Literature*, Leiden 1968.

Lieberman, S., *Tosephta kiPh'shutah* (Orders *Mo'ed*, *Zera'im* and *Nashim*), New York 1955–67.

Greek in Jewish Palestine, New York 1942.

'Roman Legal Institutions in Early Rabbinics and in the Acta Martyrium', *JQR* vol. 35 (1944–5), pp. 17ff.

Loewe, R. J., 'The "Plain" Meaning of Scripture in Early Jewish Exegesis', *Papers of the Institute of Jewish Studies*, vol. 1 (ed. G. J. Weiss), Jerusalem 1964, pp. 140ff.

Löw, I., 'Lexikalische Mizellen', *Festschrift zum Siebzigsten Gebürstage David Hoffmanns*, Berlin 1914, pp. 119–38.

Löwenstamm, S. E., *The Tradition of the Exodus and its Development* (Hebrew), Jerusalem 1965.

Mann, J., *The Bible as Read and Preached in the Old Synagogue*, vol. 1, Cincinnati 1940; vol. 2 (completed by I. Sonne) 1966.

Marmorstein, A., 'The Background to the Aggadah', *HUCA* vol. 6 (1929), pp. 141–204.

Mayer, A., *Das Rätsel des Jacobusbriefes*, Giessen 1930.

Melamed, E. Z., *M'phar'shei Ha-Miqra*, Jerusalem 1978, vol. 1 pp. 5ff.

Mowinckel, S., *The Psalms in Israel's Worship*, trans. D. R. Ap-Thomas, 2 vols., Oxford 1962.

Pope, M. H., *Job* (The Anchor Bible), New York 1965.

Pritchard, J. B. (ed.), *Ancient Near Eastern Texts*, Princeton 1954.

Rabinowitz, L. I., *Peshat, EJ* vol. 13, 329–31.

Rönsch, H., *Das Buch der Jubiläen*, Leipzig 1874.

Sandmel, S., 'Philo's Place in Judaism', *HUCA* vol. 26 (1955) pp. 151–332.

Schirman, J., 'The Battle between Behemoth and Leviathan According to an Ancient Hebrew *Piyyut*', *Proceedings of the Israel Academy of Sciences and Humanities* vol. 4 (1969–70), pp. 327–369.

Seeligmann, I. L., 'Voraussetzungen der Midraschexegese', *VTSup* 1 (1953), pp. 150ff.

Segal, M. H., *Parshanut Ha-Miqra, S'qira al Tol'doteha v'Hitpathuta*, repr. Jerusalem 1980, pp. 7ff.

Sidebottom, E. M., *The Epistle of James, The Century Bible* (New Edition), London 1967.

Spiegel, S., 'Me-Aggadot Ha-Aqedah', *Alexander Marx Jubilee Volume* (Hebrew Section), New York 1950, pp. 471–547 (published separately in an English translation by J. Goldin, under the title *The Last Trial*, New York 1967, repr. 1979).

Strack, H. L. and Billerbeck, P., *Kommentar zum Neuen Testament aus Talmud und Midrasch*, 6 Vols, Munich 1956.

Strack, H. L. and Stemberger, G., *Introduction to the Talmud and Midrash*, trans. M Bockmuehl, Edinburgh 1991.

Tur-Sinai, N. H., *The Book of Job: A New Commentary*, Jerusalem 1957.

Urbach, E. E., 'Ascesis and Suffering in Talmudic and Midrashic Literature', *Yitzhak F Baer Jubilee Volume*, Jerusalem 1960, pp. 48–68.

The Sages: Their Opinions and Beliefs, translated by I. Abrahams, Jerusalem 1975.

Vajda, G., *L'amour de Dieu dans la theologie juive du Moyen Age*, Paris 1957.

Vermes, G, *Scripture and Tradition in Judaism*, Leiden 1973.

Wieder, N., *The Judean Scrolls and Karaism*, London 1962.

'The "Law-Interpreter" of the Sect of the Dead Sea Scrolls: The Second Moses', *JJS* vol. 4 (1953), pp. 158–75.

Weiss-Halivni, D., *Peshat and Derash*, Oxford 1991.

Zulay, M., *Iyyunei Lashon b'Phiyyutei Yannai*, Studies of the Research Institute for Hebrew Poetry in Jerusalem, vol. 6 (1945), pp. 161–248.

Piyyutei Yannai: Liturgical Poems of Yannai Collected from Genizah Manuscripts and other Sources, Berlin 1938.

Zunz, L., *Ha-Drashot b'Yisrael*, ed. and enlarged by Ch. Albeck, Jerusalem 1954.

Index of sources

A   Hebrew Bible
B   Apocrypha and Pseudepigrapha
C   Philo and Josephus
D   New Testament and early Christian
     writings
E   Ancient Near Eastern sources
F   Talmud, *Midrash* and *Targum*

A   HEBREW BIBLE

Genesis
2:23 56n, 90n
3:24 99n
4:19 34
6:2 37
6:3 27, 176
6:4 27n
6:5 173
6:9 30, 32
6:11 35n
6:13 26, 29
7:12 37
8:2 39n
11:29 91n
12:1ff 91
12:2 125
12:5 125n, 188
12:10ff 139
12:17 140
13:13 134
13:15 127
13:17 127, 128n
14:1 113, 119
14:1ff 94, 114
14:14 114–15, 117n
14:15 113
14:17 93n, 122n, 123–4
14:18 115
14:18ff 123

15:1 89, 152
15:1ff 85
15:3 74, 87
15:5 87, 138, 151n, 152
15:6 143, 146, 151
15:7 83n, 134n
15:18f 152n
17:11 116
18:4–8 119
18:11 40
18:14 137
18:17 91, 152–3
18:18 153
18:19 117, 135
18:25ff 118
20:7 89n
20:15 134
20:18 138
22:2 144, 149n
22:5 152n
22:6 5
22:10 5
22:11 6
22:12 146, 149n
22:14 149n
22:16–17 151
22:17 151n
22:17–18 153
22:18 90n

199

22:20 91n
22:21ff 89
23:2 136
23:5 91
23:6 123
24:1 135
25:19ff 94
26:5 82, 84n, 85, 88, 189
31:13 107
31:35 40
38:18 108
39:21 74
41:18 44n
41:43 102

Exodus
2:15 60n
2:16–19 7
3:3 44
3:4 122
3:5 122
3:7 71
3:10 68
3:13 51
3:16 51
3:19 49
4:1 68
4:10 68
4:13 68
4:19 60n
4:27 61n
4:29 51
4:31 51
5:22–3 74n
6:6 5
6:12–13 48
7:3 49
7:16–17 62
7:23 49
7:27 63
8:28 49
9:12 49
9:13 63
9:19 63
9:20 25n
9:24 37n
10:1 49
10:21 48n
12:8 51n
12:21 51
14:15 181, 183
14:27 63
15:2 76n
15:3 61

15:13 76n
16:14 66
17:7 175
17:8 44n
17:16 100
18:1 121, 180
19:16 57
19:19 60, 77
20:6 190
20:15 46n
20:18 77
21:1 57, 174
22:19 66
25:6 111
28:13 100n
32:9 71
32:10 185
32:11 65
32:13 66
34:1 70
35:35 101
39:33 101

Leviticus
1:1 46
6:2 36
7:35 107n 111
18:6 89n
21:10 131
26:14 176

Numbers
1:51 122
7:89 46, 47n, 78n
11:22 74n
12:3 48n, 74, 99
13:32 73
14:17–18 74
16:26 54n
16:35 54n, 56
20:8ff 75
20:16 65
22:9 107n
22:20 67
23:10 67
25:2 74
27:15–16 184
31:2 64
36:2 184

Deuteronomy
3:24 72
3:25 73
3:26 184
3:27 73
6:5 92n, 125n, 148n

8:7 73, 135n
9:19 65
32:13 102n
32:17 57
32:18 70n
32:41 58
33:2 103n
33:5 101
33:21 100
Joshua
10:13 129
24:3ff 134
Judges
19:29 5
1 Samuel
3:14 5
2 Samuel
1:18 129
7:18 123
8:18 121
2 Kings
14:9ff 142
Isaiah
2:4 8
9:6 108n
16:5.118
19:4 105n
27:1 159n, 163, 166n
33:13 180
33:14 95n
33:15 129
41:1–13 114
41:2 114
41:3 114
41:7 117n
41:8 114
41:24 63n
57:2 45
63:15 125
Jeremiah
22:23 142
51:9 81
Ezekiel
17:1ff 142
17:22 142
17:22–3 137n
17:24 137
20:7
20:18 35n
21:31 111
Hosea
2:12 89n
9:10 138

12:12 71
Amos
8:4 182n
Jonah
2:9 71n
3:8 182
Micah
7:20 73
Habakuk
3:17 137
Zachariah
4:14 107n, 109–112, 130–1n
11:2 142
14:3 120
Malachi
2:5 74
Psalms
1:1 134
1:3 138
2:2 120
4:3 89n
11:5 30
16:6 84n
16:7 84, 135
25:15 140
29:3–9 76
29:4 77
29:4–5 46, 77n
29:7 77, 78n
29:9–11 77
29:11 76–8, 105n
33:7 157
37:14–15 129n
45:2 100
45:3 96
45:3–10 99–100
45:3–4 96–7
45:4 8, 104
45:5–6 102–3
45:6 102
45:7–8 98n
45:8 81, 95, 97, 103, 107n, 118
45:9 97
45:10 97, 104
45:11 104
45:11–12 80, 95–6
45:13 97
45:14 100
45:15 101
45:17 97
48:11 117
50:10 167
58:11 64–5

77:15 76n
78:61 78
80:15 138
89:7 160
92:8–10 137n
92:13 136, 140, 143
92:14 136
92:15 135, 138
99:3 76n
110:1 108, 118n, 124
110:1–2 117
110:1–4 113
110:2 108–9
110:3 114–15
110:4 108, 109–10, 116n, 131
110:5 108
110:6–7 112
122:8 101
128:3 138
132:8 78
149:6 99n
Proverbs
2:7 84, 129n
2:10 82n
2:14–16 82
3:4 91
3:5 92n
3:6 91–2
3:7 81
3:8 90, 91n
3:32 129n
4:2 89n
5:1 82n
7:22–23 67
8:14 70n
8:15 105n
9:8 82n
9:10 82n
10:1 94
10:8 81, 92
10:19 83n
11:30 93–4
12:18 82n
13:24 92n
14:1 94
14:14 88–9
14:16 81, 85–6
14:30 90
16:4 49n
23:2 10–11
25:6 21–2
25:20 11–12
28:2 94

30:14 5
Job
1:1 25n
1:6 28n
4:12–13 67n
4:15–16 56–7
4:19 178
4:20–1 174
4:21 57
5:12–15 53
5:19–23 53–4
5:22ff 181–2
5:5 182
5:9–11 183
6:17 35–9
6:18 40
8:11 44n
9:7 161n
9:8 156–7
9:10 157n, 180
9:11 180
9:22 73
11:6 69–70
11:9 70
11:11 70–71
12:5 39
12:11 51n
12:12 51, 82n
12:16 50n
12:23 49–50
12:23–4 48–49
12:24 49
14:7–9 135–6
15:34 54n
15:28–34 54–5
15:30 46n
17:9 73
19:29 32
21:8 175
21:9–15 28
21:11 175
21:15 36, 175–6
22:14 175
22:20 35–8
22:28 183–4
23:13 72
24:2 41
24:2–4 30–1, 177
24:7 31–2
24:11 26
24:13 35
24:14 31
24:14 and 16 173

24:16 177
24:18 32, 33n
24:20 29
24:21 34
26:9 65n
26:12 61, 155, 157
28:5ff 177
28:11 192
28:12 61, 82n
28:12–14 45
28:12ff 47n
28:21–3 45
28:25–26 46, 77n
28:27–28 47–8, 179–80
28:28 48n
32:2 137n
33:15 68n
33:15–17 67
33:22–4 65–6
33:24 66, 67n
33:28–9 68
33:29 68n
34:24 66n
34:29 174–5
35:9 29n
36:7 64
36:14 63–4
36:22 62–3
36:32 182
37:2 59–60
37:5 46–7n, 60
37:11 183
37:13 183
37:24 82n
38:8 and 10 157
38:8ff 156
40:16ff 164n
40:19 163–4, 166
40:23 164n
40:25 163
40:30–1 158n
40:31 161n
40:32 158
41:7 160

41:8 160
41:9 160
41:17 158n, 159n, 160
41:18–21 158
41:18 160
41:19 160
41:20 160
41:22 161n
41:23 64n
41:23–4 158n
Canticles
1:1–2 125–6
1:3 80, 124–5, 130, 131, 190
1:4 126, 129–30, 190–2
1:13 144n
1:17 143
4:6 97, 144
4:12 101
5:15 143
8:8 191
8:8–10 80, 133–4
Ecclesiastes
2:3 82n
2:13 82n
2:14–16 93
4:13–14 93
7:1 132–3
7:19 81
9:2 73
10:2 93
Ruth
3:8 40
Esther
6:11 102n
7:10 39n
Daniel
4:28 33n
8:2 119n
Nehemiah
9:8 150
2 Chronicles
6:41 78n
18:25ff 142n
20:7 150n

B APOCRYPHA AND PSEUDEPIGRAPHA

Ben Sira
44:20–1 151
1 Enoch
5:6f 27n
8:2–3 27n

20:7 164n
2 Enoch
10:1–6 37n
34:1–2 27n

Jubilees
3:30 31n
7:20 31n
7:20ff 29n, 32n
17:15–19:9 145–6n
18:11 147n
18:16 147n
19:3 151n
19:8ff 84n
19:8–9 128
21:2–3 149n
1 Maccabees
2:52 150–1

4 Maccabees
14:20 148n
Testament of Job
10:14ff 161n
Testament of Levi
3:2 37n
Sybilla i
177–201 29n
204ff 32n
Zadokite Fragments
p. 3, lines 2 and 3–4 150
Genesis Apocryphon
col. 19, p. 41 139–40

C PHILO AND JOSEPHUS

Philo
De Abrahamo viii, 46 82n
De Abrahamo x, 48 148n
De Abrahamo xv, 68–71 88n
De Abrahamo, xviii, 81 88n
De Abrahamo, xviii, 82–3 88n
De Abrahamo xxxii, 170 147n
De Decalogo 29 69n
De Sobrietate 55–6 153n
Life of MosesII, x, 53 178n
Life of Moses II, xlvii, 263 178n

Quis Haeres Sit iv, 19ff 74n
Quis Haeres Sit vi. 19ff 74n
Quis Haeres Sit vi, 28ff 148n
Quis Haeres Sit, xix, 94 151n
Josephus
Antiquities, v, i, 13 185
Pseudo-Philo
Liber Antiquitatum Biblicarum 18,5 152
Liber Antiquitatum Biblicarum 32,4 147n

D NEW TESTAMENT AND EARLY CHRISTIAN WRITINGS

Mark
12:36 108n
14:62 108n
16:19 108n
Luke
20:42 108n
Acts
2:34 108n
4:25f 120n
13:33 120n
1 Corinthians
15:25 108n
Hebrews
1:5 120n

1:8–9 98n
1:13 108n
5:5 120n
5:5ff 108n
7:1ff 115n
7:2 107n, 112n
7:17 and 21 108n
10:13 108n
James
2:21–3 145
Revelations
12:7 164n
Jerome
Epistola 73, 2 (Migne 22, 677) 166n

E ANCIENT NEAR EASTERN SOURCES

Aramaic Incantation Bowls, Orientalia 10, p. 273, lines 6–7 156n
Aramaic Incantation Texts, p. 121, lines 3–4 156n

Enuma Elis i
lines 136–9 162n
Enuma Elish ii
lines 23–26 162n

Enuma Elish II
line 50ff 159n
Enuma Elish III
lines 27–30 162n
Enuma Elish III
lines 85–8 162n
Enuma Elish IV

line 95 165n
line 97 165n
line 129 156n
lines 136–37 155n
lines 139–40 156n
The Book of Knowing
the Creations of Re 159n

F *TALMUD, MIDRASH* AND *TARGUM*

1 *Mishnah*

Shabbat
6:4 8
Ta'anit
3:8 186
Nedarim
3:11 189
Sotah
5:5 147n
Qiddushin
7:4 76n
Bava Qama
6:1 55n
Bava Meziah
4:2 33n

Sanhedrin
9:3 178n
10:3 178n
11:2 70n
Eduyot
2:10 36
Avot
1:3 73n
4:12 132n
5:2 83
5:3 128n
5:22 169n
Middot
1:8 56n
Niddah
9:11 137n

2 *Tosephta* (ed. Zuckermandel)

Pe'ah
4:18 (p. 24) 188–9
Yoma
2:6 (p. 184) 56n
5(4):13 (p. 191) 68n

Avodah Zarah
3:2 (p. 463) 32n
Hullin
3:27 (p. 506) 163n

3 *Avot d'Rabbi Natan* (ed. Schechter)

Version A, 2 (p. 12) 116n
Version A, 6 (p. 29) 192
Version A, 12 (p. 52) 177
Version A, 27 (p. 83) 64n
Version A, 32 (p. 93) 27n, 176
Version A, 33 (pp. 93–4) 83n

Version A, 33 (p. 94) 82n
Version A, 34 (p. 100) 109
Version A, Addendum 2 (pp. 156–7)
45n
Version B, 4 (p. 21) 142n
Version B, 10 (p. 26) 75n
Version B, 38 (p. 101) 57n

4 *Mekhilta d'Rabbi Ishmael* (ed. Horovitz-Rabin)

Bo, Pisha 13 (p. 43) 50n
Beshallah, Va-Yehi 1 (p. 84) 50n
Beshallah, Va-Yehi 2 (p. 91) 50n
Beshallah, Va-Yehi 6 (p. 111) 64n

Beshallah, Va-Yehi 6 (p. 112) 72n
Beshallah, Shirta 3 (p. 126) 76n
Beshallah, Shirta 3 (p. 127) 190
Beshallah, Shirta 6 (p. 135) 113

Beshallaḥ, Shirta 6 (p. 138) 64n
Beshallaḥ, Shirta 9 (p. 146) 76n
Beshallaḥ, Va-Yassa 3 (p. 165) 67n
Beshallaḥ, Va-Yassa 3 (p. 166) 66n
Beshallaḥ, Va-Yassa 6 (p. 175) 176
Beshallaḥ, Amaleq 1 (p. 176) 44n
Yitro, Amaleq 1 (p. 188) 77
Yitro, Amaleq 1 (p. 190) 8n, 121n

Yitro, Amaleq 1 (p. 195) 53n
Yitro, Ba-Ḥodesh 1 (p. 205) 77
Yitro, Ba-Ḥodesh 1 (pp. 205–6) 54n
Yitro, Ba-Ḥodesh 2 (pp. 208–9) 99
Yitro, Ba-Ḥodesh 3 (p. 214) 191
Yitro, Ba-Ḥodesh 5 (pp. 220–1) 76
Yitro, Ba-Ḥodesh 6 (p. 227) 190
Yitro, Ba-Ḥodesh 9 (p. 235) 77
Mishpatim 1 (p. 246) 58n

5 *Mekhilta d'Rabbi Shimon bar Yohai* (ed. Epstein-Melamed)

Exodus 12:29 (p. 28) 50n
12:40 (p. 34) 25n
14:2 (p. 48) 40n
14:21 (p. 61) 178

15:7 (p. 85) 133n
15:7 (p. 87) 64n
16:14 (p. 110) 66n
17:7 (p. 118) 44n

6 *Sifra* (ed. Weiss)

Baraita d'Rabbi Ishmael, (p. 3a) 65n
Leviticus
1:1 (p. 4a) 77n
7:35 (p. 40a) 110n

11:10 (p. 49b) 163n
18:3 (p. 85b) 32n
26:14 (p. 111a) 176

7 *Sifrei Numbers* (ed. Horovitz)

6:26, 42 (p. 46) 76
11:9, 89 (p. 90) 66
15:31, 112, (p. 121) 4n

27:12, 134 (p. 180) 72
27:12, 135 (p. 182) 184
31:2, 157, (p. 209) 64n

8 *Sifrei Zutta (Numbers)* (ed. Horovitz)

7:84 (p. 253) 110n

7:89 (p. 254) 47n

10 *Sifrei Deuteronomy* (ed. Horovitz-Finkelstein)

1:1, 1 (pp. 3–4) 82n
1:6, 6 (p. 15) 142n
1:10, 10 (p. 18) 99
3:24, 27 (pp. 43f) 72n
3:25, 28 (p. 45) 142n
6:5, 32 (p. 54) 125n
6:5, 32 (p. 55) 149n, 190
6:5, 32 (p. 58) 149n

6:5, 32 (pp. 58–9) 148n
6:7, 34 (p. 60) 102
11:15, 43 (p. 93) 37n
32:11, 314 (p. 356) 60n
32:17, 318 (p. 364) 57n
33:2, 343 (p. 395) 60n
33:2, 343 (p. 398) 78
34:5, 357 (p. 428) 64n

11 *Midrash Tannaim* (ed. Hoffmann)

Deuteronomy
3:23 (p. 14) 186n

11:16 (p. 36) 28n
34:5 (pp. 224–5) 44–6

12 *Seder Olam Rabbah* (ed. Ratner)

Chapter 3 (pp. 13–14) 25

Chapter 20 (p. 83) 99n

13 *Babylonian Talmud*

Berakhot
5a 89n
5b 44n
7b 120n
31b 185
31b–32a 185
32a 185
61b 190
Shabbat
55a 39n
63a 8, 102–3, 104
88b 65n
98a 179
116a 176
118b 143
156a 87n
Eruvin
54a 70n
64b 82n
Pesahim
119a 38n
Yoma
28a 84n
86b 68n
Sukkah
5a 65n
29b 50n
Rosh Ha-Shanah
4a 104
11b–12a 37n
12a 39n
17a 82n
Ta'anit
5b-6a 139n
7b 59n, 182
8a 182–3n
23a 184
Moed Qatan
25b 143
Hagigah
5b 160n
15b 104
Yevamot
11b 10n
24a 10n
Ketubot
12a 75n
28a 75n

62b 34n
Nedarim
31b 189
32a 65n, 87n
32b 115n
Sotah
11a 25, 53n
21a 82n
31a 146–7
49a 29n
Gittin
62a 105n
Qiddushin
2b 33n
Bava Batra
15a 24, 25n
15b 128n
16a 128n
16b 86n
74b 155, 159n, 161, 164n
74b–75a 158n, 163
75a 158n, 162n
Sandhedrin
19a 32n
24a 130–1n
44a 185
82b 185
89b 146n
100a 143
108a 28n, 39n
108a–b 33n
108b 39
109a 173
109a–b 177
111b 127
Avodah Zarah
17b 62n
25a 129
Menahot
88b 102n
Hullin
6a 10
91b 164n
133a 11
Temurah
16a 62n
Tamid
32a 12n

14 *Palestinian Talmud*

Berakhot
9:7 (14b) 148–9
Pe'ah
1:1 (15b) 188
2:6 (17a) 69n
Shabbat
16 (15c) 17n
Sheqalim
6:1 (49d) 69n
Rosh Ha-Shanah
1:3 (57a) 71n
Ta'anit
3:3 (66c) 183n
3:12 (67a) 184n
Ḥagigah
2:1 (77b) 176

Yevamot
1:1 (2b) 33, 139n
6:5 (7c) 33
Ketubot
12:3 (35a) 17n
Sotah
1:10 (17c) 129n
5:7 (20c) 148–9
5:8 (20d) 137n
5:8 (20c) 25n
5:8 (20d) 24n, 25n
Sanhedrin
10:1 (28a) 185
10:1 27d 55n
10:3 (29b) 39n
10:3 (29c) 177
Avodah Zarah
4:12 (44b) 39n

15 *Midrashim*

Genesis Rabbah (ed. Theodor-Albeck)
1:14 (p. 12) 4n
3:4 (p. 19) 162
3:6 (p. 21) 162
5:2 (p. 33) 157n
6:9 (p. 49) 129n
13:3f (pp. 115ff) 183
13:4 (p. 115) 183
23:2 (pp. 222–3) 34
24:5 (pp. 234f) 47, 179
26:5 (pp. 248–9) 32n, 37n, 40n
26:6 (p. 252) 174, 176
26:7 (p. 255) 27n, 58–9
27:3 (p. 257) 173, 178
28:7 (p. 266) 38
28:9 (p. 267) 39n
30:2 (p. 270f) 32–3
31:2 (p. 278) 26
31:4 (p. 297) 29–30n
31:5 (p. 279) 174
31:6 (p. 280) 35n
32:5 (p. 292) 37n
32:7 (p. 294) 37n
33:5 (p. 310) 29
36:1 (p. 334) 175
36:4 (p. 346) 119n
39:1–6 (pp. 365–8) 80–1
39:2 (p. 366) 124–5
39:8 (p. 370) 117
39:11 (p. 374) 131

40:6 (pp. 385f) 119n
41:1 (pp. 386ff) 140–1
41:2 (p. 399) 119n
41:3 (p. 410) 97
41:4 (p. 409) 119
42:1 (pp. 397–8) 129n
42:2 (p. 416) 118n
42:3 (p. 417) 119n
43:1 (p.420) 97
43:3 (p. 418) 117n, 118n
43:5 (p. 419) 123
43:6 (p. 420) 116n
43:9 (pp. 423–4) 119n
44:2 (p. 425) 81, 86, 88
44:7 (p. 430) 117n
44:10 (p. 432) 86–7
44:12 (pp. 432f) 87, 152–3
44:13 (p. 435) 134n
44:14 (p. 435) 83n
45:1 (p. 448) 97
48:6 (p. 481) 95n, 129
49:2 (p. 498) 129
49:2 (p. 501) 60n
49:8–9 (pp. 506–11) 186
52:3 (p. 542) 81
52:3 (p. 542f) 92
52:5 (p. 544) 68n
53:1 and 3 (pp. 554ff) 137–8
55:6 (p. 589) 122–3
55:7 (p. 592) 144

55:8 (p. 594) 119n
56:3 (p. 598) 5
56:7 (p. 602) 6
56:7 p. 603) 147
56:8 (p. 604) 186
56:9 (p. 605) 119n
57:1 (pp. 612–13) 90
57:4 (p. 615) 25n
59:5 (p. 633) 96
61:1 (p. 657) 84n
61:1–2 (pp. 657–9) 134–6
64:4 (pp. 703f) 82n
64:4 (p. 704) 60n
68:11 (p. 783) 143
78:1 (p. 916) 164n
85:9 (p. 1043) 108
95:3 (p. 1189) 89
98:4 (p. 1253) 122n
Exodus Rabbah
1:1 92–3, 120n
1:32 7
2:6 101n, 123n
3:2 71–2
3:8 50n
5:9 60–1
5:22 186
6:4 127n
7:2 68
9:9 62
12:1 63
15:10 48
15:15 50n
16:1 51
20:7 26n
21:2 183–4
27:4 76n
28:5 61–2
30:7 71n
30:11 57
37:1 55n
38:6 87
40:1 48n, 179
41:7 65n
42:2 65n
43:8 71n
44:3 65n
46:1 69n
47:1 69n
52:1 101
Leviticus Rabbah (ed. Margulies)
5:1 (pp. 98f) 175
7:6 (p. 161) 36, 39
10:1 (p. 197) 96n

16:4 (p. 354) 158n
18:2 (p. 402) 70n
19:3 (p. 423) 143n
23:2 (p. 528) 4–5
23:9 (pp. 538ff) 32n
23:9 (p. 539) 40n
24:4 (p. 556) 109n
25:5 (p. 580) 115
25:6 (p. 580) 115
25:8 (p. 583) 143n
27:11 (p. 646) 120n
31:4 (pp. 719 and 721) 101n
32:2 (p. 740) 101n
32:5 (pp. 745f) 30n
36:6 (p. 851–2) 89n
Numbers Rabbah
1:3 100n
2:10 50n
3:12 50n
8:3 64n
13:16 69n
14:2 89n
14:10 69n
14:22 47n
15:17 50n
18:8 55n
18:12 186
18:15 54–5
18:22 156n
18:23 108n
19:9 53n
19:10 75n
19:26 70n
20:12 68n
22:5 64n
Deuteronomy Rabbah
2:7 122, 123n
2:33 123n
7:3 130n
Canticles Rabbah
1:1 12n
1:2 126n
1:3 103n, 125, 126n
1:4 158n
1:13 144n
4:6 144
5:14 69n
Lamentations Rabbah (ed. Buber)
2:2 (p. 100) 192
Ecclesiastes Rabbah
2:3 82n
2:13 82n
2:14–15 93

4:8 101n
4:13 123n
4:13-14 93
7:1 132n
10:2 93
Esther Rabbah
9:9 182
Midrash Tanḥuma (Old Version)
Bereishit 12 35n, 37n
Lekh Lekha 9 120n
Lekh Lekha 13 123-4
Shemot 1 92n
Shemot 20 71n
Shemot 25 60n
Shemot 26 60n
Shemot 29 50n
Va-Era' 1 127n
Yitro 4 101n
Yitro 15 179-80
Ki-Tissa 17 100
Wa-Yiqra 1 46n
Zav 2 36n
Shemini 11 50n
Behar 1 101n
B'midbar 3 100, 105n
B'Ha'alotekha 13 50n
Qoraḥ 5 55n
Huqqat 1 156n
Huqqat 9 53n
Huqqat 10 75n
Huqqat 21 70n
Balaq 8 68n
Mattot 4 64n
Shophetim 11 87n
Nizzavim 4 159n
Midrash Tanḥuma (ed. Buber)
1, p. 19 99n
1, p. 23 36
1, p. 24 40
1, p. 36 38
1, p. 54 29-31
1, pp. 57-8 85
1, p. 60 114-15
1, pp. 70f 120
1, p. 71 119n, 129n
1, pp. 71-2 84n
1, p. 74 118n, 124n
1, p. 75 86
1, p. 76 119n
1, pp. 78-9 96-7
1, p. 85 97
1, p. 88 69n
1, pp. 88-9 91

1, p. 90 186
1, p. 93 178
1, p. 110 119n
1, pp. 114-15 186
1, p. 124 94n
1, p. 130 97
1, p. 177 68n
2, p. 13 60n
2, p. 14 60n
2, p. 16 50n
2, p. 20 23n
2, p. 33 62n
2, p. 37 23n
2, p. 58 23n
2, p. 69 23n
2, p. 95 23n
2, p. 96 23n
2, p. 103 23n
2, p. 113 85n
3, p. 2 46
3, p. 13 36n
3, p. 58 50n
3, p. 104 101
4, p. 7 70n
4, p. 13 23n
4, p. 32 23n
4, p. 58 66n
4, p. 89 55n
4, p. 96 185
4, pp. 97-8 156-7
4, p. 120 53n
4, p. 121 75
4, p. 128 70n
4, p. 137 68n
4, p. 159 64-5
5, p. 7 73n
5, pp. 8-9 73n
5, p. 32 50n
5, p. 51 65n
5, p. 55 76n
Pesiqta d'Rav Kahana (ed. Friedmann; ed. Mandelbaum cited in parenthesis)
6, p. 58a (p. 112) 167n
6, pp. 57b-58a (pp. 112-13) 158n
8, p. 70b (pp. 139f) 181
9, p. 77b (p. 156) 63n
11, p. 97b (p. 165) 37n
12, p. 102b p. 207) 99n
12, p. 107a (p. 219) 70
18, p. 134a (p. 293) 89n
24, p. 158b (p. 354) 63n
29, pp. 187b-188b (pp. 455-7) 158n
29, p. 187b-188a (p. 455) 158n, 161

29, p. 188a(p. 456) 160
ed. Mandelbaum, p. 50 176
ed. Mandelbaum, p. 342 149n
Pesiqta Rabbati (ed. Friedmann)
10 (p. 37b) 65n
10 (p. 38b) 65–6
21 (p. 104) 64n
Pirkei d'R. Eliezer
Chapter 3 70n
5 156n
7 138n
8 116n
21 33n
22 31n, 38n, 39n
24 84n
25 153n
41 46n
46 65n
Sepher Ha-Yashar
Noah 117n
Aggadat Bereshit (ed. Buber)
24 (p. 49) 117
37 (p. 73) 87n
Bereshit Rabbati (ed. Albeck)
Genesis 23:16 (p. 99) 84n
Midrash Psalms (ed. Buber)
1 (p. 12) 89n, 134n
7 (pp. 65–6) 65n
9 (p. 89) 112n
10 (p. 95) 117
11 (p. 100) 36n
18 (p. 157) 108n
45 (p. 271) 99–100
46 (p. 272) 99n
110 (p. 465) 116
110 (pp. 466–7) 107n
111 (p. 467) 112n
Midrash Mishlei
2:10 82n
5:1 82n
9:10 82n
Yalqut
Bereishit 34 99n
Hayyei Sarah 109 135n
Va-Era' 176 127n
Beshallah 262 44n
Qorah 752 100n
Huqqat 763 108n
Balaq 766 90n
Mattot 785 64n
Va-Ethanan 811 73n
Samuel 161 36n
Isaiah 508 36n

Psalms 667 84n
Psalms 845 136
Psalms 869 108n, 112n, 116n
Proverbs 932 89
Proverbs 961 94n
Job 907 73
Job 909 175
Job 910 39n
Canticles 982 126n
Ecclesiastes 973 132n
Midrash Ha-Gadol Genesis
(ed. Margulies)
4:19 (pp. 125–6) 34n
6:5 (p. 141) 35
6:13 (pp. 155–6) 33n
8:1 (p. 175) 39n
11:28 (p. 206) 117n
12:1 (p. 211) 81
12:1 (pp. 211–12) 93n
12:1 (p. 217) 129–30
13:29 (p. 229) 93n
14:17 (p. 236) 123n
14:20 (pp. 237f) 118n
15:1 (p. 243f) 138n
18:1 (p. 289) 93–4, 188
18:9 (pp. 253–4) 83n
18:11 (p. 300) 138
18:17 (p. 303) 153n
19:1 (p. 316) 92n
26:5 (p. 447) 189
49:3 (p. 836) 122n
Exodus (ed. Margulies)
6:3 (p. 93f) 127n
15:7 (p. 298) 113n
17:7 (p. 339) 44n
19:14 (p. 386) 103
32:10 (p. 682) 186
Leviticus (ed. Steinsalz)
7:35 (p. 193) 111
Tanna d'Bei Eliyahu (ed. Friedmann)
Seder Eliyahu Rabbah
18, p. 94 107n
29, p. 158 31–2
Seder Eliahu Zutta
p. 46 138n
Midrash Leqah Tov (ed. Buber)
Genesis 14:3 (p. 63) 123n
Exodus 10:10 (p. 45) 50n
Exodus 25:6 (p. 177) 111
Midrash Sekhel Tov (ed. Buber)
p. 28 153n
Midrash Shir-HaShirim (ed. Grunhut)
1, p. 13a–b 71n

Midrash Va-Yosha (Jellinek, *Bet
    ha-Midrasch*, vol. 1)
  p. 46 156n
Midrash Yelammedenu 35n, 36, 40n, 64n,
    73n, 84n, 89, 90n, 100, 108, 112
Midrash Zutta (ed. Buber)
  Canticles 1:2 (p. 8) 191
  Canticles 1:3 (p. 8) 130–1n
  Canticles 1:4 (p. 11) 126
  Canticles 1:4 (p. 11) 128, 190–1
  Ecclesiastes 7:1 (p. 133) 132n
Agadath Shir Ha-Shirim (ed. Schechter)
  1:3 (p. 12) 130n
  1:4 (p. 14) 127n
  1:4 (p. 15) 128n
Mishnat R. Eliezer (ed. H. G. Enelow)
  13 (p. 256) 103n
Midrash Abkir 131n
Midrash Aggadah (ed. Buber)
  Exodus 6:3 (p. 134) 127n

Midrash Alpha Betot (ed. Wertheimer,
    Batei Midrashot, vol. 2)
  p. 434 165n
  pp. 437–8 163–4
  p. 438 167
Midrash Hallel (Jellineck, *Bet
    ha-Midrasch*, vol. 5)
  p. 97 192
New Midrash on the Torah (ed. Mann,
    The Bible as Read, vol. 1, Hebrew
    Section)
  p. 157 129n
  p. 244 70n
Mayan Gannim (ed. Buber)
  Job 5:22f (p. 21) 181
  Job 24:13 (p. 77) 35n
  Job 24:24 (p. 79) 34n
  Job 28:27–8 (p. 90) 48n
  Job 40:19 (p. 130) 166n
  Job 41:22 (p. 133) 161n

16 *Targumim*

Targum Onqelos
  Genesis 15:7 134n
  Exodus 14:15 182
  Exodus 18:1 8n, 107n, 121
  Exodus 18:11 53n
  Leviticus 7:35 107n
  Leviticus 25:30 38n
  Numbers 22:9 107n
Targum Pseudo-Jonathan
  Genesis 6:2 31n
  Genesis 14:18 115n
  Genesis 15:6 150n
  Genesis 15:7 134n
  Genesis 22:5 152n
  Exodus 9:20 25n
  Exodus 12:12 50n
  Exodus 14:2 50n
  Exodus 14:15 182
  Exodus 18:1 107n, 121
  Exodus 18:11 53n
  Leviticus 7:35 107n
  Leviticus 25:30 38n
  Numbers 16:19 55n
  Numbers 20:17 33n
  Numbers 21:22 33n
  Deuteronomy 33:5 101n
Fragmentary Targum
  Genesis 14:18 115n
  Genesis 15:7 134n
  Genesis 18:17 91n, 153n

Exodus 14:15 182
Exodus 18:1 121
Numbers 20:17 33n
Targum Jonathan
  1 Samuel 28:13 91n
  1 Kings 5:13 142n
  Isaiah 41:2–3 114n
  Jeremiah 22:23 142
  Ezekiel 17:22 142
  Ezekiel 21:31 111n
  Ezekiel 38:13 164n
  Zachariah 4:14 107n
  Zachariah 11:2 142
Targum to Psalms
  29:1 159n
  29:11 76n
  45:1 99n
  45:7 100n
  78:61 78n
  82:6 91n
  86:8 91n
  110:1 107
  110:4 107
  132:8 78n
Targum to Job
  1:6 159n
  2:1 159n
  5:12–15 53
  5:19–23 53–4
  6:17 39n

7:12 52n

12:6 52n

14:19 52n

15:29 52n

24:20 41n

24:24 41n

26:12 155n

34:20 52n

36:22 63n

36:30 183

36:32 182–3

37:11 183

37:11–13 183

37:15 183

37:21 59n, 183

38:7 159n

38:23 52n

Targum to Ecclesiastes

7:1 132

Index of names

Aaron 68
Abbaye 11
Abraham 80, 83–94, 95–8, 106, 115–32,
 133–44, 145–53, 171, 186
Abraham Ibn Ezra 3, 155n, 164n
Adam 162n, 179
Aḥa 47–8, 52, 81, 95–6, 98
Alexandri 85
Altmann, A. 65n
Amalek 44n
Amir, J. 148n
Ammi 182
Anat 166
Annu 159
Antigonus of Sokho 75
Apophis 159n
Aqiva 4n, 16, 27–9, 41n, 72n, 116n,
 128n, 190–1, 192
Asher b. Yeḥiel (Rosh) 11
Avigad, N. 79n
Azariah 34, 82, 95, 144n

Bacher, W. 21, 41n, 52n, 128n, 131n
Balaam 67, 68n, 171
Bar Kippuk 143
Bar Qappara 32n, 133
Baron, S. W. 34n
Ben Azzai 47n, 60n, 191
Berekhiah 38, 63, 80, 90, 123, 124, 133,
 144, 159n
Berliner, A. 161n
Billerbeck, P. 146
Bloch, P. 21
Bowker, J. 151n
Brock, S. P. 25n
Brockmuehl, M. 15n
Buber, S. 128, 131n
Büchler, A. 29n, 75n, 80n, 147n
Budick, S 1

Cassuto, U. 154–5
Churgin, P. 41n

David 107
Dimi 11, 13, 163n
Driver, G. R. 24n, 150n

Ea 159
Easton, B. S. 146n
Edels, S. (MaharSha) 102n, 103n
Einhorn, Z. W. (Maharzu) 125n
Elbogen, I. 187
Eleazar b. Abina 119
Eleazar b. Jose 127
Eleazar (b. Pedath) 35, 38, 102, 112n,
 185–6
Eleazar Ḥisma 44n
Eleazar of Modi'in 8n, 67n, 77, 86n, 121
Eliezer (b. Hyrkanos) 6, 8, 10, 37n, 104,
 129n, 175
Eliezer b. R. Jose the Galilaean 99
Elihu 25, 58–9, 67, 161
Elisha b. Abuya 176
Enkidu 167
Epstein, L. M. 34n
Esau 171
Ezra 192

Finkelstein, L. 75
Frankl, Z. 24–5n
Friedlander, G. 31n
Fruedenthal, J. 24n

Gabriel 163–5
Gabriel and Michael 167
Gaster, T. H. 154n, 159n
Geller, M. J. 156n
Gelles, B. J. 3n
Geniba 105n

Gertner, M. 145
Ginzberg, H. L. 109n
Ginzberg, L. 24n, 31n, 35n, 38n, 40n,
  51n, 55n, 66n, 82b, 88n, 91n, 93n,
  99n, 105, 106n, 109n, 111n, 115n,
  121n, 145n, 154n, 155–6, 157n,
  162n, 164n, 171, 177–8, 185
Gotthold, Z. 109n
Gunkel, H. 154n

Ḥamma 108
Ḥananiah (nephew of R. Joshua) 69n
Ḥanina 5, 29n, 104, 173
Ḥanina b. Ḥamma 26n
Ḥanokh Zundel b. Yoseph (Etz Yoseph)
  136n
Hartman, G. H. 1
Heinemann, J. 17n, 21–2, 81, 96, 133
Ḥelbo 123
Hermes 180
Hertzberg, A. 109n
Ḥisda 39, 41n, 105
Ḥiyya 6, 11, 12n, 32n
Ḥizkiyah b. Ḥiyya 87
Ḥoni (the Circle-Drawer) 186
Hoshaiah Rabbah 59, 65
Huna 40
Hunia 125n

Idi 40
Isaac (Nappaḥa) 49, 80, 90, 95, 96, 98,
  130–1n, 139n
Isaac b. Jacob Al-Fasi (Rif) 11
Isaiah di Trani 166n
Ishmael (b. Elisha) 4n, 16, 37n, 39,
  115–16, 122n, 186
Ishmael b. Isaac 86–7

Jacob of Caesarea 138
Jaffe, S. (Y'pheh To'ar) 90n, 135n, 136n
James, M. R. 25n, 152
Jastrow, M. 56n, 58n, 66n, 71n, 127n
Jeremiah (Amora) 102n, 161n
Jesus 108
Job 25–6, 147
Johanan (b. Nappaḥa) 27n, 39, 59, 87,
  125n, 152–3, 158n, 178
Johanan b. Zaccai 37n, 129n, 147n
Jonah (b. Abraham) Gerondi 128n
Jonathan (b. Eleazar) 85, 163n
Jose b. Durmaskith 37n
Jose (b. Ḥalaphta) 32n, 138, 139n,
  143

Jose of Caeserea 33n
Joseph (Amora) 11–12, 59n
Joshua b. Ḥananiah 37n, 44n, 75n
Joshua b. Hyrkanos 147n
Joshua b. Levi 36n, 181
Joshua b. Qorḥa 114–15, 122
Joshua b. R. Joḥanan 129
Joshua Falk (Binyan Yehoshua) 109n
Joshua Ha-Garsi 128n
Judah (b. Ezekiel) 11
Judah (b. Ilai) 75n, 99n, 110, 112
Judah b. Nehemiah 178
Judah (b. R. Simon b. Pazzi) 33–4, 143
Judah the Patriarch 27, 29, 31, 34n, 176
Justin Martyr 115n

Kahana (Amora) 8–10, 104
Katz, Y. B. (Matnot Kehunah) 126n, 140n
Kimron, E. 161n
Kisch, G. 152
Kohler, K. 25n, 80n
Komlosh, Y. 41n, 80n
Korah 54–6

Lauterbach, J. Z. 3n, 44n
Lerrer, Y. N. 131n
Levi (Amora) 36, 87, 88–9
Levy, J. 71n
Lieberman, S. 34n, 161n, 175
Loewe, R. J. 3n
Lot 89, 93
Löw, I. 66n
Lowenstamm, S. E. 61n
Lowy, S. 34n
Luria, D. (R'dal) 39n, 56n, 90n, 135n

Maarsen, I. 102n
Malchizedek (= Shem) 115, 116n
Mann, J. 22, 49n, 70n, 80n, 94, 97, 114,
  125, 134
Mar, the son of R. Huna 8–10
Marcus, R. 109n
Marduk 156
Margulies, M. 130n
Marmorstein, A. 38n, 62n
Meir 10, 27n, 31, 82n, 104, 126n, 146–7,
  148n, 174–5, 176, 190
Melamed, E. Z. 3n
Menahamah 138
Meyer, A. 150n
Miriam 48n
Monobaz 188–9
Mordechai 171

Moses 7, 44–6, 55–6, 73–5, 99–101, 105,
121–2, 183–6
Moses b. Maimon (*Rambam*) 70n
Moses b. Naḥman (*Ramban*) 101n, 155n
Moses b. Samuel Ibn Tibbon 192
Moshe Ha-Darshan 85n
Mowinckel, S. 98n

Naḥman 139n, 185
Naḥman of Yafo 138
Naḥum of Gimzo 4n
Nehemiah (Tanna) 175–6
Nissim b. Reuben (*Ran*) 189
Noy, D. 17n, 21n

Pappos 72n
Philo 74–5
Phineas 171, 185
Pinḥas b. Yair 29n
Pinḥas ha-Kohen b. Ḥama 161
Pope, M. H. 155n, 158n, 166n, 167n

Qaliri (Eleazar Ha-Qaliri) 24n, 161n,
164–5, 192
Qimḥi, David b. Joseph (*R'daq*) 98n,
155n

Rabbinovicz, R. 128n
Rabin, Ch. 150n
Rabinowitz, L. I. 3n
Rahab (see also *Yam*) 155, 157
Rashi 3, 10n, 11n, 32n, 34n, 39n, 50n,
57n, 62n, 102n, 104n, 105n, 107n,
111n, 120n, 121, 129n, 152n, 161n,
164n, 166n, 182
Rav (Abba Arikha) 11, 104, 155–6,
159n, 185
Rava 10n, 11
Rava b. Ulla 164n
Ravina 143
Reuben (*Amora*) 116–17
Rönsch, H. 147n

Saadiah Gaon 164n
Sandmel, S. 153

Saphra 11
Sarah 84n, 94, 137–8, 139–40
Schechter, S. 126n, 128n, 192
Schirmann, J. 165n
Segal, M. H. 3n, 151
Shemuel b. Isaac 161n
Shemuel b. Naḥman 123, 181
Shemuel b. Naḥmani 85, 183
Shimon b. Menasia 132n
Shimon b. Yoḥai 84n, 132, 135, 178,
191
Sidebottom, E. M. 146n
Simai 25n, 32n
Spiegel, S. 152n
Stemberger, G. 15n
Strack, H. L. 15, 18n, 19n
Strashun, S. (*R'Shash*) 103n, 126n

Tanḥum bar Abba 101
Tanḥum b. Ḥiyya 130
Tarphon 66–7, 176, 192
Tiamat 156, 162
Tineus Rufus 128
Tur-Sinai, N. H. 156n, 164n

Urbach, E. E. 68n, 75n, 147n, 150n

Vajda, G. 145n, 148n
Vermes, G. 79n, 80n, 86n, 142n
Vilna Gaon 109

Weiss, J. G. 3n
Weiss, R. 41n
Weiss-Halivni, D. 3n, 9, 10–12
Wertheimer, A. J. 35n, 84n
Wieder, N. 24n, 33n, 60n

Yadin, Y. 79n
Yam (the genius of the sea) 155–6
Yannai 17n, 34n, 91, 94, 130n, 131–2,
137n, 191
Yudan 103

Zeriqa 102n
Zulay, M. 24n, 34n, 91n, 94n, 131n

Index of subjects

Adiabene 189
Aggadat Bereshit 187–8
Angels 65n
Antediluvians (*see* Generation of the Flood)
Aqedah 5–7, 145–153, 171
Audience 14, 80

Bar Cochba Uprising 175
Behemoth 166–7
Behemoth and Leviathan 160, 162
Bible (rabbinic perception of the) 4
Bold speech 72–5, 185–6
'Breasts' (= teachers) 133, 190–1
Bull of Heaven 166
Burial of Sarah 127–8

Canticles 23
Cedar 136–7, 139–44
Circumcision 116
Climatic Exegesis 4–5, 57n, 76, 108–9, 122–3, 134n, 174
Clouds 54n
Combat myth 155–67
Creation drama 15

Decalogue 57
Divine Justice 71, 72–3

Early teachers of the Church 14
Egyptians 48–50, 53, 62–3, 64n
Elders 51
Exegetical *Midrash* 15–16

Ferocious bullock of El 166
Flood 3

Generation of the Flood 2, 26–42, 173–8
Genesis Apocryphon 139

Genesis Rabbah 16–17
Gentiles 51–2
Gilgamesh 167
Gnostics (Gnosticism) 62, 68n
God 47–8, 63–4, 68n, 112, 156–7
Golden Calf 71

Halakhic *Midrashim* (*see* Tannaitic *Midrashim*)
'Ḥamas' (violence) 174
Haphtarah 22, 124
Haphtarah list for the triennial cycle 114
Homiletical *Midrash* 18–19

Jethro's title 'Kohen' 7–8, 121
Jewish Heretics 175–6
Jewish-Christian polemics 111n, 116n, 124
Job, Book of 2–3, 24–6, 72
Job, *Targum* to 52–3
Job, Testament of 25

Kidneys (= teachers) 84

'Law-Interpreter' 180
Lectionary Cycle (of hagiographic texts) 92, 98, 114n, 187–8
Leviathan 158–66
Leviticus Rabbah 17–18
Lotan (in Ugaritic texts) 158
Love of God 74–5, 125n, 128–9

Ma'aseh Merkavah 71n, 158n
'Man' 48n, 89, 134
Manna 66–7
Marcionites (*see* Gnostics, Gnosticism)
Mekhiltah of Rabbi Ishmael 16
Mekhiltah of Rabbi Shimon bar Yoḥai 16

'*Melammu*' 162
Messiah 98–9, 108–12
Midrash 3
Midrash Ha-Gadol 19–20
Mother Hubur 162

Oaks of Mamre 93–4

Patriarchs 67, 126n
Peshat (*see also* Plain Meaning) 3, 9,
    11–13
Petiḥah 2, 26n
Pharaoh 49
Plain meaning (see also *Peshat*) 1–2, 5–6,
    8–9, 104–6
Post-talmudic *Midrashim* 16–19
'Priest' (= King) 107n, 121
Priestly office 109–12, 121–3
Primordial light 162n
Prince of the sea (see also *Yam, Rahab*)
    155–7
Proemial verses 21–4, 80–1
Proof-texts 21–4
Psalm 29 46–7, 75–8
Psalm 45 95–106
Psalm 92 135–6n, 140–2
Psalm 110 106–124
'*Pulhu*' 162

Rain-fall 59, 182–3
Revelation (*see also* Sinai) 70
Rod of Jacob 108

Role models 169–70

'Sage' (= Torah sage) 82
Seder 2, 21–2
Sifra 16
Sifrei 16
Sinai (Revelation at) 46, 57–8, 59, 61–2,
    75–77
Sodomites 62, 95–6, 117–18, 177–8

Tablets of the Covenant 69–70
Tanḥuma (*Midrash*) 18–19
Tannaitic *Midrashim* 16–17
Targum 79–80
Ten Plagues 48
Torah Scholars 101–3
Tower-builders 62
Traditions (early rabbinic) 14–15, 41,
    79–80, 168–9

Voice of God 46–7, 60–1, 76–7

'Wisdom' (= Knowledge of Torah) 82
Woman (agricultural epithets for) 33n,
    137n

Yalqut 19
Yelammedenu 18–19

Ziz (the monster-bird) 162
Zikhronot 149